MIGHTY
HANDS

Persevere!
James 1:12

MIGHTY HANDS

Victory over Adversity through
the Grace of God

For my Friend & teammate, Mike

War Eagle!

Paul Ed

Paul T. Entrekin

To order additional copies of this book, contact:
Xlibris Corporation
1-888-795-4274
www.Xlibris.com
Orders@Xlibris.com
105057

CONTENTS

For

Charlie, Katie, Lindy and Logan

"ONLY GUARD YOURSELF AND GUARD YOUR SOUL CAREFULLY LEST YOU FORGET THE THINGS YOUR EYES SAW AND LEST THESE THINGS DEPART YOUR HEART ALL THE DAYS OF YOUR LIFE AND YOU SHALL MAKE THEM KNOWN TO YOUR CHILDREN AND TO YOUR CHILDREN'S CHILDREN."

Deuteronomy 4:9

"FAR BETTER IT IS TO DARE MIGHTY THINGS, TO WIN GLORIOUS TRIUMPHS, EVEN THOUGH CHECKERED BY FAILURE, THAN TO TAKE RANK WITH THOSE POOR SPIRITS WHO NEITHER ENJOY MUCH NOR SUFFER MUCH, BECAUSE THEY LIVE IN THE GRAY TWILIGHT THAT KNOWS NOT VICTORY NOR DEFEAT."

President Theodore Roosevelt

FOREWORD

When you first meet him, he is short, rather small frame, unassuming with a wide grin. I can still remember when I first met him. I had heard he was a pilot . . . an unusual pilot in that he owned his own "MiG". Not being an aviator nor very familiar with flying, I was not particularly impressed. I had also heard he was involved in "air shows", whatever that meant.

That was shortly after my family and I moved to Pensacola, Florida in January of 1998.

Many know Pensacola as "The Cradle of Naval Aviation". In my studying about the community, I learned of the vitally important role of the military in the life of Pensacola. But just like meeting *Mr. MiG*, I did not fully understand what that meant until I became a part of the community! I brought with me to Pensacola a deep and profound patriotism. My grandfather retired from the Coast Guard. My father served in the Air Force in the Korean conflict. My father-in-law was an infantryman in the Army during World War II. I love my country, but did not understand the life of a military person nor military aviation until moving to Pensacola.

I recall with great vividness the blue lights of the Deputy Sheriff's cars and the red flashing lights of the ambulance. My wife and I were returning home. As we crested the hill of the entrance to our neighborhood, we were stunned to see them gathered at my new acquaintance's home. I learned several days later the reason for their gathering was this man's 18 year-old son had taken his own life.

I share all of this in an effort to communicate when I first met Paul; I had no idea of whose hand I was shaking. Oh, I understood he had done some unusual and extraordinary things in his life. What I did not realize was I was face to face with a great man!

And now, having read the manuscript of his life's story, I again realize how undiscerning I have been. Paul's modesty cheated me of being able to fully understand just what a great man he is.

When he asked me to read this manuscript which he was self publishing, I assumed it would be the boring details of an average man's life who had a need to be remembered by his family. I assure you, this book is anything but that!

As for boring . . . I had the manuscript with me while visiting some friends in their mountain home in North Carolina. I had left the manuscript on the front porch where I had been reading and went into the house for a snack. When I returned, my host had the manuscript in her hands. Holding what you are about to read, she looked up at me with excited eyes and a smile saying, "Wow, this is a real page turner!" And indeed it is!

As for "an average man", you will discover Paul is anything but an average man. I have known Paul on several levels. I have interacted with him while he served with distinction as President of his Rotary Club. He has been my neighbor. I have been his pastor. He has been my friend.

As a Georgia Bulldog, I have had to overlook his allegiance to Auburn. The first time he told me he had played football at Auburn, I considered his size and determined he might have played intramural or played on some freshman team. But not varsity at a Division I powerhouse school like Auburn. But he did.

When he mentioned having been a captive, I discounted it as maybe he played the part of a POW during his aviation training. But he was.

When he told me about flying his MiG, I thought maybe he had an old bi-plane that had been used by Russian crop dusters. I was wrong.

As you read this book, I hope you have the same awakening I did. While I had always had a deep and abiding love and appreciation for Paul, I did NOT realize just how great a man he really is. This is not the self-aggrandizing of an aging soldier. It is the recollections of a thoughtful person who has much to share.

While he speaks of his personal experiences, he is actually addressing what his God, his family, his country and community mean to him. And should mean to us all.

As much as I admired and appreciated Paul prior to reading his manuscript, I am now honored to count Paul not only as among my friends but also as one of my heroes!
You are about to be impressed and inspired!

Dr. Robert J. Mills, Senior Pastor, 1998-2004
First Baptist Church, Pensacola, Florida

INTRODUCTION

As an airline pilot it is not uncommon to drone along for hours making only an occasional heading, altitude or airspeed change. This allows for lots of conversation between the pilots. As "the MiG guy" it was typical for me to be asked lots of the same questions from trip to trip. I was happy to wax eloquent about my many stories in the MiG which were usually followed by comments from listeners that I should write a book.

What followed was more than a decade of struggle over what to write, attempting to avoid the label of a vanity publication. Should it be an autobiography? Would my target audience be only pilots? I've heard it said that we all have a book within us. The real question is, would anybody want to read it? Who cares? Just do it.

After an acquaintance, a talented professional writer who did a story about me for an airplane magazine, forwarded my original manuscript to an editor, I was thoroughly and harshly taken to task for my ineptitude (and rightfully so) as a wordsmith. Hemingway I'm not. My objective is not to sell books so I'll stick to my day job which would probably suit professional writers just fine.

Frankly, I still don't know who my target audience really is. What I do know is that my life has been punctuated by an ongoing series of events; the results of which have become a testament to my faith.

And finishing this book has proven to be a real catharsis. Having chronicled the details that would, no doubt, fade into the shadows of my memory over time, I have accomplished the primary objective of providing my children with an admittedly unabashed view of their dad.

If you, the reader, are so inclined, I'll tell you the stories behind those events and gladly share with you what some, apparently, think are worthwhile vignettes that deal with one man's struggles with failure and victories over adversity.

Also included are historical accounts of war and politics that have helped form my opinions and reflect my philosophies on some, personally, very important topics. I've pretty well covered all the taboo subjects that should never be broached in polite conversation for fear that someone will take issue or offense with the political incorrectness. So, I guess I've just about guaranteed to offend some.

I've turned on the seat belt sign so strap in and hang on!

PROLOGUE

Life is full of beautiful lies. Life is full of ugly truths.

I never have much cared for the beach, and I especially don't care for the desert. Some consider the pristine white sands of the Pensacola Beach area to be their little slice of heaven; hurricanes and all. Others cheat Mother Nature, too, by living in stark, arid, climates that they find strikingly beautiful.

As I lay face down in the talc-like, fine powdered sand second guessing nearly everything I'd ever done that helped to get me there, I had a very real feeling that I could get very dead very quickly.

I had come to Syria under the guise of brokering airplanes and as such had a real need to be around wherever they were, including off-limits military bases. Once there with a few days growth of beard, sunglasses and a kafia, I could blend in very well even though I didn't speak the language. Supposedly, I wouldn't need to. As an operative for the Defense Intelligence Agency I was equipped with most essentials needed to accomplish my objective—everything except luck, which was up to me.

Intelligence gathering, for the most part, is pretty tame. Be somebody you aren't, to get you into someplace you aren't supposed to be.

Syria was and still is a Palestinian training camp for terrorists providing state sponsored support and equipment. Our intelligence agencies knew where some of that equipment was located but needed to know what and how much. That is truly all I can share even though the specified statute of limitations has expired. Methods are still very similar since there is often no substitute for human intelligence even with the exponential evolvement of modern technology.

I started near Aleppo, about 200 miles from Damascus. Mosque call to prayer occurred daily at 4:30 am. Many of the people spoke French in the Jdeide quarter where I stayed. The Baron Hotel was in a primarily Christian district that had a reputation for getting along well with the Muslims. Ironically, though, we knew that both Islamic Jihad and Hamas had offices there. Being a police state country, it didn't really matter. As long as a westerner had a local "fixer" with Baath Party connections you could go almost anywhere and buy almost anything from the dealers and brokers. It was easier to start in the north, a few hours from my real destination, and then travel south.

What would transpire was ironic considering Paul's biblical road to Damascus.

"Who are you? Where are you from? Who do you work for? Are you Mossad (Israeli intelligence)? Talk or I kill you!"

In SERE (survival, evasion, resistance and escape) school, we were taught that it's just mind over matter. You can withstand a lot more interrogating than you think. Well, that's true to a point. A logical presumption would be that captors would only use the force necessary to get what they want. Not necessarily, when one considers the prevailing Muslim jihadist attitude in the Middle East. Add another element, the human factor, and sometimes things just depend on what kind of mood the guy's in. To be perfectly honest with you, if I'd been sitting on a lump of coal I could've made a diamond.

He was in a bad mood and I was in a bad way. No bargaining power. I was there under false pretenses and already knew that the U.S. would deny anything about my being there. So I tried to be a tough guy. The theme of the hero.

My interrogator decided to get my attention right away by heating up a wire coat hanger. After he applied his pliers to some of my toe nails and played tic tac toe on the bottom of both feet, I told him exactly who I was and why I was there.

I collapsed back in the room where I was being held and felt the perception of shame. I could endure the physical pain. That wasn't optional anyway. But the thought that I had jeopardized my mission was emotionally overwhelming.

After a couple of days I was loaded aboard a truck and told I would be taken to a "holding facility" for further questioning. The driver and I were the only occupants and, surprisingly enough, my only restraint was having my hands tied in front. I suppose I looked pitiful and clearly not a threat. He had a pistol which he pointed at me occasionally with a scowl just to maintain the intimidation factor but otherwise seemed emotionless.

He mumbled "Mushkila" (problem) and gave me a dirty look as he pulled over to the side of the road. I don't know if he thought we were running out of gas or what, but he stopped the truck, got out and waved his little pistol at the first vehicle that came by. The highway out of Dar'a had no traffic in sight.

Ironically, he hopped into a passing tanker truck without saying a word and left me just sitting there! It was kind of like a scene out of the old television show *Candid Camera*. OK, where is it? I'm gonna get out and somebody's gonna shoot me, right? After a few short minutes of contemplation my pulse began to race and I figured it was time to do something.

I knew which way was south and figured I was less than 20 miles from safety in Jordan. I couldn't miss the highway running east and west across the border and never thought for a second about the pain in my feet or the hunger in my belly as the adrenaline hustled me along. Except for the handicap of being dehydrated and a pair of sore feet filling a bloody pair of socks, my evasion was simple. I stayed just far enough off the road to keep it in sight but close enough to follow it as a lifeline to safety. I did not see another person or vehicle until, as it turned out, I was well inside the Hashemite Kingdom of Jordan.

Why in the world did that guy just leave me there? Was he just stupid? I haven't a clue. I do believe that the Man upstairs decides who, what, when, where, how and, most of the time, why. That's the story of my life.

Today, on my wall hangs the blood chit that I carried with me that summer in 1986. It contains a message in thirteen languages and reads:

I am an American. I do not speak your language. Misfortune forces me to seek your assistance in obtaining food, shelter and protection. Please take me to someone who will provide for my safety and see that I am returned to my people. I will do my best to see that no harm comes to you. My government will reward you.

It all started back on active duty in the Marine Corps. I was recruited to participate in covert activities and continued to do so even after my return to civilian life. The resignation of my regular Marine Corps officers commission involved being, what is referred to as, "sheep dipped". The way it works is that, although you are for all practical purposes a civilian again, a special top secret intelligence file is maintained and your military career continues. Provided you continue service, you are promoted with your contemporaries. Sheep dipped personnel know up front that any and all information about their activities will be disavowed should they be killed or captured. Although pay problems were common, it was clear that our families would be adequately provided for. So, I elected to do what patriots do.

This was but one of several adventures that would forge my faith and bring me to the realization that my life was, truly, in His *Mighty Hands*.

In his book *Wild at Heart*, John Eldredge writes "The paradox of courage is that a man must seek his life in a spirit of furious indifference to it; he must desire life like water and yet drink death like wine.

God rigged the world in such a way that it only works when we embrace risk as the theme of our lives, which is to say, only when we live by faith."

That is, for the most part, the drum beat to which I have marched.

CHAPTER 1

ROOTS

SCOTLAND THE BRAVE

In the southern highlands of Dumfriesshire lies the parish of Durisdeer. Nearby is the tiny area known as Enterkinfoot. A few hundred years ago my ancestors lived in this area as evidenced by the influence of the name. Enterkin Burn (the Scottish name for a stream) meanders about seven miles from the hills along Enterkin path down to Enterkinfoot in the south. I have stood there on Enterkin Bridge at Enterkin Mill as the stream empties nearby into the River Nith. It is definitely Entrekin country, although a couple of letters in the name were switched at some time over the years.

Nothing exists there now except for three small cottages. It is a beautiful land of steep grades and rolling hills with sheep-filled pastures all about. Around an hour's drive south of Edinburgh through a few small towns and pastoral scenery, I wondered why they had left. Could the king of England have been so brutal that they sought refuge in another land? Perhaps they fought with William Wallace and some died fighting for their freedom. There is no one left to ask, but it's easy to speculate that there must have been extraordinary circumstances to cause them to leave such a beautiful place.

Standing there, on that hallowed ground, where those hundreds of years ago my ancestors pondered their future, I was moved by the significance of the moment. I had returned home.

Could they ever have imagined what their progeny would accomplish? Generations later, I saw what their eyes had seen; the purple heather softly carpeting portions of the hillsides like a patchwork quilt, the thistle down that lines every path and roadway blowing with the soft summer breeze and the majesty and power of the rugged landscape all around. As I allowed my soul to drink in my surroundings, it occurred to me that, while I had great reverence for where I was, I recognized that my heart was truly at home, in America.

I must admit, though, to feeling a passion in my blood when I read the stirring words written by Robert Burns and etched on my Sgian Dubh:

> "My heart's in the Highlands,
> my heart is not here;
> My heart's in the Highlands,
> a chasing the deer—"

And as a Trinitarian Christian I am honored to carry the Masonic title of Knight of The Royal Order of Scotland.

It's hard to describe the passion I feel for my country. On my mother's side, my ancestors fought the British for our freedom during the Revolutionary War. Being such an efficient genealogist, Mom traced our family back to the 1700s and afforded me the privilege of membership in the Sons of the American Revolution.

She also found that our family had fought on both sides of the Civil War which, considering myself a Southerner, made it possible for me to join the Sons of Confederate Veterans.

So, you see, my family has fought for our right to be here, living free. So much blood has been shed throughout the centuries. And they did it for us, their children. They did it for me.

THE BOYS OF SUMMER

Shortly after joining my family in Michigan, we moved back to Alabama and I've always been an Alabamian at heart. I love the South and stand out of respect whenever I hear *Dixie* played. Of course the same is true for *The National Anthem*, *The Marine Corps Hymn*, *Scotland the Brave* and *The Doxology*; all parts of the fabric of my being.

Having tried his hand at such jobs as a steeple jack and crane operator, Dad figured life was better back in Cullman County. We moved back to the country, close to where Dad grew up. I have some very fond memories of those times.

I had a pet hen named Hilda who followed me around like a dog. I "fished" in our newly dug well and terrified my mom that I'd fall in and drown. One of my favorite things was to run and sit on the washing machine on our back porch during its spin cycle. It was so off-balance that it would literally walk off the porch without our extra weight on it. My only unhappy memory from that time was learning that a particularly delicious fried chicken dinner we enjoyed was provided courtesy of Hilda.

At age five we moved to the Louisville, Kentucky area which was where I entered first grade. During the next five years we moved once more and I continued to spend each summer on the farm with Grandma and Grandpa back in Alabama. Those were certainly the happiest years of my childhood.

I remember sleeping under a mountain of quilts in their drafty old farm house, camping out and playing with my cousins (I always cried when Uncle Earney's coral '57 Chevy pulled away with James, Paula and Rodney curled up in the back seat, window and floorboard on their way home), chasing the chickens in the chicken house, helping Grandma wash the watering jugs, fishing in the creek, squirrel hunting with Grandpa, playing in the barn loft and helping Grandpa pick corn and throw it in Homer Alvis' mule-drawn wagon. I learned the meaning of gee and haw and how to drive the mules.

I remember how my Uncle Larry used to give me a quarter to fetch things for him. He was my favorite uncle; a bachelor, and I vowed to be just like him when I grew up.

I remember the pond being dug and how muddy it stayed, playing in the cool red clay under the house, the iron rich water and how it stained the blue porcelain in the new toilet, sink and bathtub when they got indoor plumbing. Prior to that, I remember how much I hated choosing between corn cobs and the Sears catalog in the outhouse.

Back in Kentucky the winters were cold, dreary, gloomy seasons and my memories include waiting for the bus in freezing weather and walking the two miles to school when I missed it, riding my sled down the ice-covered street when it was impossible for cars to drive and skating on pond ice. We looked forward to the spring when Dad always planted a garden.

It was during this period that my folks decided it was time for me to have a sister, so in 1961 Lori joined us and we became a family of four.

Being a kid in the 60s was not quite what today's kids would think. Basically, life in general was simpler but without many of the comforts that we enjoy today; digital television (in color), cell phones, computers, video games or microwaves. Both of my parents were heavy smokers which made riding in the car with them miserable, especially in the winter when the windows were up. The windows were usually down in the summer and that helped but it was hot, miserably hot, and there was no escaping it. Suffer the smoke or suffer the heat. Either way, you suffered.

There was a lot more emphasis on corporal punishment then, too. My spankings, which were frequent, usually involved a switch from Mom or a belt from Dad. Believe me, I got my share of whippin's.

My father injured his back when he slipped on an icy step while driving a truck and then had to take a position as a safety investigator for the same truck line. This required even more lengthy absences and a pay cut so Mom had to take a job to supplement their income.

This was also around the time that Dad brought home a German Shepherd puppy that we named Heidi. She was my loyal companion for many years. Others came and went such as Moe, a black mutt who was hit by a car and Poncho, a Chihuahua who ran away from home. Heidi was special.

My best friend during my first through third grade years was my next door neighbor, Rip. He and I used to hold .22 caliber rifle bullets with pliers and smack the casing with a hammer on the sidewalk just to hear the pop.

My friends and I climbed trees and knocked down most of the neighborhood bagworm nests, joined Cub Scouts, rode our bikes and experienced the youthful thrill of stealing a watermelon.

One of our favorite activities was BB gun battles. In the cold weather, we were all bundled up and the BBs just bounced off. We never considered the dangers of a ricochet or a BB in the eye. It was kind of like paintball without the protection. One day, just after a snowfall, I was stalking the enemy and caught one unaware. He was busy answering nature's call as I adjusted for windage and elevation and squeezed off a shot that hit him in the most exposed part of his body. He danced a jig and hollered while I laughed 'till I nearly wet my pants.

All of us kids in the neighborhood played sandlot baseball. There was always a field big enough to play on and close enough to get to. Gloves were left in the field so that we had enough to go around. Bases were whatever we could find, sometimes just an obvious dirt spot. We usually had a selection of two or three bats, always choosing the newest one unless a particularly sweet bat was available, but we nursed our baseballs to last. We collected shoe boxes full of baseball cards and kept our favorite players. All the others were traded or relegated to slow destruction in the spokes of our bicycles. Their distinctive noise crescendoed the faster we pedaled.

In the summer evenings, about nine o'clock, when it became too dark to see the ball and after our mothers had called us in for supper which we inhaled so as to rush back out to the game, we diverted our attention to catching fire flies or "lightnin' bugs". We were the boys of summer.

I loved to roam and explore our nearby woods and kept many of the critters that I found pickled in a jar full of vinegar. Mom absolutely hated the snakes.

I had a couple of grocery bags full of fossils and geodes which I carefully cracked open to discover each unique crystal formation inside.

Without a doubt the highlight of that time period was learning to play the drums. I absolutely loved it and drummed on everything all the time. It was a natural physical activity to me so I joined the Overdale Elementary School band when I started fourth grade. This was to be a pivotal decision for me as, later in life, music became an integral part.

One thing I have to mention about this time period was the *April fool* that I played on Mom. She came home about the same time every day and I was determined to meet her at the driveway to exercise "operation road kill". Normally she would have appreciated the greeting but this time it was a nightmare. I was slathered in carefully applied ketchup to simulate blood and curled up in a ball with my bike next to the street. As she drove up, she was convinced that I was horribly mauled and dashed out of the car in tears, only to find me grinning. I think she would've killed me if she hadn't been so glad that I was alive.

My biggest childhood nightmare, however, began near the end of the summer before my 6th grade year.

CHAPTER 2

SWEET HOME ALABAMA

Mom had an interesting childhood. Her mother died when she was a little girl and, in keeping with the times, her father remarried a much younger woman. Even though she had two brothers, a sister and then a half brother, they were not a close knit family and she had it pretty tough.

Dad, though, was the oldest of six and a jack-of-all-trades learned from a father who was a carpenter, farmer and a blacksmith. He was a tall, handsome, Chuck Connors look alike. He was an outstanding baseball player and sang bass in a gospel quartet.

Both Mom and Dad worked hard to earn a living and I believe that Dad's extended absences were just more than Mom could bear. They gradually grew apart and, to them I suppose, divorce was inevitable.

The process started while I was spending the summer in the country with Grandma and Grandpa.

I could tell it was time to head home by all the back to school commercials on television. After insisting that somebody tell me why no one had come to pick me up, I was finally told what was going on and that I'd be living with my grandparents indefinitely. Needless to say, I was devastated. I felt so betrayed by my parents; especially since they hadn't had the courage to tell me themselves.

My sadness evolved to anger and it was intense as I settled into my sixth grade year. I made the most of it but I was bitter about having all of my things tossed away in the ensuing confusion of the divorce and move. I learned to live out of a suitcase.

The homes my grandparents had for the next three years began with a big antebellum house and ended in a housing project with cinder block walls. At some point the farm had to be sold for reasons I never knew.

I was fortunate to be able to have Heidi with me. She was a big dog and intimidated most people by her size. We had a special bond, though, and I was always allowed into her dog house when others couldn't even come into the back yard. When she had a litter of pups I would crawl into the hay with her and snuggle with her and her babies.

I was small by 11 year old standards so athletics were not much of an option. I made one effort at peewee football and played a little basketball with RA's at church but had to realize that my size was too great an obstacle.

I did find success in Scouting and got some surrogate parenting on the side. My Aunt Judy and Uncle Larry still lived at home with my grandparents so I had plenty of adults around to keep me on the straight and narrow there, too.

Mom made a valiant effort to take both Lori and me the next year (seventh grade) but it was short lived and I ended up with my grandparents in Cullman again. At this point I came to feel that I was mostly on my own.

Having mentioned some of my aunts and uncles, it's important to note that they all played a positive part in my adolescent development. Each in their own way made some significant contribution to my character.

Even more important was a gift my Aunt Judy gave me before I learned to swim.

I was playing near the deep end of my Great Aunt Velma's pool while Judy read a book in a lounge chair. She warned me numerous times to be careful as I inched too close to the drop-off and, inevitably, I finally slipped over the edge. Even though she couldn't swim, she dove in and pulled me out.

Although cancer has taken her now, I will never forget how she gave me a second chance at life.

Living in Cullman afforded me the opportunity to get to know almost every paternal relative in my family and that was very special. Conversely, I hardly knew my maternal aunts and uncles and have met those cousins only once or twice in my life.

By the time I was 14, Dad had remarried and both my sister and I went to live with him in Jackson, Mississippi.

My 9th grade year was still junior high (now middle school) in Jackson so I never really was a high school freshman. I must admit that although I looked forward to being a part of a real family again, I hated to have to leave Cullman. I had been selected to be the drum major for the band and was finally coming into my own. I figured I'd just have to go all out in Jackson so that's exactly what I did.

I gave little league baseball a try with very limited success but discovered I had some speed on the track team. Still, my size was a factor so I focused completely on Boy Scouts and band.

I became President of the band and the first drummer ever to letter at Peeples Junior High.

Once again, though, we pulled up our shallow roots and moved.

Dad informed us that we had a choice between Opelika and Decatur, Alabama. I didn't know where Opelika was but I knew that Decatur was close to Cullman! I had friends there and voted for Dad to commute the 30 miles to work. I found out that my vote counted for squat as we moved to Decatur anyway and I lamented being so close to Cullman yet so far.

I gradually came to dislike my stepmother, Carolyn. She adored Dad, though, and that was a small consolation. She was quite vocal about having already raised her child, a step brother (about 10 years older) named George, and not relishing the idea of raising two more. Even though she knew going into their marriage that we were, at least for the short term, a package deal there was little affection.

Over the years she has, perhaps, come to terms with her shortcomings as a step-parent and has mellowed; occasionally calling to inquire as to our well-being following severe weather. We swap Christmas cards but that's really the extent of our relationship today.

Thinking that my 16th birthday would be special, I was in for quite a surprise. Under pressure from my stepmother, Dad informed me that I was expected to get a job. So, I did—two as a matter of fact and I worked my tail off.

A few weeks later, they saw an ad on television describing the symptoms of drug abuse in teenagers and they were convinced that I was a doper. They didn't consider that perhaps I was tired everyday because of my 3:30 am paper route after working at McDonalds until 10 pm the night before.

Dad had a physical problem that gave him almost no tolerance for alcohol. Only three beers could make him intoxicated to the point of appearing drunk. He was a big man and unfortunately, never understood his problem thinking his body could tolerate more alcohol than he truly could. When he had a couple of pops after cutting the grass, we all stood by for the worst and on one such occasion I became his target. He decided to confront me with the revelation shared by Carolyn and him. I denied their accusations as passionately as I could and couldn't help but show my resentment at their suspicion. Dad ended up on top of me on the floor with a fist.

Our little three bedroom house was crammed to the rafters since my stepbrother, along with his wife and baby, had moved in with us and evicted me from my room. George was a lazy, low-life moocher who worked sparingly and mostly laid around the house and stuffed his fat rear end with junk food. Once again I found myself living out of a suitcase and sleeping on a couch.

I was learning the hard way, and my independence would serve me well later in life. I never asked Dad for anything except a place to sleep, up until I left for college. At that point I no longer asked for anything.

Decatur High School was a turning point in my life; for it was there that I gained the confidence that I could do whatever I set my mind to.

High school was a magical time for me.

I knew I had musical talent because the offers began coming in on a regular basis. I played for local Junior Service League productions and an occasional gig at the Redstone Arsenal officers club.

In addition, I became somewhat of a thespian. I enjoyed taking drama class and had roles in both the junior and senior class plays. In one, *A Remarkable Incident at Carson's Corner*, I had the lead as Mr. Kovalesky, the school janitor. I recall a classmate who was looked upon as the class star and how everyone just assumed he would get the lead (including the teacher). We read for parts as a formality and when it was my turn I told her I wanted to read for the lead part. She humored me and let me read. After I read a few lines with my version of an eastern European accent the whole class erupted in cheers and applause and she gave me the part instantly. I joined the International Thespian Society and considered what the future might hold but after high school was never to act again.

Music played such a pivotal role in my development and that was due in no small part to my wonderful band director Mr. Jerry Countryman. He has a unique talent for drawing out the best in his students by insisting on a stubborn perseverance for perfection. He never, ever settled for mediocrity and pushed us to dig deeper than we thought possible.

We were exposed to an incredible range of music from classical to Broadway show tunes and I was fortunate to be able to play both snare drum and timbales in the marching band, a drum kit in our stage band and tympani in concert band.

During his 30 plus years in the public school systems he impacted thousands of young lives in a profoundly positive way. His baton smacked many a rear end as he liberally applied discipline as necessary. He was not quick, however, with a compliment. Regardless of his style, the fact that he was enshrined in the Alabama Bandmasters Hall of Fame speaks for itself.

Although unaware at the time, his example would prove to be of substantial benefit to me in many ways throughout my life. That baton in his "thundering velvet hand" was always pointing me in the right direction.

Our marching band was outstanding and our concert band was remarkable during those years. The Decatur High School band still holds the distinction of having more Superior ratings at state contest than any other high school band in Alabama. I suppose I was getting a pretty good musical reputation and from all appearances, I was becoming a real purveyor of the arts.

Although apparently contradictory, I finally discovered that I had some athletic talent as well.

As I mentioned earlier, I was not the biggest guy in my class. As a little kid playing sandlot football, I found that I sometimes had near "out-of-body" experiences as I ran. Nobody could catch me. Sometimes when I dreamed, I felt that I could, literally, almost fly.

I was the first guy anyone could remember at my school to letter in band and track. I ran the 100 yard dash in 10.2 seconds, the 120 high hurdles in 14.3, the 220 in 22.3 and I high jumped 5 feet 9 inches. When I walked on stage during the athletic awards assembly to get my track letter everybody in band went crazy with applause.

The one moment that stands out the most though, happened the day we were having a meet with Cullman, my old home town. One guy I was racing in the hurdles was Johnny Mitchell. He was a real stud on the football team and I knew he was fast. I was apprehensive about the match-up and flashed back to junior high when I was a runt. I felt good, though, and managed to focus myself. Today they call it being "in the zone". I waxed his tail and won the race. It wasn't even close.

Around that time I began to second guess myself about choosing music over football but it was too late.

There were other activities, too. My junior year Air Force junior ROTC came to my school and of course I jumped right into that. The next year I held the rank of Cadet Captain and was commander of the unit. Lieutenant Colonel Wood and Master Sergeant Ledbetter were great teachers and motivators. It must have shown that I was buying what they were selling because Lieutenant Colonel Wood set me up for an interview for an appointment to the Air Force Academy. My dad and stepmom showed little interest and no confidence during the interview though, leaving the liaison with an impression of ambivalence from my family. My only other option was a shot at an ROTC scholarship, but I chose not to pursue it. It almost seemed like settling for second best.

I loved the uniform and loved to drill. Little wonder I ended up in the military.

My other uniform was that of a Scout. Boy Scouting had been a true refuge for me throughout all the turbulence in my adolescence. Earning the God & Country award and achieving the rank of Eagle Scout helped instill a sense of pride in achievement for hard work.

I developed a love for the outdoors and learned many skills that I still use today. I used to pour over my scout handbook to see what merit badges or awards I could work towards and pursued them with a passion.

Each troop I was in hiked many civil war battlefields throughout the south and I had a vest decorated with the patches, medals and pins from the hikes, camporees and other events. I loved to sit around a campfire at night smelling wood smoke and feeling the warmth of a lightered knot spitting pine pitch into the flames. Eventually I was inducted into the Order of the Arrow, a Boy Scout honor camper society. I went through my initiation ordeal at summer camp and earned my mile swim and Paul Bunyan axman awards there, too.

In between scout camp and band camp, I managed to find time for two summers to attend Ridgecrest, a Baptist retreat in the mountains of North Carolina. Someone had heard me play at church and I ended up with a scholarship to play in the orchestra. I also received a scholarship to play at Glorietta, New Mexico, but couldn't afford to get out there. Unfortunately, the scholarship did not include transportation but the bus ride to North Carolina was relatively inexpensive.

My first experience playing with strings such as violins and cellos was extraordinary. I couldn't believe how beautiful our music sounded. At least one of our performances was recorded and I still have the album. I also have albums of our spring band concerts each year.

It appeared that the die was cast for me to go into music and, even though my best friend, Randy Countryman (the band director's son), had beaten me out for drum major (Mr. Countryman said it was because he was taller) I was thrilled to receive the Carl Schwuchow Memorial Scholarship given to an outstanding senior band member planning to major in music. I don't remember how much it was, just a few hundred bucks, but it helped to supplement the money I'd been saving from my high school jobs.

I graduated from Decatur High School on May 29th, 1972, and later that summer received scholarship offers from the music departments at William Jewell College in Liberty, Missouri and the University of South Alabama in Mobile.

There was one very important factor that influenced my ultimate decision, though. My girlfriend, Kaye, was going to Auburn University to study textile chemistry.

During the summer of '72 I worked for Kaye's dad at Peebles Oil Company, the local Shell Oil distributor owned by Mr. Shine Peebles.

I learned how to break down and move a full fifty five gallon drum, repair gas pumps, use a jackhammer, drive a 5000 gallon gas truck and whatever else Mr. Gosline decided he needed done. He treated me like a son and I loved him and Mrs. Gosline like they were my own folks.

CHAPTER 3

WAR EAGLE

"WHAT COUNTS IS NOT NECESSARILY THE SIZE OF THE DOG IN THE FIGHT. INSTEAD, IT'S THE SIZE OF THE FIGHT IN THE DOG."

President Dwight D. Eisenhower

The fall of '72 found me adjusting to college life fairly easily. I certainly wasn't home sick. I participated to some extent in fraternity rush and got a bid from Theta Xi. They had a great frat house and the guys seemed to be my type but there was no way I could afford it.

My wonderful Uncle Howard had helped me out once more by setting me up for a job with a local Chevron service station. With my savings and my wages I could get by.

Fate was about to intervene at another pivotal point in my life.

Even though I was majoring in music I was *not* in the marching band. I had come down to Auburn for an audition earlier in the year and been tentatively selected. The band director, Doc Walls, told me that more of the seniors than he anticipated had returned for graduate school and he just couldn't (to me it was *wouldn't*) accommodate another freshman drummer. That was his story and he was sticking to it. Obviously I was angry and upset. I was a music major for cryin' out loud! *Strike one.*

Additionally, my percussion instructor tried to get me to change my stick grip and I never could seem to play to his liking. In my humble opinion he was a lousy teacher because I was an above average drummer. All this guy did was ridicule and criticize and I was going to have to spend four years matriculating with him. I was not having fun! *Strike two.*

AUBURN FOOTBALL

In the words of my friend, teammate and fellow walk-on, Thom Gossom, "Some things in life are destined. Auburn didn't choose me. I chose Auburn."

One afternoon, during the first two weeks of fall quarter, I went to watch a freshman football practice. I was fairly unimpressed with what I observed and, basically, said so. My comments were followed by the challenge from a friend "Why don't you try out for the team if you think you can do any better?" I actually had the delusion that I could and the gauntlet was laid down.

The next day I went to see the head freshman coach, Doug Barfield. I walked into his office unannounced and said that I'd like to tryout as a walk-on. Surprisingly his first question was "What position?" I never expected him to ask me that for some reason and I was stumped. I couldn't think of any positions! After a brief silence, I said I was fast and would make a good punt returner. He said he could always use a quick defensive back and then inquired as to where I had gone to high school. When I replied, "Decatur", he said "Weren't you guys state champions last year?" "Yes sir", I said, and if he was having any reservations about giving me a tryout that sealed it. *Strike three.*

It was clear to me that my relationship with the music curriculum was not destined to last, so I decided right then and there that I would change my major to physical education and focus on athletics.

What happened next is hilarious now but was terrifying then.

On my first day of practice I got so much gear I didn't even know how to put it all on. Everything combined must have weighed thirty pounds and I had to watch the other guys in the locker room stuff the pads here and there to figure out where everything went. When we started the warm-up drills, I had no clue how to do most of them and probably looked like an idiot.

As a youngster of 17, I felt the fear and trepidation of preparing to butt heads with grown men 22 and even older. I really was a boy among men.

My learning curve went straight up.

Speaking of straight up, if you've never tried to catch a punted football wearing shoulder pads and a helmet, you can't possibly appreciate how awkward it is. It's much more difficult than it appears and is definitely an acquired skill. Although I was comical, I must have shown some promise because rather than summarily booting me from the team, something prompted Coach Barfield to call the Decatur head football coach, Earl Webb, to inquire about me.

After about two weeks I was called to Coach Barfield's office. He started by telling me that he had called Coach Webb for some information about me and how disappointed he was that I had lied to him about playing for Decatur.

Obviously, Coach Webb (who knew of me from the track team) exposed the fact that I hadn't played for him at all but he must have offered some complimentary remarks about my sprinting abilities.

At that point I quickly reminded Coach Barfield that he had merely asked me "where" I went to school and "Weren't you (we) the '72 state champs"—he never asked me if I *played.*

He paused for a minute and then tried to hide a small grin on his face as he dismissed me from the room.

The truly coincidental thing about this story is that Coach Shug Jordan's Auburn football career started nearly the same way when he watched a practice and then walked-on in 1928.

That first season was brutal.

We practiced for two and a half hours a day in the sizzling sun. Our pads were stinking and heavy; soaked with sweat. Helmets stayed on and chinstraps stayed fastened unless you were on your hands and knees at the spigot during a rare water break.

I received my first broken nose in the Georgia game when I ran onto the field during a brawl without my helmet. I never made that mistake again.

I did make a lot of mistakes, though, as I was constantly reminded by a couple of the scout team coaches who will remain nameless. Their techniques were Neanderthal and they were despised by most of us.

One of their favorite drills was to have a defensive back anticipate the snap of a field goal or extra point attempt by running and jumping onto the nose tackle's back. The tackle would then try to launch us straight up into the air to block the kick. The drill was never used in a game (and is now illegal) but it was great amusement for the coaches. Although the ball was seldom even touched the coaches enjoyed watching the poor soul tumble several feet down to the ground and land in a heap.

One tackling technique, particularly for a smaller player, was to lock-up a ball carrier low around the legs, thus avoiding all the energy from his upper body and a potential stiffarm. Usually this was effective and at least allowed you to slow the man down until help arrived from a linebacker or defensive end.

Lord how I hated to attempt to tackle Dan Nugent. I say attempt because I was seldom successful. He was a big, lumbering, fullback whose running style was to lift his legs like a thoroughbred horse. His thighs were massive and could send an adversary to dreamland if you missed locking him up. To give you an idea of just how big he was, the Washington Redskins drafted him as an offensive lineman!

With all the attention paid to football players being knocked unconscious these days, it's a wonder that many of us from the 70s are still ambulatory and able to speak in complete sentences. That gratitude notwithstanding, I truly can't remember the number of times I awoke in a supine position, inhaling the dank smell of sweat, grass and sometimes blood with the Auburn sky gradually coming back into focus. Those times *were*, however, numerous.

The knockout that many of my teammates and I will probably *never* forget, though, occurred on the practice field one afternoon toward the end of a typical grueling day.

During a first team offense, first team defense scrimmage, Rick Neel was covering a wide receiver down the sideline at full speed. The ball was thrown deep. The receiver was concentrating on the ball and getting open while Rick's attention was on the receiver's eyes. At the point of the catch, both were looking over their shoulders. To those of us on a knee in our little cluster of defensive backs, the anticipation of what was about to occur next was palpable.

Our team trainer, Kenny Howard and Coach Jordan were standing in the general proximity of his golf cart and engaged in conversation with their backs to the playing field. Most eyes were on the football as we shouted encouragement to Rick and began to stand to better see the culmination of the play. As the inevitable unfolded, there was no time to warn of the impending collision. The two players missed Kenny, who barely managed to step aside at the last second, but bored into Coach Jordan's back with the force of a small truck.

Coach Jordan went down hard and didn't move.

We all remember the acreage of those combined practice fields but even with their enormity, the place became as quiet as church.

Kenny attended to Coach Jordan as the assistant coaches regained control and Rick and his cohort trotted back to their respective huddles, stunned and scared. We all were.

With a little help and after a few minutes, Coach Jordan eventually sat up and then made it to the seat of his cart indicating to us that, at least, there was apparently no significant injury.

He was well into his sixties and rumors had already started about his failing health so, clearly, there was unspoken concern about the effects of the blow.

A short time later, just before practice ended, Coach Jordan called the team together and in a serious tone with everyone gathered around him, inquired as to who was responsible for mowing him down. Rick slowly stepped forward, head down and helmet in hand, to accept his fate. Then, as one would expect from a man of such character, Coach Jordan put his arm on Rick's shoulder pads, pulled him close and said "Son, you do that on Saturday, you hear?!" He grinned at us all and that reassurance made us all smile back; especially Rick.

To give another example of how brutal practice could be, one of the scholarship guys, Lee Beeler, had made a tackle and ended up on the bottom of the pile. We heard a blood curdling scream and when the bodies unstacked, discovered his arm was broken in three places. He never played again.

While I don't want to belabor the point, I think it's important for those who've never played the game at this level to have an appreciation for just how tough NCAA Division 1 college football at a major SEC university can be.

In his book *War Eagle, A Story of Auburn Football*, Clyde Bolton refers to us being " . . . as tough as a dollar steak . . ." and then writes the following:

> "It began in spring practice, and players recalled April 22 as a key date. The drill was fundamental that day. The coaches simply put their eleven best offensive players against their eleven best defensive players. The offense had only three plays. For hour after hour, the equivalent of two ball games, the offense ran these three plays. There were no punts, no passes, just ole-timey, nose-bloodying football.
>
> "It was a rotten day," Captain Mike Neel recalled. "I can't remember how long we stayed out, but I remember

how tough it was. After we went through that day, I think the whole team realized we could go through anything."

Those spring ordeals became commonplace, and Auburn's football players grew as hard as their plastic helmets."

That was the spring of my freshman year.

A couple of years before my arrival at Auburn there were two famous players who basically embodied the Auburn spirit—Pat Sullivan (of Heisman Trophy fame) and his favorite receiver, Terry Beasley. Gusty Yearout called out Sullivan to Beasley passes during radio broadcasts with excited frequency every Saturday that they played. Pat went into coaching and Terry . . . well, Terry is another story.

Terry Beasley is permanently disabled from football injuries. He lives on a farm in rural Alabama suffering from short-term memory loss, decreased blood flow to the brain and severe fatigue. His adrenal glands don't work and the right side of his face twitches. He's been diagnosed with congestive heart failure and has had emergency kidney surgery. He is permanently disabled and will never work again due to the vicious blows he took. Even though he suffers the ultimate price for his heroism on the gridiron, Terry doesn't lament the loss. He is a true Auburn hero.

As I alluded to earlier, concussions were my bane. It wasn't until many years later while studying diligently to not only memorize but retain the plethora of procedures necessary to instantly recall as an airline pilot, that it was clear my retention was lacking. There had also been occasional tinnitus (ringing in my ears) and sleeplessness but the memory loss was frustrating. While studies continue regarding the harmful long-term effects of concussions there is little doubt that those minimally protective suspension helmets we wore afforded false confidence that we could hammer away at our opponents with impunity.

In 1972 we beat Alabama 17-16 in one of the most memorable college football games of all time. That was my first Iron Bowl and, although most of us freshmen didn't play, all of us were there. It has become known as the "Punt Bama Punt" game because in the fourth quarter Bill Newton blocked two of Greg Gantt's punts which were returned for touchdowns by David Langner.

The defenses we ran were relatively simple. The "52" defense involved five down linemen who stunted from time to time, two linebackers and four defensive backs (two corners and a strong and free safety) in man to man coverage. The "44" defense was our primary run defense with four down linemen, four linebackers and three defensive backs in a three deep zone. We kept it simple and just won.

Coach Jordan said "I have always hesitated to put one of my teams ahead of any of the others, but today I'm putting this team at the top of the list". This postseason comment is forever etched in the annals of Auburn football.

A SPECIAL TEAM

We finished the season 9-1 and then beat 13th ranked Colorado in the Gator Bowl making us the 2nd team in Auburn history, following the '57 National Championship team, to win 10 games. We were ranked 5th in the nation and Coach Jordan was voted SEC Coach of the Year (for the 3rd time).

Our team was devoid of perceived "stars". We knew each others strengths and weaknesses and learned how to compensate for either. Practice scrimmages were typically the first team offense against the first team defense. It was 20 and 21 power for an hour straight. The coaches would even tell us what play the O was going to run! The collisions were things of legend.

Randy Walls was our quarterback and Terry Henley the primary running back. It was Henley up the middle for 3 and a cloud of dust.

Our first game was in Jackson, Mississippi against Mississippi State. I remember Johnny Simmons' pre-game speech in the locker room. He got tears in his eyes and had us all fired up to the point we were punching the lockers.

All season long David Beverly would launch the most beautiful, high spiral punts you ever saw and our kicker, Gardner Jett, seldom missed splitting the uprights.

In the Tennessee game Coach Jordan told David "I want you to go in there and punt that thing dead on the one yard line!" And what did David do? He punted it dead on the one yard line. As David trotted off the field Coach Jordan said "Now, that's good coaching."

Our only loss came at Baton Rouge where LSU quarterback Bert Jones picked us apart with 3 touch down passes and ran for another score. Even though we lost 35-7, that was probably the defining moment of our season because the coaches reaffirmed that they still believed in us. The entire next week we dressed in shorts and head gear so we could get our legs back under us.

Our final regular season game was against Alabama. We were ranked 9th in the nation with Bama 10-0 and number 2 behind Southern Cal. It was the 37th Iron Bowl.

Just how good was the Crimson Tide?

Alabama had won 3 national championships in the 1960s under Bear Bryant (and later won back-to-back titles in 1978 and '79). They had become not only a perennial contender but a psychological juggernaut as well. It was exceptionally difficult for an opposing team to even *think* that they might stand toe to toe with a team whose predecessors had made their program a thing of legend.

The offense's failure to execute kept us in a hole but the defense repeatedly kept us in the game. Defensive coordinator Paul Davis and my secondary coach Sam Mitchell preached an aggressive defense all week prior to the game. We were determined to live up to Coach Bryant's mantra—"Hit 'em in the mouth then help 'em up and tell 'em you'll be right back."

David Langner, our right corner, layed a lick on wideout Wayne Wheeler the first play of the game. A fight ensued and set the tone for the game.

Bama ran the wishbone which picked apart most defenses but our answer was to have a defender take out one aspect of the triple option. Then it's not a triple option anymore.

Benny Sivley was a great defensive tackle and had few problems taking out the fullback. A defensive end keyed on the quarterback and that left an outside linebacker and corner to cover the pitch man.

Alabama had averaged about 400 yards per game but we held them to about 250. They averaged less than 4 yards per carry.

We held the previously undefeated, number 2 team in the country to two touchdowns (with one blocked extra point by Roger Mitchell) and a field goal. Our offense only generated a field goal but in the 4th quarter the defense got lucky when the Alabama line confused their assignments and allowed Bill Newton to come straight up the middle to block Greg Gantt's punt at the 40 yard line. The ball bounced right into David Langner's arms and he sprinted into the end zone from the 25 yard line and scored.

We had worked all week with a machine that simulated punts using pressurized air to spin rubber wheels. It could be made to spin either way depending upon whether the punter was left or right footed (Gantt was a lefty) and that seemed to make a difference to us punt returners. We never dreamed that anybody would be returning *blocked* punts.

With two minutes left in the game Alabama failed to convert on 3rd down again and lined up to punt. The result was a carbon copy of the first blocked punt. We were actually expecting a fake because Gantt was only lined up

10 yards deep (again) instead of the normal 15. Coach Davis had warned us to watch for a screen or a draw. After that, with time running out, Terry Davis tried to force a pass but Langner picked it off to ice the game. Final score Auburn 17, Alabama 16. Punt Bama punt!

The "Amazin's" as Coach Jordan called us, had no stars on the team. Just 80 or so hard-headed guys that refused to quit and refused to believe we weren't good enough. Sure, we had some prima donnas who liked to think that they carried the team and to this day they still bask in the glory of that season and especially the Bama game. For those few it's all they have to cling to and I feel sorry for them.

To his credit Coach Jordan recognized that we got where we were because of a team effort supported by some excellent coaching. That and the fact that the good Lord smiled on the Auburn football team in 1972.

I would be remiss if I didn't mention one of the, long since departed from, traditions of Auburn football. After the end of the third quarter of all home games, the crowd would stand facing the Confederate flag while the band played Dixie. The cheers were deafening.

The spring of '73 was interesting. Doc Walls, the beloved band director, was finally ready for me to participate in the marching band, starting with our spring game, A Day. I think it came as quite a shock to him that I chose football when he gave me an ultimatum. (Whether they'll admit to it or not, there has always been a rivalry between band directors and football coaches, even in high school.)

Coach Jordan's loyalty was unfailing. Doc's loyalty was not. End of story.

I did continue music to a lesser extent by playing tympani in the university orchestra for a couple of years. It was fun; like music was supposed to be.

I also made my first sport parachute jump that spring. Coach Jordan had rules for his players, intended to prevent needless off-field injuries such as no motorcycle riding and even no wearing of flip flops, so I knew he wouldn't have been thrilled at my new extracurricular activity.

The Auburn University Sport Parachute Club met at the student union building and jumped on weekends at a little place called Society Hill near Tuskegee. Most of my jumps were uneventful . . . with a couple of exceptions.

As a new skydiver, you depend on the jumpmaster to "spot" you. That is, he determines the point at which you should leave the aircraft so as to arrive at the appropriate point in the drop zone. Most of the time the guys did an adequate job but occasionally they misjudged the wind. On one such occasion, I was following the commands with eager anticipation. "Sit in the door." "Get out." "Go!"

I counted to "three one thousand" as the static line performed as expected. I looked up at a good canopy and then down to check my spot. The drop zone wasn't even close! I turned the canopy into the wind and hoped to gain some ground, back in the right direction. No cigar.

I had to make a quick decision as to the *least bad* place to land. There were a lot of trees around and they aren't very accommodating to parachutes and their passengers. I saw a farmhouse with a small area nearby that appeared big enough to land in, so I steered in that direction as I descended. As I got closer, I noticed some lightning rods on top of the farmhouse and knew that I'd come close to them if I proceeded in that direction.

I changed course to the only other clearing in sight where I noticed a power line running from the house to the barn. It didn't matter. I was committed.

Approaching the power line, I pulled my legs up to my chest and thrust them down in an attempt to break it when I made contact. With the kick and my rate of descent, the line broke and I landed safely. Fortunately, the house was abandoned and the electricity was off.

It was a long walk back to the drop zone.

My only other parachuting incident happened when I jumped a high performance canopy for the first time. I was just getting into freefalls and was still doing ten second delays. One of the other jumpers had loaned me a paracommander which had panels cut out in strategic places allowing for greater steering control.

My exit from the plane was uneventful and I had no problem stabilizing in the freefall. I counted to ten and reached for the ripcord.

I neglected to remember that when reaching for the ripcord, you must bring the other hand toward your chest also in order to maintain aerodynamic stability. As the pilot chute deployed, I rolled over onto my back and the suspension lines fed out between my legs.

The canopy was inflating as I continued my freefall going almost feet first.

At the opening shock, the heel of my boot got caught in one of the risers and my leg was jerked up causing my knee to impact my nose.

There I was, with a good canopy, hanging upside down in the harness and blood from my nose running into my eyes. Knowing I couldn't steer and most certainly couldn't land head first, I managed to wiggle my way up to the riser and free my boot. I flopped down into the twisted harness, wiped my nose and couldn't wait to land in the nice, soft pea gravel.

Why did I jump out of airplanes? Lindbergh said it with eloquence:

> "I watched him strap on his harness and helmet, climb into the cockpit and, minutes later, a black dot falls off the wing two thousand feet above our field. At almost the same instant, a white streak behind him flowered out into the delicate wavering muslin of a parachute—a few gossamer yards grasping onto air and suspending below

them, with invisible threads, a human life and man who, by stitches, cloth and cord had made himself a god of the sky for those immortal moments.

A day or two later, when I decided that I, too, must pass through the experience of a parachute jump, life rose to a higher level, to a sort of exhilarated calmness. The thought of crawling out onto the struts and wires hundreds of feet above the earth and then giving up even that tenuous hold of safety and of substance, left me a feeling of anticipation mixed with dread, of confidence restrained by caution, of courage salted through with fear. How tightly should one hold onto life? How loosely give it rein? What gain was there or such a risk?

I would have to pay in money for hurling my body into space.

There would be no crowd to watch and applaud my landing.

Nor was there any scientific objective to be gained. No, there was deeper reason for wanting to jump, a desire I could not explain. It was that quality that led me into aviation in the first place—it was a love of the air and sky and flying, the lure of adventure, the appreciation of beauty. It lay beyond the descriptive words of man —where immortality is touched through danger, where life meets death on equal plane, where man is more than man and existence both supreme and valueless at the same instant."

Lindbergh was right. The adrenaline rush of cheating death each time was exhilarating. I continued to jump until several members of the club sustained sprains or broken bones. Parachuting injuries were not conducive to playing football and I figured I owed it to Coach Jordan to stay healthy.

Skydiving with the Golden Knights

Coach Ralph "Shug" Jordan was as fine a man as I have ever known. I not only learned how to play football with "reckless abandon" but also a lot of those life lessons that we hear so much about coming from sports.

Football players go back to school several weeks before the other students to get ready for the fall season. During that time a group of reporters known in the southeast as the Skywriters, toured all of the SEC schools.

One day, walking off the practice field, I thought I recognized the sports reporter from my home town paper, the *Decatur Daily*. As I walked past I said, "Hey, aren't you Billy Mitchell?" I think he was a little flattered that I had recognized him and he said, "How'd you know?" When I told him I was from Decatur he knew he had a good story. I still have a copy of the article he wrote about the midget drummer who had the nerve to walk-on at a major SEC powerhouse.

I sweated and bled on that practice field for four years with no accolades or recognition whatsoever. It seemed that folks were only interested if you were a "starter". Each year I'd ask myself why I kept on playing and each year the answer was the same. It was hard—harder than anything I had ever experienced but I just couldn't quit. I knew I'd never be an All American. I knew I'd never start. I was happy just to be in the same company with some of those athletes!

On more than one occasion I thought the freshman defensive back coach wanted me to quit. After about a month under his tutelage, he had given me a new nick name, Dammit, because every time he said something to me it started with "Dammit Entrekin!"

I was a full time student and worked evenings after practice at Mr. Bailey's Chevron gas station across from the Sani Freeze. I had just worn myself out between school, work and football and didn't go to practice one afternoon during that first year. Missing practice was an unforgivable sin and it was the excuse that my coach had been looking for to clean out my locker. I had to appeal to the defensive coordinator, Coach Paul Davis, to be reinstated. I always felt I could talk to him and admired him. It was a shame that he didn't succeed Coach Jordan.

Then, I made it to the varsity and . . . let's just tell it like it was. I was no super star. I was a grunt—a guy who played on the scout team just hoping to dress for the game on Saturday and get in for a kickoff coverage or a punt block attempt. We had outstanding defensive backs who never seemed to get hurt.

Our coach was Sam Mitchell. All of us were pretty much cut from the same mold—around five foot nine or ten, 175 to 185 pounds and we were known as "Mitchell's Midgets". It was a moniker we accepted with pride because we *midgets* busted a lot of heads on the gridiron. How did we do it? Physics.

Albert Einstein theorized $E=MC^2$ or energy is mass times acceleration times speed. Whether you refer to it as energy or force or power, it is achieved by mass times acceleration. At a buck eighty five I wasn't going to knock anybody over by mass alone. But give me a running start and I could knock a running back or wide receiver on their butt. During winter workouts when we were timed in the 40, I ran a 4.4 (indoors, in the coliseum, on concrete, wearing Converse All Stars); second on the team behind running back Secedrick McIntyre.

Even today when the subject of my football past comes up, I'll get an occasional condescending comment about my size from an armchair quarterback who never strapped on the pads a day in his life.

For the sake of comparison, Emmitt Smith is 5'9", just like me. I had Walter Payton on a flight once and we stood together talking football for a few minutes and we were eye to eye. I'm not comparing my abilities with either of those two fine players but if we're talking size, we were equals.

It didn't take long for Coach Mitchell to convince me that I had been elevated to a more divine position, too, because his words of encouragement were always preceded by, "Jesus Christ Paul!"

I played much better during my junior and senior year, having been switched from corner to safety, but I still didn't start. I was thrilled just to be on the depth chart behind a guy like Mike Fuller, an All American who went on to play in the NFL for the Chargers and Bengals.

And I was a walk-on. Why buy the cow when you're getting the milk for free? No need to give me a scholarship. They needed cannon fodder and knew I wasn't going to quit.

After the Miami game, we led the nation in total defense allowing a little over 130 yards and 2.5 points per game. Nobody had scored a touchdown on us from scrimmage.

You've probably seen or heard of the iconic football movie *Rudy*, about a guy who played football at Notre Dame at the same time I played at Auburn. Except for the fact that Rudy was only at Notre Dame for two years, the similarities were remarkable and I wept when I saw it because the preponderance of that film is *my* story, too.

My number changed every year and, since I was non-scholarship, I sometimes wasn't even included in the program. I truly don't know what my incentive was or what motivated me but quitting was *never* an option. Perhaps it was because, even then, I knew it was a privilege to play football at Auburn University

My most meaningful reward was that, after four years of sacrifice, Coach Jordan recognized my effort by lettering me my senior year. I vividly remember when he called me into his office and told me to go down to the equipment room to pick up my senior football—a memento that we all received. I was able to keep my helmet, also, due to the fact that it had a crack and it was no longer usable.

Running a close second, though, were the times that I was honored to take my sons to bask in the glory of Auburn football.

Twenty years later, our 1974 team was recognized at half time. Charlie walked onto the field with me during the introduction. I'm not sure what awed him most; the size of the crowd or the size of my teammates.

Our '74 team had finished the season 6th in the nation and had soundly defeated Texas 27-3 in the Gator Bowl. Even the massive legs of running back Earl Campbell couldn't manage a touchdown against the Auburn defense.

In 2002 Auburn had a thirty-year reunion for the 1972 team. Part of the festivities included participating in the "Tiger Walk", a now traditional pre-game procession by the team through thousands of fans from the athletic complex to the stadium. (When we played, it was more of an informal stroll from the athletic dorm, Sewell Hall.) The throng of well-wishers cheer and reach out to touch the players as they make their way to the locker room at Jordan-Hare. Every smiling face and touched hand displayed the sincerity of the Tiger faithful that had supported us so many years before.

We were allowed to bring along a family member so Logan held my hand as we slowly passed by the massive sea of excited, screaming Auburn fans. Our pride swelled as we walked that gauntlet of gratitude.

It was a privilege to play on Coach Jordan's teams. During my four years there, we played in three bowl games and left our mark on Auburn football history.

My personal contribution to Auburn football does not exist in the record books. It only exists in my legacy of persistence, determination and stubborn perseverance.

Coach Jordan didn't letter guys easily and nothing was guaranteed. In fact, the Auburn Athletic Department says today's criteria is much more relaxed than in the Jordan era.

He didn't tell me he was going to do it and I didn't expect it but I beamed when he told me I had lettered. Today it's one of the proudest accomplishments of my life.

What a ride it was.

By the grace of God, I am humble and honored. Both literally and figuratively, I have stood on the shoulders and walked in the shadows of giants. It was great to be an Auburn Tiger.

Auburn football Senior picture

RUSSO

Some of the funniest stories of my Auburn days involved my good buddy Manny Russo. He was my best friend all through college.

Unfortunately, Manny had some serious vision problems that rendered him legally blind. He had a souped-up little Mustang that he eventually had to sell, but he never lost his sense of humor. It was by far the thing that I liked most about him.

He kept me in stitches telling me stories such as the time he and his buddy, Clark, were fishing in a little boat that they had tied to a low-hanging branch. He wondered for several minutes about the humming sound that he heard, but it wasn't until Clark saw the hornets nest that they figured it out. Manny gunned the motor which broke the branch that followed them all the way across the pond . . . nest and all.

At that same pond, Manny and his Aunt Buggii (pronounced Boojie) were catfishing with worms. Manny had laid his pole down for a minute, baited hook and all, when a resident duck proceeded to enjoy the free meal. About that time Manny picked up the pole and made his cast sending that duck out into the pond. He said he eventually just had to cut the line.

My favorite story, though, was the one about his dad relieving himself during a deer hunt. The story goes that while his dad was in that compromising position with his pants and drawers down around his ankles, a buck moseyed along and, while his dad was struggling for his rifle, the buck began trotting away. All the while keeping an eye on Mr. Russo, the buck ran faster and faster until it rammed into a good-sized tree, breaking its neck. I saw that deer's head hanging in the Russo's house.
If it *aint* true, Manny sure spun a good story.

I remember the time that Manny and I were hanging around the dorm one day, bored to tears. As we stared out his window at a nearby oak tree, we both noticed a busy little squirrel going about his business. I looked at Manny and he looked at me and we both knew we were thinking the same thing.

We grabbed a small garbage can, some rope and a bed sheet and off we went. Manny climbed the tree and chased that little sucker all the way to the top.

Realizing that Manny's intentions were serious, the squirrel started back down the tree trunk right for him.

They had a Mexican standoff for a few seconds until the critter faked him out and shot down the tree and up another. Not to be outdone, Manny followed in hot pursuit and cornered the squirrel at the top. Even though that tree must've been fifty feet tall, the squirrel jumped all the way to the ground. I heard him grunt when he hit and couldn't believe that he ran back up the other tree again. Ol' Manny had him figured out by now and was right behind him again. This time the squirrel made a tactical error and went out on a limb. I positioned the garbage can right under the squirrel while Manny bounced on the limb for all he was worth. Eventually the tuckered-out squirrel fell and I caught him. We covered the can with the bed sheet and tied the rope around the top. Next we tried to figure out what to do with one very tired and very agitated squirrel.

We ended up putting him in an old grapefruit crate that somebody got from the grocery store. We kept him a few days and then, after he wouldn't eat, turned him loose.

A few months later we did the whole thing all over again because some of the guys accused us of making it up. I don't think we caught the same one though. He probably moved to Tuscaloosa.

Since I had a composite major/minor in health, physical education and recreation, I diversified my athletic experiences to sports other than just football. I ran intramural track each year and enjoyed some success. Although I was fast, I was nowhere near the likes of some of our track guys. Harvey Glance, for example, ran and medaled in the 1976 Olympics. For a time he replaced Coach Mel Rosen, one of my teachers and one of the all-time greats, as Auburn's Track & Field coach.

I also competed in the intramural powerlift competitions and won my weight class. I could bench press 280, squat 380 and dead lift 500 pounds.

Although I worked part-time at school, the bulk of my financial resources were earned during my summers off. When I reflect on those days, I find it hard to understand how I made it through college in only four years. The overloaded combination of academics, athletics and a part-time job was a recipe for failure.

Even though Mr. Gosline was kind enough to keep a job open for me, I needed desperately to maximize my earnings and, in 1975, a business associate of my dad's gave me a good job at a truck stop as a dispatcher for his trucking agency in Birmingham.

I learned some valuable lessons in that filthy place while dealing with some pretty rough characters. I came to understand that doing my best to take care of the drivers earned their respect and they, in kind, took care of me.

Dan Sivley took a chance in giving so much responsibility to a college kid but it paid off in spades for him. He made record profits while I was there and, before I left for school, Dan had a small dinner party for me at a swank restaurant where he gave me a plaque that read "For Paul, Summer of '75, He has done so much with so little for so long, now he can do nearly anything with nothing at all." I was truly touched by Dan's gratitude and remained in touch with him for several years after. In fact, he was the one who planted the seed for me to become a "gyrene jet jockey".

During my senior year, I did a lot of instructing. I suppose that was good preparation for a future leader.

I taught a mountaineering course called "Wilderness Skills" which included introductions to climbing, rappelling, orienteering and the like. We usually went up to Cheaha mountain in the Talladega national forest.

I also taught a beginners swimming course where I met my future wife, Julie.

My final student-teaching experience took place back at my old high school in Decatur and it truly ended with a flourish.

In addition to classroom teaching I did some assistant coaching as well.

On the sideline one night during a home game with our cross town rival, Austin, I watched as a player tackled our quarterback, Benny Perrin, out of bounds no more than five yards from me. The closest official, who had turned his back to the players after they went out of bounds, didn't see the late hit. The official was about two feet from me and I hadn't moved at all. He was marking the spot with his foot on the sideline as I spoke to him. I didn't shout but in a conversational tone said, "Hey ref, did you see that?" I don't know what his problem was but he instantly threw a flag and called unsportsmanlike conduct on the bench; *me*! Of course Coach Webb went ballistic claiming that I wasn't even *really* a coach.

He never bothered to ask me what happened and it didn't matter at the time because the penalty was enforced anyway.

We won the game and on Monday morning I was called to the principal's office and was told that the superintendent wanted to see me right away. He was very upset about the penalty on Friday night but I figured that if I had an opportunity to explain what had really happened (and the game film would back me up) he would understand.

Unfortunately the superintendent never gave me an opportunity to say a word but proceeded to berate me for a few minutes telling me he would make sure I never taught in Decatur or anywhere else in the state if he could prevent it.

Although I harbored resentment toward him for years, I eventually came to realize that he really did me a favor.

Despite whatever power he may have thought that he had, I graduated anyway knowing that I could teach in the future on my own terms, not his. For me, high school was no place for a new teacher fresh out of college anyway. The hours were long; 7am to 7pm. All for the meager sum of $13,000 a year which included the coaching supplement.

After graduation, with time to totally reassess my life, I drove a forklift on the graveyard shift at a chemical company for a few weeks before answering an ad in the paper for an insurance job. It seemed like a respectable career so I proceeded to sell life insurance like it was going out of style. I sold over a million dollars worth for Metropolitan but hated the day to day office grind. I had always said I'd never have a job where I was stuck in an office and forced to wear a tie.

There was no team spirit among the agents. In fact, there was no team. It was every man for himself. Forget esprit.

Once again, it was no place for an ambitious kid fresh out of college.

CHAPTER 4

SEMPER FI

"TO BE A MARINE PILOT IS TO BE THE CHOSEN OF
THE CHOSEN."

Once again fate intervened.

In Birmingham, my future wife, Julie, and I had gone to visit her roommate from Auburn, Lynn DeShazo. Her roommate's dad, unknown to me, was a lieutenant colonel in the Marine Corps reserve. The girls were off to themselves which afforded an opportunity for some conversation with Lynn's dad. During the small talk he asked me what I planned to do with my life. Hearing that I had no particular direction, he inquired as to whether I had given any thought to the military. I said no but that if I ever did, I'd only be interested in the Marines. Still sandbagging me, he inquired as to why. I proceeded to tell him of my grandfather's exploits in Haiti in the 1920s and how he had won the Navy Cross* and that my dad and uncles had all been in other services. I told him of how I had promised Grandpa as a child that I would join the Marines and be like him.

While he was grinning, he pulled a business card from his wallet and said, "You need to talk to this man." That man was Captain Tony Gain who became my Officer Selection Officer (OSO) and started me on my military career. I'll be forever indebted to Lieutenant Colonel Tom DeShazo for his guidance.

Captain Gain sent Staff Sergeant Young up to Decatur to give me a battery of tests within a few days of my call. Having made some prerequisite score, he asked if I'd be interested in taking the aviation tests as well. After I stupidly said I had "no interest in the Air Force", he smiled and assured me that the

Marines had aircraft, too. Feeling rather foolish, I said I'd like to take the tests and found that they were relatively simple. The next thing I knew, I was in Birmingham raising my right hand to be sworn in with an aviation guarantee, provided I could make it through the flight physical and OCS, Officer Candidates School.

> *His citation reads: "For extraordinary heroism in the line of his profession in Haiti, May 19, 1920. With total disregard of personal danger he attacked, with Captain Jesse L. Perkins, and two other enlisted men, a band of about seventy five armed bandits of the Mirebalis District, resulting in the death of the greatest bandit leader, Benoit Batraville, and the practical suppression of banditry throughout the District."

That brief description doesn't do justice to the significance of Grandpa's achievement, so let me give you a quick history lesson.

Sometime during 1919 in Haiti, Charlemagne Massena Peralte was in control of a rebel army of Cacos. To assist the Haitian government with regaining control of the countryside, the Second Marine Regiment of the First Marine Brigade was sent there along with a detachment from Squadron E flying seven Curtiss HS-2s and six Curtiss Jennies.

Shortly after their arrival, two recon Marines and a gendarme (a Haitian government soldier) got past six Caco outposts and into Charlemagne's camp where they killed him. The Marines lashed his body across a mule and packed him down to the city of Cap Haitien. Benoit Batraville took his place.

On 14 January, 1920, Batraville infiltrated three hundred men into Port-au-Prince. By the morning of the 15th, sixty six were dead and twice that many wounded. Over three thousand Cacos eventually surrendered during January and February but Batraville would not concede.

Marine pilots were experimenting with bombing by dropping them out of mail sacks tied to their landing gear spreaders. Eventually they had bomb racks and achieved good accuracy at forty five degree dive angles. In March, two Marine aircraft caught Batraville on a hilltop near Mirebalais and drove him into the gunfire of the converging Marine ground patrol. Batraville escaped but lost two hundred more men. On 4 April, 1920, Batraville ambushed a Marine patrol and, later, ceremonially ate the heart and liver of the lieutenant in charge. Word made its way back to the Marines who were then, more than ever, anxious to seek out and destroy the enemy. A few weeks later he had the misfortune of making the acquaintance of my grandfather and his patrol which put the kibosh on him, banditry and the revolution.

THE PHYSICAL

The physical at Maxwell Air Force Base in Montgomery was quite an ordeal. I was so apprehensive that the corpsman checking my blood pressure said there was concern. It was right on the border. When I asked how close, he said "About like Laredo." That scared me even more.

The next thing that happened involved the vision tests. I was told that my eyes had to be dilated and have a certain number of drops in each one at a precise interval. Now, I don't know very much about eyeballs, but I do know that two different corpsmen were giving me too many drops and by the time I was tested I almost couldn't see anything! I ended up having to get a civilian ophthalmologist to verify my vision which turned out to be twenty/ten in both eyes.

Even though my appearance was rather scraggly (I had an awful looking beard at the time), Captain Gain somehow saw through all the hair. With my scuba diving, parachuting and outdoors background, not to mention some pretty glowing references from Dan Sivley (also a former Marine), Mr. Gosline and Lieutenant Colonel DeShazo, I was found to be "air droppable and stream fordable".

In seven months I would experience one of the most glorified and heralded, cursed and dreaded rituals that a man could endure—United States Marine Corps Officer Candidates School.

OCS

The cowards never showed up. The weak left. Only the strong remained.

On October 3, 1977, I reported to Officer Candidates School at Quantico, Virginia referred to as "the land that God forgot . . . where the mud is eighteen inches deep and the sun is blazing hot."

My greeting at Washington National airport was unforgettable and it seemed that I got little or no sleep for the next few days.

We were hustled into formation and soon came to believe that we all probably were "slimy civilians".

I learned to eat faster than any creature known to man. To this day I still get accused of eating too fast. We did everything on the double. We could also get into and out of the shower (or "rain room") almost without getting wet. Our toiletry habits were colorfully described in *The Tumbling Mirth* by J. Douglas Harvey:

>   " . . . A long row of sinks was topped by a very narrow shelf where you could lay your razor, toothbrush and so on. Above the shelf was an equally long and very

thin continuous mirror that stretched the length of the room. In the early morning traffic jam, every basin was occupied and there was a line of frantic guys jostling for position. Time was of the essence . . .

During inspection, a French-Canadian guy was asked, "Did you shave this morning?" He put his hand to his chin, rubbed it and said, "I taught I 'ad sir, but der were so many face in d'mirror dat I might 'ave shave somebody else!"

I felt sympathy for those who, in all the commotion, had forgotten their left from their right. "That's your right foot, maggot", Staff Sergeant Winger said as he stomped on it. "It's the one that hurts!"

I learned to do the Marine Corps "daily seven" (calisthenics) and do them in a way that pleased Sergeant Mellinger, my sergeant instructor.

I learned to starch a cover. (The army wears hats—Marines wear covers.) And I learned to fire, disassemble and clean an M-16A1 rifle and every piece of 782 or "deuce" gear that was issued.

To say that Marine Corps boot camp is the challenge of a lifetime is an understatement.

Although playing football at Auburn was both mentally and physically challenging (and I had even played some semi-pro ball with a Decatur area minor league team) I was not prepared for the constant barrage involved in the Marines "breaking down" process. No one is. Their philosophy was to reduce each individual to his lowest point by whatever means and then gradually build him into a Marine. All the while they were analyzing us to determine our character and grit. The scrutiny for officers was exceptionally so. It was easy to tell early on who had it and who didn't.

I remember one kid whose dad was the friend of some congressman. He was a slacker and we disposed of him (with some guidance from our platoon sergeant) by tossing him down a ladderwell (stairway) in a wall locker. His broken leg landed him in casual platoon where he soon submitted his DOR (dropped on request).

On December 16th, Dad pinned the gold bars of a second lieutenant on the shoulders of my winter service alpha uniform. It was a proud day for us both.

After a couple of weeks on leave, I was assigned to report to The Basic School in January.

The oath of a Marine officer:

> *I do solemnly swear*
> *That I will support and defend the Constitution of the*
> *United States of America against all enemies foreign*
> *and domestic;*
> *That I will bear true faith and allegiance to the same;*
> *That I take this obligation freely, without any mental*
> *reservation or purpose of evasion;*
> *That I will well and faithfully discharge the duties of the*
> *office on which I am about to enter*
> *So help me God.*

THE BASIC SCHOOL

TBS was much more low key and with an aviation guarantee in my pocket, I didn't have to compete with my classmates for an MOS (military occupational specialty).

During the time that I had been planning a Marine Corps career, my high school sweetheart, Kaye, had grown impatient with me. She would have liked nothing better than for me to continue to sell insurance and settle down in Decatur. When

I chose the Marine Corps she felt that I had excluded her and she soon sent me a "Dear John" letter. I philosophized that perhaps the Corps was right. If they had wanted me to have a wife they would have issued me one.

Realizing that for the next six years, at least, I would have a roof over my head and three square meals a day, I decided to invest in my first new car, a 1978 "captain blue" Jeep Cherokee Chief. It's been repainted and restored but I still have it.

Upon graduation from TBS I was "stashed" at Camp Upshur working with PLC (platoon leaders class) candidates who were college juniors. My duties as Camp Commandant primarily consisted of insuring that the roadside was kept clear of trash.

I was next attached to my former OSO, now Major Gain, for recruiting duty. That involved cruising some of the southeast and gulf coast college campuses in his corvette. We became fast and lifelong friends during that time. One little episode almost did us both in, however.

While in Panama City, after a full day of recruiting, he and Gunny Hamilton and I had gone to an early happy hour at a place called the Treasure Ship. We were quite the heroes in our sharp uniforms and ended up staying rather late. Since we had been so well received by the locals, not to mention having had several of their well known "fertility drinks", we decided it would be appropriate to leave them with a fond memory. On our departure, after stepping outside the front door momentarily, we backed in and "dropped trou" (meaning we mooned 'em). Our little prank was received with thunderous applause and laughter.

They loved us . . . or so we thought.

Unfortunately, not everyone found humor in our debauchery. Somebody with friends at Headquarters Marine Corps was not amused and passed the word all the way to Washington. By the time it got back down to the colonel in charge of the district, he was ready to fry us. He called Tony to his office in Atlanta and inquired as to his knowledge of the situation.

Tony explained that he was the senior man involved and therefore accepted full responsibility. He wouldn't implicate the Gunny and me no matter what.

I think the colonel was so impressed with Tony's loyalty, he settled for a good butt chewing. Shortly thereafter, he presented Tony a medal for being the best OSO in the country.

———◦◦◦———

"In the beginning was the Word, and the Word was God. In the beginning was God—all else was darkness and void, and without form. So God created the heavens and the earth. He created the sun and the moon and the stars so that light might pierce the darkness. And the earth God divided between the land and the sea, and these He filled with many assorted creatures.

And the dark, salty, slimy creatures that inhabited the murky depths of the oceans, God called sailors, and He dressed them accordingly.

And the flighty creatures of the air, He called airmen. And these He clothed in uniforms that were ruffled and fowl.

And the lower creatures of the land, God called soldiers. And with a twinkle in His eye and a sense of humor that only He could have, God gave them trousers too short, and covers too large, and pockets to warm their hands. And to adorn their uniforms, God gave them badges. And He gave them cords and he gave them ribbons . . . and patches . . . and stars . . . and bells. He gave them emblems . . . and crests . . . and all sorts of shiny things that glittered . . . and devices that dangled.

And on the seventh day, as you know, God rested. And on the eighth day at 0730, God looked down upon the earth and was not happy . . . God was not happy!

So He thought about His labors, and in His infinite wisdom, God created a divine creature and this He called a Marine. And these Marines, whom God created in His own image, were to be of the air, the land, and the sea. And these He gave many wonderful uniforms.

He gave them practical fighting uniforms so that they could wage war against the forces of Satan and evil.

He gave them service uniforms for their daily work and training, that they might be sharp and ready.

And He gave them evening and dress uniforms. Sharp, stylish, handsome things so that they might profile with the ladies on Saturday night and impress the hell outta everybody!

And at the end of the eighth day, God looked down upon the earth and saw that it was good. But was God happy? No! God was still not happy! Because in the course of His labors, He had forgotten one thing . . . He did not have a Marine uniform! But He thought about it and thought about it and, finally, satisfied Himself in knowing that, well, not everybody can be a Marine."

Author unknown

Blasphemous attempt at humor aside, for my tenure as a parent I've attempted to instill character in my children. As it says in the dedication to this book, it's primarily written for them. No path in my walk through life has done as much to instill character as that time that I've spent as a Marine.

On Leadership and Marines:

*If you're riding at the head of the herd, look back every
   now and then and make sure it is still there.*
Never enter an hour-long gunfight with 5 minutes of ammo.
There are three types of leaders:
*Those who learn from reading, those who learn from
   observation and those who still have to touch the
   electric fence to get the message.*

> *Anything worth shooting is worth shooting twice. Ammo is cheap.*
>
> *I like the fact that if you are a self-declared enemy of America, we will locate, close with and destroy you. Running into a Marine unit in combat is your worst nightmare and your health record is about to get a lot thicker or be closed out entirely.*
>
> *I like the fact that most civilians don't have a clue what makes us tick. And that's not a bad thing. Because if they did, it would scare the hell out of them.*
>
> *I like the fact that we're a brotherhood of warriors, not a fraternal organization, and that we're in the butt-kicking business. Unfortunately, today business is good and our message to our foes is, and always has been, "We own this side of the street. Threaten my country or our allies and we will come over to your side of the street, burn your hut down, secure your heart beat and whisper in your ear "Can you hear me now?"*

I like being a Marine and being around Marines.

A DIFFERENT KIND OF LEADER

For my sons in particular, Charlie and Logan, I hope I impart some wisdom regarding my own philosophies on leadership that you will find of value in the future.

Excellence isn't always what preceeds success. Often times what does is a talent for maneuvering; pleasing your superiors or choosing a powerful mentor and riding his coattails. *Followers* don't usually take risks like questioning how things are done or try to effect change. They don't question authority.

I guarantee that you will encounter people like this and find yourself in environments where conformity is rewarded above all.

Moreover, the world is full of technocrats—people trained to be exceptionally good at one specific thing. They have no interest in anything beyond their isolated area of expertise. Be a renaissance man. Think for yourself. Be a visionary. If you can think for yourself you will have the confidence and the moral courage to stand up for what you believe and espouse your ideas even when they aren't popular; even when they don't please your superiors.

True leadership means being able to think for yourself and act on your convictions.

Thinking means concentrating on one thing long enough to develop an idea about it; not memorizing *other* people's ideas. To think you must concentrate, gather your thoughts and focus.

When you have questions or doubts, confront them directly. The answers to most of your dilemmas are introspectively found within—not from social media or peers.

When one continuously exposes oneself to social media in particular you're being inundated with a stream of other people's thoughts; conventional wisdom.

Emerson said "He who should inspire and *lead* his race must be defended from traveling with the souls of other men, from living, breathing, reading, and writing in the daily, time-worn yoke of their opinions."

Leadership often means finding a new direction.

What I suggest should not be taken as a directive to be alone. To the contrary, seek counsel and allow yourself the vulnerability to have long, individual, introspective conversations with close friends. That will help you to discover what you believe in your heart and soul as you articulate your thoughts and feelings out loud. Your 1568 *Facebook* friends don't count.

I refer to your handful of true friends like the ones I have in Steve Bacon, Tony Gain and Howard Smith.

Will you have the guts to do what's right? Think now about morality. Don't wait for the time that you'll have to make a split second decision that could determine whether or not you or others will live or die.

A leader is ultimately, intensely solitary. You are the one who has to make the tough call and all you really have is yourself.

Former Commandant of the Marine Corps, General Charles Krulak, addressed a graduating class at Pepperdine University and spoke on the subject of character. These are some of his words:

> "I can tell you from personal experience that combat is the most traumatic human event. It strips away an individual's veneer, exposing their true character. If a character flaw exists, it will appear in combat—guaranteed.
>
> This morning I will tell the story of an American who's true character was tested and exposed in the crucible of war. I will then draw some conclusions that are applicable to how the rest of us should live our lives . . . lives where combat will, hopefully, never play a role.
>
> He was a nineteen year old Marine—about the same age as most of you in the audience this morning. His name was Lance Corporal Grable. He was a man of courage, a man of character . . . and this is his story.
>
> Vietnam . . . it was 0600, the third of June, 1966. I was in command of "A" Company, Second Battalion, First Marine Regiment.
>
> I was a first lieutenant at the time and had been given this command because the previous commander had been killed about one week earlier. My company had been given a simple mission that began with a helicopter assault. We would land in a series of dried up rice paddies about six football fields in length and three

football fields in width. These paddies were surrounded by jungle-covered mountains with a dry stream bed running along one side.

We were supposed to land, put on our packs and do what all Marines do: find the largest mountain and climb to the top. There we would put ourselves into a defensive perimeter and act as the blocking force for an offensive sweep conducted by two battalions.

The helicopters landed, unloaded my company of Marines and had just started to leave when the world collapsed. Automatic weapons, mortar fire, artillery—it was hell on earth.

Fortunately, a good portion of my company had managed to move into the dry stream bed where they were protected from most of the fire.

However, one platoon had landed too far west to move immediately to the cover of the stream bed.

As they tried to move in that direction, the fire became so heavy they had no alternative but to hit the deck. One particular squad found itself directly in the line of fire of a North Vietnamese heavy machine gun.

In a matter of seconds, two Marines were killed and more were seriously wounded.

As I watched what was happening from my position in the stream bed, I knew that it was just a matter of time before that machine gun would systematically "take out" that whole platoon—squad by squad. If I didn't act immediately, they would be lost in just a matter of minutes. I made a call to the commander of the first platoon that had made its way into the stream bed, directing him to move up the stream bed so he could attack across the flank of the gun position—not having to assault it directly from the front.

At the same time, I directed another platoon to provide suppressing fire that might diminish the volume of fire coming from the machine gun position. All this was happening in the midst of smoke, multiple explosions, heavy small arms fire and people yelling to be heard over the din of battle.

Suddenly, my radio operator grabbed me by the sleeve and pointed toward the middle of the rice paddy where a black Marine—a lance corporal by the name of Grable—had gotten to his feet, placed his M-14 on his hip and charged the machine gun, firing as fast as he could possibly fire. He ran about forty meters directly toward the machine gun and then cut to the side, much like a running back might do during a football game. Sure enough, the machine gun, which had been delivering heavy fire on his squad, began firing at Grable.

Seeing the fire shift away from them, the squad moved immediately to the cover of a small rice paddy dike. They and the other two squads were able to drag their casualties to a position of safety behind this dike.

Grable didn't look back. He didn't see what happened. He kept on fighting and dodged back and forth across these paddies, firing continuously. He would run out of ammunition, reload on the run and continue forward—dodging back and forth as he ran.

BAM! Suddenly he was picked up like a dishrag and thrown backward—hit by at least one round.

The rest of the platoon charged. My radio operator grabbed me again.

Saying nothing, he just pointed to the middle of the rice paddy.

That young Marine—Lance Corporal Grable—had gotten to his feet.

As he stood, he didn't put the rifle to his hip; he locked the weapon into his shoulder, took steady aim—good sight picture, good sight alignment—and walked straight down the line of fire into that machine gun.

About four minutes later, my command group and the rest of the unit finally arrived at the, now silent, machine gun position. There were nine dead enemy soldiers around the gun . . . Lance Corporal Grable was draped over the gun itself.

As only Marines can do, these battle-hardened young men tenderly picked up Grable and laid him on the ground. When they opened his flack jacket, he had five massive wounds from that machine gun.

FIVE . . .

About seven months later, I traveled back to Headquarters Marine Corps in Washington and watched the Commandant of the Marine Corps present Lance Corporal Grable's widow with the nations second highest decoration for valor—the Navy Cross. In this woman's arms was the baby boy that Grable had only seen in a Polaroid picture.

Grable displayed great physical courage. Somewhere in his character was another kind of courage as well—moral courage—the courage to do the right thing. When he had the chance to do something else, he chose to do the right thing.

His squad was in mortal danger. He had a choice to make and he did what was right, at the cost of his life. Let me remind you, this was 1966. Grable was a black Marine from Tennessee who couldn't even buy a hamburger at the McDonalds in his home town.

Grable . . . moral courage . . . personal courage . . . character . . .

So, what of your character? Who are you? No, not the way you look in the mirror or in photographs . . . but who are you, really? What do you stand for? What is the essence of your character? Where is your moral compass pointing? Which course do you follow?

Everyday we have to make decisions. It is through this decision making process that we show those around us the quality of our character.

The majority of the decisions we have to make are "no brainers". Deciding what we are going to have for breakfast is not going to test your character . . . judgment maybe, but not character.

The true test of character comes when the stakes are high, when the chips are down, when your gut starts to churn, when the sweat starts to form on your brow, when you know the decision you are about to make may not be popular . . . but it must be made. That's when your true character is exposed.

The associations you keep, the peers you choose, the mentors you seek and the organizations you affiliate with all help to define your character. In the end you will be judged as an individual, not as part of a group.

Success in combat and in life has always demanded a depth of character. Those who can reach deep within themselves and draw upon an inner strength, fortified by strong values, always carry the day against those of lesser character.

Moral cowards never win in war. Moral cowards never win in life. They believe that they are winning a few battles here and there, but their victories are never sweet. They never stand the test of time and they never serve to inspire others. In fact, each and every one of a moral coward's "supposed victories" ultimately leads them to failure.

Those who have the courage to face up to ethical challenges in their daily lives will find that same courage can be drawn upon in times of great stress, times of great controversy, in times of the never-ending battle between good and evil.

All around our society you see immoral behavior . . . lying, cheating, stealing, drug and alcohol abuse, prejudice and a lack of respect for dignity and the law.

In the not too distant future, each of you is going to be confronted with situations where you will have to deal straight-up with issues such as these. The question is, what will you do when you are? What action will you take? You will know what to do—the challenge is will you DO what you know is right?

It takes moral courage to hold your ideas above yourself. It is the DEFINING aspect of your character.

When the test of your character and moral courage comes, regardless of the noise and confusion around you, there will be a moment of inner silence in which you must decide what to do. Your character will be defined by your decision and it is yours and yours alone to make. I am confident you will each make the right one."

The United States Marine Corps is the only U.S. military service that recruits men to *fight*.

The Army emphasizes individual development. "Be all that you can be"—"An Army of one".

The Navy promotes adventure and sight-seeing. "It's not just a job . . ."—"Let the journey begin".

And the Air Force promises a good career. "It's a great way of life".

All recruit for the peace time military.

Consider the Marine's Hymn. Yes, a hymn—not a song. It focuses on why the Marines exist. "We *fight* our country's battles", "First to *fight* for right and freedom", "We have *fought* in every clime and place", "We've *fought* for life and never lost our nerve".

War fighting; that's what the Marine Corps is all about.

Now consider the Army's "Caisson Song"—a pleasant jaunt over hill and dale. Or the Navy's song "Anchors Aweigh"—espousing the joys of sailing. And, of course, the "Air Force Song" is full of lyrics about pretty blue skies and engine noise.

It's a clear choice. Join the Navy to go to far away ports of call. Join the Army to go to adventure school. Join the Air Force to go to high tech school. Join the Marines to go to war.

Army, Navy and Air Force recruits are soldiers, sailors or airmen as soon as they sign on the dotted line. Marine recruits are not called Marine until they earn the right to claim the title.

Ask a member of another service to recount some glorious tradition of their branch and you'll probably be greeted with a blank stare. Ask a young Marine the same question and he'll regale you with the exploits of Belleau Wood. He'll tell you how the Marines charged a superior number of well-entrenched Germans across an open field and into history as "Devil Dogs".

Every Marine who ever lived is living still; because the Corps lives on.

THE TUESDAYS

I was very apprehensive about starting flight school having reviewed all of our programmed texts during the summer after TBS. I knew that I didn't have the background necessary by the difficulty I had with them, but I was in Pensacola now and determined to give it my best shot. Prior to my AI (Aviation Indoctrination) class, every student was required to take *and pass* a battery of inventory pre-tests. Unfortunately, I didn't know a logarithm from a luggage rack.

For some unknown, wonderful reason, beginning with my class the tests were still given but *passing was not required.* Our classes consisted of aerodynamics, engineering, navigation and such. For a very intense period of a few weeks I went to class, ate and then came back to my BOQ (Bachelor Officer Quarters) room and studied. It was almost as though I entered a Zen-like state of detachment because when it was over and I snapped out of it, I had absolutely no recollection of anything . . . and I had passed!

"SOMEBODY'S PRAYIN'
I CAN FEEL IT
SOMEBODY'S PRAYIN' FOR ME
MIGHTY HANDS ARE GUIDING ME
TO PROTECT ME FROM WHAT I CAN'T SEE

LORD, I BELIEVE
LORD, I BELIEVE
SOMEBODY'S PRAYIN' FOR ME"

Those are words from a Ricky Skaggs song that bear a great deal of meaning for me. There have been a few times in my life that it has been crystal clear I have experienced divine intervention. This is in no small way due to the efforts of a Ft. Lauderdale ladies prayer group known as the "Tuesdays". Julie's mom was a member of the group which met every Tuesday to intercede for those in need. I had met most of them at one time or another and they were quite a bunch. Educated, witty and caring, they prayed for me for a long time and I'm quite sure that I made it through AI thanks to their prayers.

There were other challenges beyond academics, not the least of which was water survival training, and some of it was actually fun.

There are several teaching aides designed to simulate the types of emergency situations that naval aviators might encounter. The dilbert dunker, helo dunker and parachute entanglement devices (all made famous in the movie *An Officer and a Gentleman*) were but a few.

My biggest challenge was the mile swim, a mandatory prerequisite for pilots.

Although I was able to swim a mile as a Boy Scout, this was different. We were wearing flight suits and boots. My body fat has always been low so I don't have much natural buoyancy. Actually, I float like a rock. Being the *enterprising* young man that I was, however, I managed to come up with a little assistance. By renting the lower half of a wet suit at a local dive shop and slipping into it under my flight suit, I was able to generate just enough flotation to enable me to do the swim.

Sometimes I think we were tested on our creativity and problem solving skills as much as anything else. Improvise, adapt, overcome.

Our final physical at NAMI, the (now closed) Naval Aerospace Medical Institute, was no cake walk either. There we experienced some of the most exotic medical tests known. It wasn't exactly like some of the comedic astronaut physicals in the movie *The Right Stuff,* but it was close.

The closest I came to being NPQ'd (found "not physically qualified") was having a Doc notice that my nose was not quite straight. "Deviated septum", he said as he walked down a line of us in our skivvies. Some guys were reduced to tears as he just arbitrarily said "NPQ'd" for some minor thing he noticed either on their body or in their medical jacket. Generally, there was no appeal. His word was final. "How'd you break that nose", he asked as he held a pencil along its length. "Auburn football, sir", I said figuring that I was about to become a casualty. He grinned and said, "War Eagle" and walked on. Another opportunity to be attrited from the program had been averted. Somebody *up there* had determined that I was going to be a pilot.

Speaking of attrition, I was told that it was broken down something like this. Of the initial officer candidate applicants 30% failed the entrance exams, 20% attrited from OCS, 20% were failed physically and 20% were attrited from training for academic/flight failures. They told us that if we got our wings we were in the *top 10%* of young men in our age group in this country. That was pretty good company.

JULIE ROSS

By this time, Julie was attending the University of South Alabama just a short drive away in Mobile. We had been seeing each other regularly (since Kaye gave me the "deep six") due to the fact that she was living in the Triangle, Virginia area while I was at Quantico. Julie lived in a mobile home with her dog, Punkin, and was trying to find work as a rehabilitative counselor with the aid of contacts from some local friends of her family. The winters were hard and the job market was soft so she decided to go back to school to become a physical therapist. USA had an excellent PT school and it was close to Pensacola. On weekends we got together to share our experiences and talk about life and the future. We had become best friends and at that point in my life I saw no need to continue looking for the right mate. I prayed a little, talked to Dad and ultimately decided she was a great choice for a wife. I was elated when I asked her to marry me and she said yes. So, in March, I went with her to Ft. Lauderdale to ask her folks permission.

That scenario, itself, was comical.

I was trying to be casual but sincere as we sat and chatted in the living room with Julie's parents. Being a southern gentleman, it was imperative that I properly ask for Julie's hand. When the time was right, I led into my well-rehearsed dissertation. Mrs. Ross had astutely figured out where I was going and listened intently on the edge of her chair. Mr. Ross, however, was casually reading his newspaper and nodded politely from time to time, pretending he was interested. When Mrs. Ross could take no more, she interrupted and scolded Mr. Ross saying, "Julian, will you *please* pay attention to the young man! This is *rather* important!"

When I asked for their blessing Mr. Ross nodded his head and grunted something that sounded affirmative and Mrs. Ross went off on some soliloquy of her own, eventually saying that she thought it was wonderful. I was about to turn blue.

FLIGHT TRAINING

The next big step took place on May 29th, 1979, when I had my first training flight. Upon reaching that phase of training, I knew I wanted to be a pilot for the rest of my life. I absolutely loved it. Even the smell of jet fuel exhaust and the musty odor of the seats got into my blood. It was an evocative scent; a distinct mix of oil, metal, fuel, fabric and sweat.

I quickly learned the pilot's art of compartmentalization: the ability to concentrate on the task at hand and not dwell on or drift back to distractions.

My biggest initial obstacle was the grief I took from my on-wing instructor, Captain Tom Stanmore. He went crazy when I spoke on the radio with my slow southern drawl and threatened to give me a below average grade in communications procedures if I didn't change. I suppose that's why today I have very little accent . . . unless I want to.

In less than a month my training was interrupted by Major John Fogg (later to become the mayor of Pensacola) who informed me by message that my father had died of a heart attack.

I went home for a short time, saluted Dad smartly in my dress blues and proceeded to do what I knew he would have wanted.

Having been an Army Air Corps cadet himself when the war ended, I knew he truly wanted me to get my wings. When friends would ask "How's that boy of yours doin' in the Marines?" Dad's standard answer was "I think he's gonna make a pilot." He had been tough on me, forcing me into the workplace and making me put myself through college. Deep down, I know he would have helped me financially if he could, but I was better served by his forcing my self sufficiency.

At 57 he had a stress-induced heart attack while home in his own bed.

We were closer than ever then as father and son. I had asked him to be my best man.

They say that when God closes a door, somewhere he opens a window. My guiding light came shining through God's window in the form of my Uncle Earney, Dad's next younger brother. Not only did he gladly fill in for Dad as my best man, he also assumed the role of the father figure which I still very much needed. In the years since, he was always there for me as a counselor and his sage advice was invaluable.

He also took it upon himself to be a grandfather for my children even though he had a passel of his own.

T-34C first solo

He was also my spiritual leader and guide since the time he taught a Sunday school class of little boys who all sat on the edge our chairs as he taught us the story of Shadrach, Meshach and Abednego from the book of Daniel. I found particular strength from that story in later years for, as an officer of Marines, I would do what was right, regardless of the commandments of my seniors. He fathered me for over twenty years, nearly as long as Dad, and words cannot express how much I loved him. He has gone on to glory, now, but Earney Entrekin is my candidate for father of the millennium.

On July 20th I flew my first solo in the T-34C.

It's a neat little turbo prop that was a thrill for us junior pilots to fly. I had a choice between it and the T-28 (which I have since flown) but chose the T-34 because it was air-conditioned. It was a good call. I had been through training in the dead of winter and the heat of summer and it was time for some creature comforts. Besides, I "sweated" the training flights enough as it was.

At that point in training, the flying was coming easy and about the only time I got in trouble was for smiling too much. Some crusty instructor didn't think I was taking the program seriously enough but, after he flew with me, he gave me three above averages and *knew* why I was smiling.

Julie and I were married in August and honeymooned in the Virgin Islands. It was quite a trip. We did a little scuba diving our first few days on St. John and, just as we moved over to St. Thomas, hurricane Frederick hit. We spent the next few days learning to play backgammon while waiting for our flight home.

We made it back to Ft. Lauderdale just in time to pack up the Jeep before it hit there and, by the time we made it home to Milton, we had just enough time to get the plants in.

One hurricane three times was more than our share.

I think Julie was ready to come home anyway because during our years of diving together I had run her out of air more than once.

It started with our very first open water dive when I used up my own tank and then swam over to use her octopus rig (spare regulator) to continue looking around. We were ascending, at about fifty feet, when her tank emptied and we came up directly under the boat, starving for air.

Our buoyancy compensator backpacks were fully inflated since we came up a little faster than we should have and they stuck to the bottom of the dive boat with us in them. I loosened my straps and managed to get to the surface for a big gasp of air but there was no sign of Julie for at least ten more seconds.

It seemed longer, but she finally surfaced, too. During that last part of our ascent, Julie had bumped her head on the bottom of the boat and the reddish paint was coating her hair. I just knew that she had cut open her scalp as we scrambled into the boat to avoid attracting sharks. Relieved that we didn't get the bends and that neither one was hurt, we laughed-off our close call. We learned our lesson seriously, though, and thereafter she watched her tank pressure more closely. If I got anywhere near her octopus she started to surface.

The last time I ran out of air was in Morrison Spring while diving with some flight school buddies. We had briefed the dive like a flight and went into the cave in two groups of two. There was a log laying across the narrow entrance into the main cavern and a strong current surged out in a venturi effect. To enter, it was necessary to grab the log and pull over or under it and then swim through the opening. While swimming under the log, I managed to bump the J valve on my tank which removed its feature of providing a five hundred pound (psi) remaining warning.

We had briefed that the first guy that breathed his tank down to five hundred pounds would signal the others and we would surface. When my regulator had provided my last breath, I reached to pull the rod which activates the J valve but the valve was already down and I was completely out of air. I calmly swam over to my buddy, Chip Moehlau, pulled my regulator from my mouth and gave the cut sign indicating my problem. He did not have an octopus so we started buddy breathing by sharing his regulator and we headed out of the cave. The strong current shot us out of the opening and as soon as I saw sunlight and the surface I knew we would be safe. I'm convinced that a good briefing and diving with a cool-headed buddy prevented a potential disaster.

While flight training could be fun at times, I don't want to give the impression that it was easy.

The precision aerobatics, formation and night flying were some of the more enjoyable flights but the radio instruments syllabus was a real challenge for a novice. Stick and rudder skills were no substitute for knowledge of procedures.

I had one RI (radio instruments) flight where I flew so poorly the instructor just incompleted the hop and headed straight for the administration office to check my records before grading me or giving me a down (unsatisfactory flight). In the debrief he said he couldn't believe he had flown with the same guy he had just read about and gave me a day off to get myself together. He didn't say it exactly that way but I sure knew what he meant.

As it turned out, I never got a down in flight school and my grades were very good. They were certainly good enough to get jets and I was dying to fly the F-4 Phantom.

Unfortunately the jet pipeline was closed when I came up for selection and all of us Marines were assigned to helicopters. It was a real kick in the teeth to see our Navy counterparts with poor grades get assigned to jet squadrons. Sometimes the luckiest can be mistaken for the fittest and I had to accept my fate, temporarily exchanging my dream of flying fast for being able to fly backward.

With apologies for the paraphrasing to Delta Captain Robert Gandt . . .

It is deeply ingrained—If you ain't a fighter pilot, you ain't (expletive deleted). At the apex of the caste system, wallowing in glory and exhibiting the most highly developed sense of snobbery and elitism, are the fighter pilots. They gaze down in disdain on the rest. Many fighter pilots believe that they are where they are, and the helo pilots are where they are because of an innate difference in quality.

The top students were rewarded with their first choice of assignments. This was almost always pointy-nosed jets. *Almost* always. The bottom ranking students got last choice, which was almost always helos. *Almost* always.

My devastation was short lived due to some encouragement from the VT-3 Marine instructors like Captain Ken Sluis. They typically would single out certain guys that they would like to have in their fleet squadrons and spend time talking up their particular aircraft.

Even in advanced helo training, I met guys like Captain Vic Vangrowski who encouraged me to consider the UH-1N Huey because of its versatility, and that was what I eventually chose. (Vic and I later owned a cabin cruiser together that we kept at the Del Mar marina near Camp Pendleton. We became friends and squadron mates there in HML-267.)

In the Marine Corps, being a helo pilot is the closest thing to being a grunt. Every grunt story starts and ends with a helicopter; talking about cussing us for hauling their butts into deep kimchi or being ready to kiss us for hauling them out of it. There isn't a grunt anywhere who doesn't feel the hair stand up on the back of his neck when he hears the *whup whup whup* of rotor blades.

We ate the same sorry rations and slept in the same miserable tents while the fighter jocks dined indoors and slept in air-conditioned comfort. I still recall times leaving a remote LZ, pulling pitch, with the grunts grinning and giving me the bird and, at times, I've given them a parting farewell by dusting them with desert sand as fine as talcum powder.

The truth is, for Marines anyway, that the truer you were to being a Marine pilot, the closer to the ground you flew. It didn't matter if you were fixed wing or rotary wing. We were a band of brothers, a fraternity wearing the eagle, globe and anchor and we could do anything, anywhere, anytime. We let the Air Force pukes have their silk scarves & elite mentality and they cocked their heads to the side like a puppy dog, not understanding, when we laughed at them and their silly bias.

Lord, how I loved the grunts. Their tenacity and valor. Their determination.

In his book *Bonnie-Sue, A Marine Corps Helicopter Squadron in Vietnam*, author and Marine pilot Marion F. Sturkey summed up this august group:

> "As the grunts neared the crest of the mountaintop, they ran into the main NVA lines of defense. The airborne controller radioed the grunts and told them to stop their attack. Marine air and artillery wanted to pound the peak for an hour to soften-up the defenders. There was no need to needlessly sacrifice the lives of more of the grunts in a frontal assault against the waiting and entrenched North Vietnamese Army soldiers.
>
> Perhaps the maddening frustration and fury of the past three months overwhelmed the grunts. They were too close now and they refused to stop. The grunts fixed bayonets and swarmed up the slope toward the North Vietnamese.
>
> Their battalion operations officer, Major M. P. Caulfield, saw what was happening and he frantically radioed to his company commanders and told them to stop their men. The radioed reply:
>
> "Sir, I can't stop them!"

Hill 881 North, 1428 hours: With fixed bayonets the grunts swept through the enemy trenches and bunkers. Within fifteen minutes the fighting died out. Most of the tan-uniformed NVA soldiers had been killed and the rest of them now were fleeing down the north side of the mountain. The grunts shot a few of them, but they did not pursue the others. They had retaken the last North Vietnamese stronghold, and that was enough.

Lieutenant Colonel John Studt explained what happened next:

I watched the jungle utility-clad Marine shinny up a shrapnel-torn tree whose limbs had been sheared from the intensive prep fires, and affix the stars and stripes.

Helicopters began landing on the mountaintop to evacuate the grunts who had fallen during the assault. There was no enemy fire.

Now the former North Vietnamese fortress had been turned into a barren hill of death. It had been bombed, rocketed, shelled, mortared, blasted and denuded. One Marine said it looked like the surface of the moon.

Their job now over, the ambulatory grunts started straggling back toward Hill 881 South, roughly one mile away. Their commander proudly described them: "Near exhaustion, filthy, bearded, ragged; some wore bloody battle dressings." Then, he quickly added:

"They were all grinning."

I had my first helo flight in January, 1980 in a TH-57 (Bell Jet Ranger). I learned quickly and went through HT-8 and HT-18 with ease. Learning to hover was a challenge but fun beyond imagination.

On May 16th, my old mentor, Dan Sivley, pinned the "Wings of Gold" on my chest and I officially became a Naval Aviator.

A couple of traditions at flight school were the tie-cutting (recognition of a student's first solo) and the "fastest drinker at the bar" competition after the winging ceremony. Participation is not optional as each new pilot consumes some odd concoction as fast as he can. After chugging the drink the empty glass is held upside down on the head giving the judges no doubt as to the order of finish.

After a few elimination rounds, the final was between me and a Navy guy. Of course with Marine Corps pride on the line I *couldn't* be beaten by a squid and I still have the big winner's mug displayed prominently in my cabinet.

CHAPTER 5

THE FLEET

"A HELICOPTER DOES NOT WANT TO FLY. IT IS MAINTAINED IN THE AIR BY A VARIETY OF FORCES AND CONTROLS WORKING IN OPPOSITION TO EACH OTHER AND IF THERE IS ANY DISTURBANCE IN THIS DELICATE BALANCE THE HELICOPTER STOPS FLYING, IMMEDIATELY AND DISASTROUSLY. THIS IS WHY HELICOPTER PILOTS ARE BROODERS, INTROSPECTIVE ANTICIPATORS OF TROUBLE. THEY KNOW IF SOMETHING BAD HAS NOT HAPPENED, IT IS ABOUT TO."

Harry Reasoner

I reported to Camp Pendleton shortly thereafter to finish my training to become a combat qualified pilot in the fleet.

While house hunting and still living in a hotel, our son, Charlie, just couldn't wait any longer and, on June 9th, decided it was time to be born. He weighed only four pounds four ounces and was several weeks premature but I was thrilled to see him. It is not possible for me to explain the flood of emotions I felt when I saw his little face. He was so tiny. Except for being a little jaundiced, he was fine but we still had to wait a few days to bring him home. I remember standing in the hotel pool and holding him in my arm like a football. God's miracle had touched me deeply.

Within a month we had found a nice house in Fallbrook and used the July 4th holiday to move in. Only weeks later Julie was hospitalized with what turned out to be toxic shock syndrome. She had a close call but recovered quickly.

As a hard-charging young Marine first lieutenant I loved everything about my first squadron, HML-267.

I was in great shape and could nearly max the PFT (physical fitness test) each year. I did the eighty sit-ups within the two minutes allowed, twenty pull-ups and ran three miles in nineteen and a half minutes.

One of my CO's, whom I would've followed into hell, was Lieutenant Colonel Rick Phillips. He later became a three star general.

After the Huey and Cobra squadrons went composite*, I ended up in HMA-369 and had another outstanding warrior for a skipper in Lieutenant Colonel George Ross.

> *Prior to this time, Hueys and Cobras, primarily because of their different missions, had maintained separate squadrons like all others, but their similarities outweighed their differences and the Marine Corps decided to combine the two.

Our missions were, indeed, diverse in support of the grunts. We had water inserts, confined area landings, rappelling, medevac, VIP, guns & rockets and I made my first carrier landing on the USS New Orleans. We flew cross country flights for proficiency and saw all of the national parks from Yosemite to the Grand Canyon up close, low and slow. We chased Mustangs across the Nevada desert at Nellis Air Force Base. We landed at remote mountain lakes in the Sierras to fish. Helo flying was wonderful.

During the time I was there, none was wasted. There were obvious differences between those of us who loved to fly and fought for every minute of flight time we could get and those milk-run pilots who actually liked their squadron desk jobs. They were referred to as "seagulls" because you just about had to throw rocks at them to get them to fly.

To be designated a PQM (Pilot Qualified in Model) was the ultimate goal of every lieutenant. To be able to "sign for the aircraft" was to be the HAC (Helicopter Aircraft Commander) and that was the best.

Getting your wings is just a start. Once a new pilot arrives in the fleet, he must first go through substantial training in his assigned aircraft, learning everything pertinent to flying it in combat. In single seat aircraft the check out is critical because you're useless until you do. In dual seat aircraft the checkout is no less important but the stigma of being only qualified as a copilot is a right of passage every pilot longs to surpass. Typically, it takes a few short months.

Captain Denny Loftis gave me my check ride beginning with some bizarre maintenance questions about how to adjust the Ng idle speed set screw. He tried to rattle me with some bogus questions but I knew the Huey and could flat fly one, too.

Eventually I had about every designation that a squadron pilot could have. I was a formation section, division and flight lead and an instructor in TERF (low level terrain flying), tactics, instruments & navigation. I was day and night carrier qualified and had a special instrument rating.

I was selected to attend FAC (Forward Air Controller) school at LFTCPAC (Landing Force Training Center Pacific) in Coronado near San Diego. I say *selected* because I just happened to be walking through the ready room when the XO was scratching his head over which lieutenant to pick. I had no other collateral duties at the time and he told me it was a "good deal". Since lieutenants are always looking for a good deal, I volunteered to go. I only found out later that FAC duty was shunned by most pilots, especially jet drivers, because of the time spent out of the cockpit.

The school was fun and we learned a lot about controlling air, artillery and naval gunfire.

I was later fortunate to be assigned to spot for the requalifying of the most decorated battleship in the Navy, the USS New Jersey—45,000 tons of fighting steel. When she was brought out of mothballs in 1982, she became the only active battleship in the world. Originally, she was commissioned December 7, 1942, one year to the day after the Japanese attacked Pearl Harbor. She had seen action in World War II, Korea and Vietnam and would, next year (1983), provide fire support for the Marines in Beirut, Lebanon. She would also cruise the Persian Gulf.

Seeing nine 16-inch guns fire a two thousand pound sandbag twenty miles onto a target was remarkable. We killed a lot of wild goats on San Clemente Island that day and that tertiary

MOS (military occupational specialty) would follow me for years to come. (At that time, I had three MOS's; 7563—Huey pilot, 7596—Aviation Safety Officer and 7207—Forward Air Controller.)

As part of the "rent-a-FAC" program I was assigned to 1/5 (First Battalion, Fifth Marines) and went on maneuvers with them whenever they deployed. We frequented the ranges at Twentynine Palms where I was personally bombed, rocketed or strafed and I still have a piece of artillary schrapnel that nearly ripped off my flak jacket. I quickly learned never to use the words "surgical strike" and became a master of the Nine-Line brief.

As it turned out, it really was a good deal because the rest of the time I was free to continue flying with my squadron.

In December, the battalion was activated as part of the RDF (Rapid Deployment Force) and headed for parts unknown. We knew it was serious when the officers were issued live ammo.

Having little responsibility aboard ship with the battalion, I got to know the Navy pilot aboard that was in charge of pri-fly, the air traffic control tower used to launch and recover helicopters. The ship was an LSD with two aft landing spots that were large enough for CH-53 Super Stallions. Eventually, I learned enough about flight deck operations to handle pri-fly alone.

After a few days we had a classified briefing that disclosed we were enroute to Nicaragua, El Salvador or some such place with a carrier battle group.

It seemed that something political had flared up that would most likely require a show of force from the U.S. to support the current government. This is where I first became acquainted with some of the guys from DIA (the Defense Intelligence Agency).

They were full-time with the agency, but explained their utilization of TAD (temporary active duty) personnel.

Typically, they recruited individuals that they met, and liked, during the course of their "normal" operations.

We sat and talked for hours on end and I learned that their sense of patriotism was exemplary. Being a military pilot was great. It was fun to fly and rewarding to serve your country but I discovered another way to serve, a deeper commitment that involved even greater risk than flying military hardware. The challenge was both enticing and exciting and it was noble in my eyes to be chosen. We stayed in touch and shortly thereafter the wheels began to turn to absorb me into the world of covert operations—spooks.

During a routine day, some Sea Stallions were embarking a platoon of Marines to another ship. They were being led to the aft boarding door of the lead helo by their Lieutenant who had instructed his guys to keep their heads down and follow him. The tail rotor of a CH-53 is high enough that keeping low is not necessary but Marines are known for following orders to the letter.

This doofus was heeding his own advice and marching in a stooped over position, staring at the deck and heading straight for the tail rotor of a UH-1N Huey on the other helo spot. A Huey tail rotor, while only half as high as a CH-53, *will* grind you to hamburger, though.

The 53's crew chief was on the starboard side by the front door communicating with the pilots while this was evolving and hadn't given the command for or even seen the Marines boarding.

Viewing what was about to happen from pri-fly, I slid down the ladder and bolted for the Lieutenant. I managed to tackle him just inches from the Huey's tail rotor and the domino effect knocked a couple of the others down, too. I received a big strawberry on my right forearm, some ripped utilities and a Navy commendation from the skipper of the USS Cleveland.

THE FAR EAST

In May of 1982, my squadron rotated to Okinawa for the first of my two 6 month deployments. We became intimately familiar with the Philippines or P.I. as it is typically called. Some of our stomping grounds were Olongapo, Subic Bay, Clark Air Force Base, Angeles City and, our favorite, Cubi Point.

Olongapo was a modern day Sodom and Gomorrah rolled into one. Angeles City (just outside the Clark Air Force Base gates) was worse. Across from Olongapo, we crossed the S . . . River bridge from Subic where children begged for us to throw pesos into the coffee-colored, polluted water. Young girls, dressed in white and standing on makeshift boats, did most of the begging while the boys dove for the coins that were occasionally tossed. Among the many bars and bordellos were shops offering aircraft models, T shirts, belt buckles and the like.

At the Cubi Point Officer's Club bar, one activity in particular was a real hoot. Every naval aviator has to be able to land aboard ship. To display our prowess to our peers (without an aircraft), we would participate in "carrier quals". This involved arranging a few tables end to end to act as our deck. Then, after copious amounts of beer had been applied to the surface, we took turns running full speed toward the tables. Then, on the "LSO's"(Landing Signal Officer) command, we would leap onto the deck and slide, hoping to catch a three wire (which was nothing more than some knotted bar towels being held by two mates) with our feet. Thunderous roars of approval were reserved for the poor slob who missed the "wire" and skidded off the end of the table into a crumpled heap.

Worse was the pilot who dove for the tables before the LSO's signal and suffered a "ramp strike" with his head smacking the end of the table. Occasionally, such as at my winging back in Pensacola, stitches were required for poor "airmanship".

Eventually, in the downstairs bar, there was another device constructed that was actually a crude simulation of an aircraft cockpit that hung from a cable. The occupant was actually able to "fly" down to a simulated deck and extend a tailhook to attempt to grab a wire. Failure was met with unbearable ridicule, a dunking in the pool or both. It was great fun for aviators blowing off steam in port.

During that time, on Okinawa, I had my first inflight experience with divine intervention.

MIGHTY HANDS

I was the aircraft commander for a routine flight from our base at Futenma to pick up a brigadier general and his aide and transport them to a meeting somewhere on the island. Okinawa is quite small and we each knew the island very well. The weather that day was particularly bad with low ceilings and isolated rain showers. I had briefed my co-pilot, Curt Arndt, that we should take a coastal route after picking up the general. We landed at his LZ (landing zone) and waited a while for him to show up. As he approached the Huey, he informed us that he was very late for a meeting at Camp Schwab and to get him there ASAP. I looked at Curt, shrugged my shoulders and said "Oh well, guess we'll go direct". My plan was to stay as low as possible and fly around the only relatively high terrain we would encounter through a pass called the Awasi corridor. Curt was navigating but the low altitude made it extremely difficult to track our course. As we entered what we thought was the corridor, it appeared that the terrain was gradually rising while the ceiling was gradually coming down.

Eventually I reached the point that I could no longer maintain visual conditions and told Curt I was transitioning to an IFR (instrument flight rules) scan. He was in the process of calling Kadena approach to get us an IFR clearance and I was monitoring the instruments when I noticed something green above the glare shield. We had inadvertently flown into a box canyon and were heading straight for a cliff.

I remember pulling back on the stick and up on the collective in an attempt to go vertical. After that, I braced for the inevitable impact with the canyon wall. It felt almost as though some giant hands reached down and scooped us away from it, though, and the next thing I knew we were climbing. I was totally disoriented at that point and when I looked at Curt, he was leaning toward his door with vertigo worse than mine.

We were climbing directly into a thunderstorm and lost our TACAN (tactical air navigation) and radio as water dripped into the cockpit from the intense rain. I leveled off after about a thousand feet, squawked an emergency code on our transponder and headed out to sea. When I was convinced we were over the water and found a small hole in the clouds, I started a slow spiraling descent and pulled into a hover about fifty feet over the water. I did a slow pedal turn looking for land and headed west back toward the island.

Once we had picked up the coastline, we were able to get back to the general's LZ. Once there, we shut down and I wondered how long it would take for the general to order my court martial for trying to kill him. Instead he thanked us for trying to get him to his meeting, smiled and walked away.

His aide had vomited in the back, so we took a few minutes to clean up and collect our wits. The flight back to base was uneventful but I knew that there was no way we should be alive.

I suppose my skipper didn't lose faith in me because when the Secretary of the Navy, John Lehman, requested a Huey for some flight time around the island, I got the nod.

I recall landing at the helo pad next to the officers club at Camp Butler. It was in a beautiful spot but precarious because of its close proximity to a steep drop-off. It would be a bad spot for an engine failure on takeoff. Secretary Lehman hopped into the copilot's seat, strapped in and announced "I've got it, Captain".

A brilliant man who was a superb Secretary of the Navy, he was neither a pilot nor a naval aviator. Rather, he was a lieutenant commander still in the Navy reserves as an A-6 Intruder (2 seat attack jet) BN (bombardier navigator). Basically, he designated *himself* a naval aviator and spent his annual 2 weeks of active duty time (or, really, whenever he wanted) flying with check pilots like me.

When he saw that I was obviously apprehensive about letting him do the takeoff, he pushed up his helmet visor and then looked at me with a grin and said "No guts, no glory". I said "You've got it, sir" but followed him very closely with my hands and feet near the controls. Actually, I was pleasantly surprised with his flying skills. He was a pretty good pilot!

While we didn't get off the island much during that first pump, I did manage to get some liberty with my buddies Steve Bacon, Rick Kammer and Tom Gilroy. We went to Hong Kong on a rotating chartered 747 known as the freedom flight.

Some of us also had the "pleasure" of attending JEST (jungle environment survival training) school in the Philippines. We learned how to get water from bamboo and how to feed ourselves with the local flora and fauna. Actually, monkey and monitor lizard were pretty good compared to some of the fare available. The 100% humidity and voracious mosquitoes were awful, too.

Ernest Gann said, " . . . in most tropical regions there exists a special combination of nocturnal factors antagonistic to human sleep." Gann was right.

I flew some MEDEVAC missions from a remote outpost affectionately known as "Fort" Magsaysay where you could get sunburned in fifteen minutes. It was in the middle of nowhere but in close proximity to an operating area that required support. It consisted of a large open water tank and a dilapidated tin building.

This was not a highly sought after duty. It was scenic, though, due to its close proximity to one of the island's volcanoes (which erupted years later and completely covered Clark Air Force Base and nearby Angeles City in ash, prompting the closure of the base and the eventual collapse of the city's prurient economy).

During that rotation, Julie was pregnant with our daughter, Katie, and I was fortunate enough to get two weeks of leave bracketed around her due date. After arriving back in the states, I mentioned to Julie how much I would have liked to attend my ten year high school reunion on the approaching weekend. I had absolutely no plans to attend but Julie encouraged me to go and assured me that she felt no inclination to go into labor anytime soon. In fact, after I returned we asked the doctor to do a minor pelvic exam to sort of speed things up because we suspected that she might not deliver until after my leave. He did and Katie was born right on schedule.

CRABS

Returning to Japan thrust me right back into a busy flight schedule. We had operations in Korea and flew a lot of support on Okinawa itself.

My most enlightening trip involved an escort mission to bring an AH-1J Cobra back from depot level maintenance in Iwakuni, Japan.

Our maintenance department head, Major Denny Mann, was the flight leader. To fly over so much open water, a two ship formation was the smallest allowed so Steve Bacon and I volunteered to fly a Huey as his wingmen.

Major Mann didn't fly a lot so his formation skills were a little shaky. However, on the return trip with the second Cobra in the flight, they got worse.

We were heading for Kanoya to refuel before the long leg to Okinawa and the weather was marginal.

The formation was low over the water and it was easy to see on our map that the contour lines along the beach ahead were very close together indicating steeply rising terrain. It was obvious that entering instrument conditions was imminent but our leader pressed on. When Bits and I had all but lost the other two helos we called that we were breaking off. We climbed up and contacted approach and flew a TACAN instrument approach to an uneventful landing.

We were concerned that the Cobras might have flown into the ground when we heard that they had eventually slowed to hover taxi speed and landed on the beach. They looked like whipped puppies as a JSDF (Japanese self defense force) H-3 escorted them back to base safely.

Everybody was pretty well done for the day so we opted to spend the night there at the generous invitation of the locals. Exhausted, we slept soundly in some old run-down quarters on tatami mats and headed out the following morning.

I had a nice hot shower as soon as I got back to my BOQ room and spent the first few minutes pulling off some very tiny "ticks". I stuck a couple on a piece of tape and stopped by the dispensary to show the Doc since I'd never seen any that small before.

He quickly explained that those little critters were not ticks at all. Every crew member ended up getting treated for body lice.

My squadron was assigned our daily missions by group headquarters and each mission was called a frag (short for fragmentary order). Typically, we flew frags in support of our grunt counterparts all over the island and scheduled our own training flights in conjunction with them whenever we could. One particular frag called for me to take a crew up to the NTA (northern training area) in support of a recon patrol that needed a non-tactical extract (transportation home). We arrived at the LZ a few minutes early and shut down to take in the remote, lush, jungle surroundings. As I was enjoying the scenery and fantasizing about the dangerous snakes indigenous to the area (which the locals referred to as the Habu), the recon patrol slipped quietly out of the bush behind us. I suddenly heard a voice that made my blood run cold. As I turned to see who had said "How about a ride outta here, captain?" the smiling, camouflaged face on top of a body covered with grimy, but neat, utilities gave me a chill. The West Virginia accent took me back to Quantico. My old platoon sergeant from OCS, now Gunnery Sergeant Winger, still had the power to evoke fear with nothing more than his unique, booming voice. Still, it was great to meet up with him again in the fleet.

Needless to say, it sure was nice to get home from "the rock". Several of us had saved our per diem money for a get home gift to ourselves. I bought myself a 1982 Collector Edition Corvette.

With that and the 27 foot cabin cruiser I had bought with Vic a year earlier, my toy box was full. It didn't seem like life in California could get any better.

I had been augmented with a regular commission, promoted to captain and just assigned to the Aviation Safety Officer course at the Naval Postgraduate School in Monterey. My fitness reports kept me either at or near the top of the pack.

After a little more than a year and just as we were getting accustomed to the good life, it was time to rotate back to Okinawa and by February we were deployed to Korea for operation Team Spirit.

Our base at Pohang was a tent city. In each tent we had kerosene stoves (which had a tendency to explode) and spent as little time as possible there. Basically we lived in the cockpit and flew during the daylight as much as possible.

The missions were routine but we were acutely aware of their importance as we acknowledged the Nike missile batteries that appeared along the coast. We occasionally got liberty to Osan Air Base and flew more interesting missions around Seoul and along the DMZ (the Demilitarized Zone between North and South Korea).

The freezing temperatures on the South Korean peninsula were almost unbearable due to the constant wind and moisture. If the ground wasn't frozen it was muddy. When bathing could no longer be avoided, it was quite an odyssey to get to the shower tent which was nothing more than a water buffalo (tank trailer) with a heating unit attached. We stood on wood pallets and soaped and rinsed as quickly as we could.

While servicing the heating unit, some incompetent rube managed to drop the fuel regulating pin in a puddle, never to be found, and we were forced to endure cold showers for the rest of our time there.

Once again I got some liberty and went on a little tour of Southeast Asia. Julie came over for a week and we went to Bangkok, Singapore, Malaysia and Hong Kong.

After return to CONUS (military jargon for continental U.S.) in May 1984, I participated in my first Air Force *Red Flag*, a five time per year, Air Force directed, event held at Nellis Air Force Base near Las Vegas, Nevada: part war game and part readiness drill; the world's most complex and realistic aerial combat training exercise complete with "enemy" forces to fight.

My only buddy still in the squadron who was also participating in covert operations was Gene McCarthy.

Gene was a strapping, handsome Naval Academy graduate that the women swooned over. He was hard core and lived a real Spartan bachelor life. Gene slept on the floor of the apartment he shared with another good buddy of ours, Kim McCabe.

On one particular cross-country trip, Gene and I were flying together which was extremely rare since he was a Cobra pilot. Flying home, just west of Salt Lake, we saw the most beautiful sunset ever. As we chased the sun, the sky turned different shades of green, pink, blue and orange. It changed so quickly it looked almost liked the aurora borealis. It's impossible to explain what we saw but the two of us were both so overwhelmed, I landed the Huey out in the desert to continue to watch. It was over in minutes and afterward we both stared at each other momentarily with looks of wonder on our faces. One of us said something like, "What was that?" and without an answer we continued on our way.

Some of my squadron mates were unfortunate enough to strike some air frames from the government inventory. That's a technical way of saying that they crashed and destroyed some aircraft.

Bob Maguire and Mike Coulman were doing some instructor training at Futenma when, operating with one engine with a simulated engine out, the engine providing power failed and they rolled into a ball. Neither was injured but Bob was killed a few years later due to another mechanical failure in a Huey.

Dave Westmeyer, our best pilot, had the misfortune to experience a dual flameout followed by a night autorotation with only one minor injury. To this day I don't think anyone else in our squadron could've done what he did. He was a superb pilot.

A short time later in the Sierras, Dave and Chris Haw rolled into a mountainside after experiencing a whiteout from snow in the rotorwash. Fortunately, there were no injuries.

I had a transmission chip light once (indicating a small amount of metal in the oil) but, basically, the Pratt & Whitney engines treated me pretty good.

I'm fortunate to have had only one poor commanding officer. Because he had flown fixed-wing prior to helos (as had some of my other skippers) he thought he was special. The C.O. on my first deployment to Okinawa had been surrounded by weak field grade department heads resulting in a disastrous tour. We had several mishaps which forced his replacement when we returned to Camp Pendleton. The new, "special" C.O. proceeded to tell us how screwed-up we were and that he was the Messiah who would whip us into shape. His animus of nihilism far overlooked the elan of both our troops and cadre of pilots. His inflated ego was epitomized by what he tried to use as a call sign; the "Hostile Tomcat". We just refused to call him that on the radio so he eventually settled for something a little more tame; the "Hawk".

Even so, because of the spelling and pronunciation of his name, we referred to him as "The Schwantz". The Schwantz was a control freak but, in spite of his opinion, we had some great people who made him look really good and that was all he wanted.

Neither Gene nor I participated in any DIA activities under his command.

Our squadron was tasked to fly security and VIP support for the Olympic Games in Los Angeles and man did we have a ball. We practiced low level routes all over the city and set up LZ's (landing zones) at each venue site. It was neat to see familiar places that were normally off limits to low flight. We buzzed around the city like the helo in the movie *Blue Thunder*. We flew over the coliseum and UCLA and learned to identify ground references like the Playboy mansion at a glance.

It was a fitting swan song from the fleet but hard to say goodbye. I am not ashamed to say that I loved my squadron mates and would not have traded any one for a busload of instant Canadians, a boatload of Rhodes Scholars bound for England or a whole campus full of wimps who turned up for their draft physicals wearing pantyhose.

I will teach my sons the stories and legends about them and I will warn my daughters never to go out with aviators.

HMA-369 Huey Gunship

CHAPTER 6

THE TRAINING COMMAND

"FOR ONCE YOU HAVE TASTED FLIGHT YOU WILL WALK THE EARTH WITH YOUR EYES TURNED SKYWARDS, FOR THERE YOU HAVE BEEN AND THERE YOU WILL LONG TO RETURN."

Leonardo daVinci

By the fall, I was in Pensacola for flight instructor duty and back in a fixed-wing cockpit. I hit the ground running there, too, and was quickly instructor of the month, quarter, etc. I was the high time instructor almost every month and earned recognition as a "Hacker" for flying a certain number of students and a "Centurion" for flying over a hundred hours a month. I taught aerobatics, formation, day and night navigation, instruments and the student's initial introduction to flight, familiarization or Fam for short.

Flight instructors tended to fall into two categories, those who taught and those who critiqued. Again, I must paraphrase some from Bob Gandt throughout the next few paragraphs:

Of the two roles, easiest by far was critique: itemizing the bungling student's errors and dumping them on him like a litany of sins. They were also the screamers and the ones who threw kneeboards at their charges.

The tougher and more useful task was to teach. Good instructors taught by example. And we allowed, with a watchful eye, a student to make his own mistakes thereby enabling him to learn what *not* to do.

Most of all, instructors had to be cool; unflappable. It represented confidence in our own abilities. We had to remain calm even when it seemed clear that a particular student had been sent from hell just to kill us. Maintaining coolness was a prerequisite when you were instructing nuggets. During my time as an instructor pilot, we called them "cones"—short for coneheads.

At OLF (outlying field) Choctaw we demonstrated the carrier landing using the Fresnel lens—the optical glide path indicator that's installed on every carrier in the Navy.

The Fresnel lens is a mirror-like board at the edge of the runway (or flight deck aboard ship), next to the landing area. The mirror has a row of green datum lights on each side and an amber "meatball" in the lens that moves up and down according to the pilot's position on the glideslope.

When the pilot sees that the ball is exactly between the green datum lights on the lens, it tells him that he is on the correct descent path. If he scrupulously "flys" the ball, meaning that he keeps it in the middle of the lens—between the green datum lights—his plane will plunk into the landing area exactly on target.

If he lets the ball go high, off the top of the lens, the plane is too high on its approach path. It will land beyond the touchdown zone, missing the arresting wires of the aircraft carrier and carom off the deck back into the air.

Worse, if the ball goes low, settling off the bottom of the lens, meaning he has gone below the glide path, it means he is toast—literally. His plane crashes into the unyielding blunt ramp of the ship.

Landing aboard a ship at sea is what makes naval aviators different from our counterparts on the rest of the planet. It is the most important skill in aviation whether helicopter or fixed wing. Anticipating the results of every movement of the flight controls has been described as being like "milking a mouse".

As the instructor, I was an "onboard" LSO (landing signal officer) and, since my butt was strapped inside too, it gave an even more intense meaning to the LSO's somewhat effacing Latin motto, "Rectum non Bustus".

Some daytime FCLPs (field carrier landing practice) were done during initial training which soon progressed to night flights where a calming voice was essential for the students in such a high stress environment. How you enunciated your words was important. For example, if a guy was low you'd say "Pow-werrr"—"Eeee-zzzee." And if he continued to settle he'd hear "Pow-WERRR!" Not a gravelly baritone, but a soothing whisper followed by a firm command if necessary.

Ultimately, these young nuggets would strive for the perfect carrier landing—an okay three wire. It was my job to teach them the initial skills necessary to stay competitive on the "greenie board"—the chart where a tally of each pilot's landings is maintained during a deployment—the primary determining factor of a carrier pilot's standing in the pecking order.

Formation flying is an even more specialized hand-eye skill, like musical ability or language fluency. For some pilots it comes easily, naturally. For others, flying precise formation will always be a harrowing, sweaty-palmed ordeal.

Maintaining your position a few feet away from the lead aircraft is something akin to zooming down the freeway at a hundred and fifty miles per hour, staying three feet away from the fender of the car in the next lane. But in an aircraft you have a third dimension, the up-down axis. Tight formation flying is an internal mind game; a reflexive activity that occurs at a subliminal level of consciousness.

Flying three feet apart isn't the tough part, at least not after learning the basic skills. Aircraft rarely collide when flying formation. It is getting *into* formation that can peak your pucker factor. The join-up is called a rendezvous. With a fast closure rate, it's like ice skating toward an abyss and trying to stop a few inches from the edge.

When you do it wrong with either excessive closure rate or the wrong angle, you perform an underrun, meaning you level the wings and slide beneath the lead aircraft, from your step-down position.

It's considerably easier in a propeller driven plane because you get a quicker response to power adjustments and the prop itself acts as a big speed brake. It takes much more finesse in a jet because corrections take longer to realize.

In a helicopter you have ten feet of step *up* so as to keep the leader's rotor in sight and a botched join-up results in an overrun.

Night and instrument formation is even more demanding, the basic difference being that you can't see anything!

Fortunately, my training command skippers endorsed participation in DIA activities so I spent a significant amount of time away from the squadron on "cross-countries". Most of these trips were administrative with little actual time as an operative. The cross countries took me to some strange places but my favorites were in Canada.

One particular trip was just for fun. Gene, Steve, Kim and I went up to Moose Jaw, Saskatchewan for their annual airshow. Gene was scheduled to leave shortly thereafter for Army Ranger School and was a little up tight. We tried to help him unwind but he just couldn't do it.

Kim was enroute back to Camp Pendleton so I rode on with him in his Alfa Romeo sports car. We visited friends in Saskatoon and Cold Lake and then drove through Jasper and Banff to Vancouver. The Canadian Rockies were spectacular; more beautiful than the Tetons, Lake Tahoe or any other place I'd been privileged to see on duty. We ferried over to Vancouver Island to Comox and Victoria and then on to Seattle where I bid Kim adios and flew on home.

1985 was a good year and I had the opportunities to go to both Oshkosh for the big EAA (Experimental Aircraft Association) fly-in and to Reno for the air races. I met Pappy Boyington* at Oshkosh and linked up with some good buddies flying for the Canadian Snowbirds at Reno. I knew some of the guys from F-18s and F-5s at CFB Cold Lake and had met others during airshows around the U.S. and Canada.

The highlight of the year, though, and what really made it special, was the birth of our second daughter, Lindy.

> *Pappy was a Marine Corsair pilot who won the Medal of Honor in the South Pacific during World War II. The movie *Black Sheep Squadron* and subsequent television show *Baa Baa Blacksheep* were loosely based upon his exploits.

The timing was incredible.

As I negotiated with the monitor at Headquarters Marine Corps about my next assignment, I was told bluntly that I was slated to be an Air Officer at Camp Pendleton. That involved working with a battalion operations officer, flying a desk for the next 3 years. Since I had been previuosly told to expect to transition to a fleet fixed-wing squadron (hopefully flying the F-18 Hornet) it was quite a blow. Having just been selected for major, I knew it would be the kiss of death to be with the grunts for 3 years and then arrive back at an operational squadron as a mid to senior major having been out of the cockpit while my contemporaries were getting better and better.

No matter that my fitness reports were great which merited a good assignment, he said the needs of the Marine Corps were his first priority. I knew when someone was blowing smoke and told him so. His retort was that my only option to the orders was to resign.

One of my favorite syllabus flights as an instructor was to take the student nearing the end of his intermediate training phase on a cross country (air navigation) flight. Students loved the air navs because it was their first chance to take a military airplane to their home town or somewhere else of personal interest. We normally scheduled these flights on weekends. Occasionally, the student had no particular desire for a destination so I would suggest an airshow. The training command, like the fleet, received lots of requests for military static display aircraft from airshows across the country and Canada. Because I flew so many students, I ended up at a lot of airshows. When you see the same faces regularly, the military and civilian participants naturally become acquaintances and sometimes friends.

Having met a lot of the civilian air show performers while displaying the T-34, I'd learned what a lucrative business it was and considered it an option should I ever decide to get out of the service. Kim McCabe was interested in starting a Pitts Special team, so, when everything was considered, I decided to resign my commission and go into business with him. I ordered a Pitts from the factory forthwith.

There was a major problem to consider, however, which Kim had initially failed to disclose. He had accepted a bonus which prevented him from resigning at the same time as me so I was faced with flying a solo Pitts act for a while—a dime a dozen in the airshow world.

If I'd had the option, I would have stayed a captain in the Marine Corps and instructed in T-34s until retirement. I loved it that much.

VT-3 Instructor

I enjoyed taking a student up for his first few flights and then turning him loose to solo.

Typically, the Navy and Coast Guard students were fearful of flying with the Marine instructors. I guess our image preceded us but I got around that by forcing each student to reach into my helmet bag, just prior to strapping in, and take a "smart pill" . . . a piece of bubble gum. It usually broke the ice and, in addition, the student had a better chance of clearing his ears during altitude changes.

Some of my more memorable Marine students were Ken "Thumper" Switzer, Joe Mihalek and Pat Cook. My fellow instructors and I must have done something right because they all went on to become Blue Angels.

Fast forward to 1992. While flying my MiG in airshows, I saw Thumper in Bristol, Tennessee and was tickled to learn how much he had achieved. It was his first year on the team. He walked up to me at the Tri-Cities airshow and said "Hi, you don't remember me do you sir?" I recognized his boyish grin and we proceeded to chat about what flights he remembered us flying together back in the training command and how many above averages I gave him. Ken suggested to the boss, Greg Wooldridge, that I fly a practice show with them back home in Pensacola a few weeks later. Thumper was number 6, the opposing solo, so I had the privilege of flying with John "Gucci" Foley, number 5, the lead solo.

The rest of the diamond was rounded out by Larry "Fudge" Packer, number 2, Doug Thompson, number 3 and Pat Rainey, number 4 in the slot. Dave Stewart, number 7 was the narrator that year. Randy Duhrkopf, number 8 was the coordinator and the outstanding team flight surgeon was Pat Spruce.

I know I'm biased, but I've had the opportunity to get to know a lot of the pilots who've flown for the Blue Angels, Snowbirds and Thunderbirds during both my airshow and military careers and I can tell you that, as a team, these guys were the best. Their egos were in check. They were focused. They were professional to a man. No wonder they were selected to go to Europe for a tour of eight airshows, including Moscow; the first U.S. team ever to perform there.

They watered my eyes for forty five minutes and I felt very much a part of the team during the brief, flight and debrief. Afterwards we swapped pictures, T-shirts and some laughs. It was the ultimate ride with some really neat guys.

MID-LIFE CRISIS

I retained my reserve commission so as to be available should any future conflicts arise. I also continued to pursue flight ratings since having taken the military competency exam to get my civilian commercial pilots license right after getting my wings.

In January of 1987 I took my ATP (Airline Transport Pilot) rating.

I was discharged from active duty on February 28, 1986. My Pitts S-2B was delivered from the factory by the end of May, followed by the painting and some modifications which would take several more weeks.

I had been hesitant to take the Pitts safety course thinking I would have no trouble adapting to the little tail-dragger after all of my flight instructor experience. My little voice told me to do it anyway and I learned how wrong I would have been after flying with Dan Gray.

The things I learned about inverted flat spins and other maneuvers the military didn't teach were lifesavers. I still cringe when I hear some salty pilot say "Just show me how to start it—I can fly anything". I probably would've busted my butt. I learned I was far too inexperienced in the Pitts to just jump right into the airshow circuit.

Curtis Pitts originally designed this little biplane in the 1940s and it had grown, at that time, to become one of the most popular aerobatic airplanes in the world—primarily because of its control responsiveness. It has a mind-boggling roll rate and with a souped-up engine it's light enough to hang in the air in a hover during multiple torque rolls.

A couple of years later I was fortunate to meet aerobatic great Clint McHenry. He was a wealth of knowledge and quite a gentleman. From time to time, when I'd see him at a show, I solicited his advice and became a much better pilot for it.

My buddy, Scott Marshall and I flew the Pitts up to Langley, British Columbia from Santa Paula, California when the beautiful "Spectrum Eagle" paint job was finished. It needed auxiliary fuel tanks and some navigation instruments to make it more suited to flying from show site to site and the Ray Ban Gold Team's mechanic, Fred Beauchesne, had agreed to modify my Pitts similar to theirs.

Rod Ellis, George Kirbyson and Bill Cowan were more than kind in allowing me to use their facility. George, in particular, was a wealth of knowledge about the Pitts relating to me the story of how he had been badly burned because of a fuel leak. The Ray Bans were a class act in every sense of the word.

A very special Pitts, the Spectrum Eagle

Scott and I had a scenic and uneventful trip except for one unexpected stop. The headwinds had drastically increased during one leg and I was convinced I wouldn't make it to the destination airport. Looking for a suitable site, I found an old forestry strip that was about as wide as a driveway and not much longer; not the best place to land a tail-dragger. That is, without a doubt, one of the most precise landings I've ever made. We found a pay phone and had the FBO (fixed base operator) from our destination airport bring us some fuel which we poured into the tank with a, cut in half, quart oil can.

The air show season had passed and, when the Pitts was ready in September, I flew it to Pensacola for the winter. It was a wonderful solo flight through the Rockies and a spectacular view of our country in a biplane.

One stop was in Cody, Wyoming and I very nearly didn't make it.

Flying at 12,000 feet, I had to maneuver around a lot of peaks and my direct flight plan eventually had a lot of unplanned mileage added. Somehow, the local FBO got word from flight service that I was inbound. Since there's nothing within a hundred miles of Cody, I absolutely *had* to land there and was at minimum fuel. When I finally got close enough to see the town, a large thunderstorm was just passing. I was on fumes and desperately looking for the airport when, suddenly, the runway lights came on.

After landing, a line boy taxied me in and explained that his boss had instructed him to listen for my engine at a certain time and then turn on the lights for me when he heard me coming. They also hangared the plane and gave me the keys to a Cadillac El Dorado. He said I'd need it to get to the Hotel Irma (named after Buffalo Bill's daughter) where they had already reserved a room for me. The next day he tried to loan me a beautiful leather flight jacket fearing that I'd get too cold on my way. Those folks had never met me yet they couldn't have been kinder.

On that same trip, weather forced me to land unplanned at Pine Bluff, Arkansas where I experienced similar hospitality from some folks I would later get to know in the airshow business, Bob and Ruthie Blankenship.

By October, I had embarked on a journey that would forever change my life.

CHAPTER 7

HAVE MiG
WILL TRAVEL

"THE COCKPIT WAS MY OFFICE. IT WAS A PLACE WHERE I EXPERIENCED MANY EMOTIONS AND LEARNED MANY LESSONS. IT WAS A PLACE OF WORK, BUT ALSO A KEEPER OF DREAMS. IT WAS A PLACE OF DEADLY SERIOUS ENCOUNTERS, YET THERE I DISCOVERED MUCH ABOUT LIFE. I LEARNED ABOUT JOY AND SORROW, PRIDE AND HUMILITY, AND FEAR, AND OVERCOMING FEAR. I SAW MUCH FROM THAT OFFICE THAT MOST PEOPLE WOULD NEVER SEE. AT TIMES IT TERRIFIED ME, YET I COULD ALWAYS FEEL AT HOME THERE. IT WAS MY PLACE, AT THAT TIME IN SPACE, AND THE JET WAS MINE FOR THOSE MOMENTS. THOUGH IT WAS A PLACE WHERE I COULD QUICKLY DIE, THE COCKPIT WAS A PLACE WHERE I TRULY LIVED."

Brian Shul

My good friend, Steve Wallace, a former Canadian Snowbird, had told me of an article he'd seen in *Canadian Aviation* magazine about someone in Ottawa who was planning to import some MiG-17s.

It seemed that this fellow, David Chow, was of Chinese ancestry and still had contacts in the People's Republic of China. With some prodding from Steve and on a lark, I called Chow to inquire as to the validity of the article. He assured me that he was serious and only required a deposit to guarantee shipment. The deal was that if I wasn't completely satisfied, he'd refund the deposit which would be held in escrow. The one detractor, though, was that he would not be responsible for any maintenance.

Armed with that information, the most important thing for me to find out was how to maintain the aircraft if, in fact, it could truly be delivered. Remembering a day trip to the Chino (California) airport, I dug through a stack of business cards until I found the one I'd saved from the Combat Jet and Aerospace Museum.

Chino is the Mecca for warbirds and I had met the proprietor of the museum, Bruce Goessling, while I was there. So, I phoned him to ask about the possibilities of maintaining a MiG-17 and, obviously, he was curious to know why. I explained my intentions after which he commented that, in his opinion, the MiG-15 had much more history and was easier to maintain due to its lack of an afterburner. I recall saying, "That's really interesting Bruce, but where the heck am I gonna find a MiG-15?" After a pause he said, "You won't believe this but

I've got five of 'em sitting on the dock at Long Beach right now waiting to go through Customs."

Still not convinced that operating a MiG could be feasible, let alone possible, I decided to hold off making any decisions until I'd had a chance to poll some potential show sponsors at the International Council of Air Shows convention in December.

Since Pitts Specials are relatively common in the airshow business, I had been gearing up all year for a big blitz at the convention to book my beautiful plane.

Without any substantial credentials such as an aerobatic championship, I had to find some gimmick to set myself apart from the rest.

I was still polishing my routine and, with the help of my mentor, Byrd Mapoles, learning the ropes when the MiG came along.

I had seen Byrd fly and knew I needed guidance to break into the business.

He flew a Decathlon and did a marvelous show known as "The Flying Mayor" (he was at one time the mayor of Milton, Florida—a little town just outside Pensacola) and he was very reluctant to talk to me.

He explained that he'd seen other young hot shot pilots come and go, some to their deaths, and he wasn't interested in a protege' looking for kicks.

Once I convinced him that I was already committed and would continue even without his help, he figured it would be best if he offered some education.

So, hanging on Byrd's coattails at the 1986 convention, I was introduced to numerous sponsors to whom I posed the question, "Would you be interested in having a MiG at your show?" Clearly, the response was overwhelmingly favorable so I went directly from Las Vegas to Chino and made a deal with Bruce.

I explained that I'd spent our nest egg on the Pitts and didn't have the money to buy the jet and still have operating capital.

My business plan figured that the potential airshow revenues could be substantial so he agreed to payments. It was good for him, too, because he knew that the first question people would ask about the jet was where I got it. He had four more to sell and that would surely send warbird enthusiasts beating a path to his door. They did, and I became the first civilian in the world to own and operate a MiG.

Bruce dealt with all the administrative red tape involving certificating the MiG. The Long Beach MIDO (The FAA branch office responsible for maintenance and engineering) inspector had been reasonable with his inspection but the Riverside FSDO (The FAA flight standards district office) inspector was having considerable problems with Washington. It seemed that someone high up in the chain of command had felt compelled to issue the edict that there was "no way that MiGs would be flying around this country". That was among the first portions of crow that would later be consumed by FAA officials.

Apparently there was some misguided information about the reliability of the jet perpetuated from the Korean War days. All you had to do was write a book, print the rumors and hearsay that was handed down, and you were an expert. ("Historians" still can't even agree on what the accurate kill ratio was.) So, unfounded fears seemed to override the common sense that these jets had been flying for over thirty years around the world and there was no reason to suspect that the air in North America would change a thing.

Various FAA entities kept creating wickets for us to go through and we kept satisfying them. Eventually they ran out of reasons and gave us an airworthiness certificate in the experimental category. (That's the catch-all category for surplus military aircraft since no valid category exists.)

The operating limitations were very restrictive for the first fifteen hours and, even after, there was a geographic range limitation included for proficiency flying. Otherwise, flight was authorized only to, from and at airshow sites and for motion pictures and air racing.

There was no problem with IFR (instrument flight rules) flight since they realized, from both common sense and our data, that the jet would be cruising at high altitudes (up to flight level 510-51,000 feet) and at a speed of around .82 Mach.

Aerobatic flight was also permitted within the limits of the operating manuals which, as you will see, were something of our own creation.

The manuals themselves were extremely vague and, with the exception of some basic numbers, virtually useless. For example, range was specified at twelve hundred nautical miles but, in reality, it was actually seven hundred. Much had been lost when the manuals were translated from Russian to Chinese to English.

The airplane was built in 1954 (the same year I was born) at the Shenyang plant in China with parts manufactured in the Soviet Union. The Chinese were later able to do it all but, only a short time after the Korean War, they were still dependent upon assistance from the Russians.

It had around two thousand hours on the airframe and less than two hundred on the engine. One of the rumors about the jet was that it had short life engines, said to be around three hundred hours, which was true only of the late '40s and very early '50s jets. (Some later generation Russian/Soviet fighters, such as MiG-29s, were also plagued by minimal life engines.)

The metallurgy was substantially improved by the time mine was built and, although actual lifespan is subject to speculation, it was our expectation to get well over a thousand hours before overhaul.

The engine had regular and extensive hot section inspections and soap samples routinely taken indicated only minimal wear. (For those that may not be aviation oriented, that simply means that the innermost parts of the engine were looked at visually and that the engine oil was analyzed to check for any microscopic particles of metal.)

I flew the jet well over a thousand hours myself which, at one time, made me the high-time native MiG pilot in this country. I can't say it unequivocally due to a couple of my expatriot acquaintances, Viktor Belenko and Alex Zuyev, both now deceased due to aircraft mishaps.

The only other guy who even came close was renowned air racing legend John Penney who has flown Mig-15s and 17s quite extensively as well.

First MiG flight

TEST PILOT

Emblazoned on the fuselage, just below the canopy rail, was my name—in Russian. Again, some paraphrasing from Gandt is in order.

It was a sinister world of the enemy upon which I was intruding; consoles loaded with luminous dials, an instrument panel that displayed everything about the jet's path of flight and inner workings and a big white line down the center as a reference for the proper stick position during the panic of an unintentional spin recovery attempt; a throttle that commanded the engine and a control stick, taller than normal to allow for greater leverage during high speed with limited hydraulic boost to the ailerons and none to the elevators. The stick was large and simple with only a trigger for the nose-mounted cannons.

All labeling was in either Russian Cyrillic letters or Chinese characters. It was indeed a hostile environment. Inside the tiny, cramped cockpit, I felt as though I was getting ready for a knife fight in a phone booth.

Being single seat, I knew that high workload times would be a deadly dance in a hands-on jet with no autopilot and marginal trim so the airspeed indicator and altimeter were replaced to avoid having to translate metric indications to standard. Air Traffic Controllers wouldn't care less how many kilometers per hour I was going or how many meters high I was. We added a transponder and a single communication/navigation package making the jet ILS—Instrument Landing System—capable and I was ready to fly.

The ejection seat was another concern altogether. To activate it, the seat safe pins are pulled. Then the trigger on the right handle is pulled to fire the archaic twenty millimeter cartridge which launches the seat. This type of ejection seat had a reputation for making pilots a couple of inches shorter after significant spinal compression. No rockets, but cheerfully guaranteed to work by the sellers. They said that if it failed, they would gladly replace it with another one! How encouraging.

Part of the ejection sequence is a Rube Goldberg type of mechanical release which, prior to firing the cartridge, actually cocks the canopy through a system of levers, up into the slipstream to be caught by the onrushing air and jerked off the jet. There is no torso harness, just chest and leg straps for the parachute and a four point harness for the seat. There are foot rests to assure proper leg position prior to ejecting but nothing prevents legs and arms from flailing about during a high speed ejection. Potentially, Mr. Toad's wild ride!

Due to the questionable reliability of the ejection system I decided early on that I would land in a field or ditch the airplane before I would eject without a gyro-stabilized rocket seat.

The only exception would be an imminent explosion or a total loss of my flight controls.

An oxygen hose and radio coupling were mated separately. The hose from the G suit plugged directly into a connector which supplied the air that inflated it.

Gs are units of acceleration. One G is the force of the earth's gravity. When the jet is pulled up steeply or is pulled out of a dive, the Gs increase from the normal one G to four or five or more, increasing the pilot's effective weight by four or five times. The blood drains from the head to the lower body, causing "grayout" (a loss of vision and wooziness) and, ultimately, "blackout" (unconsciousness). With the onset of Gs, the G suit inflates around the pilot, squeezing the legs and abdomen, preventing some of the flow of blood downward from the brain and helping to maintain consciousness. Bless the Canadians for inventing it.

I didn't always use mine because I became conditioned to the four to five Gs I typically pulled during a show, but there was a time that I was glad to have it. I pulled over ten (as high as the G meter indicates) during a situation at a show in Macon, Georgia. But that's another story I'll share later.

My first flight in the MiG was at the Mojave airport in the California high desert near the test facility at Edwards Air Force Base. It was appropriate. Besides, the Feds didn't want any problems associated with flying the jet near a populated area on its first and subsequent few flights. It was a real Walter Mitty type of experience and I suppose I wasted most of the first flight just enjoying flying a real "bad guy" airplane.

Becoming a fledgling test pilot wasn't easy, especially without the benefit of attending a formal test pilot school.

The pilot Bruce had initially contracted turned out to be a shyster. He supposedly had extensive Air Force test pilot experience and had flown MiGs before. He gave us convoluted data from his joy rides that he called test flights and Bruce and I quickly discerned that we were being had. So, to get realistic data, it fell to me. With speculative numbers gathered from comparing both the F-86 and T-33, I had a ball-park idea as to what to expect. Typically, I was given a test card and went up to get specific data during each sortie.

It was truly like testing an X plane with only hypothetical numbers.

A few years later, I was privileged to join the distinguished Society of Experimental Test Pilots due to my initial work with the MiG.

Just three years prior, while gearing up for our squadron MCCRES (Marine Corps Combat Readiness Evaluation System), I had learned from recognition slides all we knew about the enemy and their equipment.

One of the things I learned as I consumed every bit of information available about the MiG-15 was that many of the so called "experts" who had written about it had done nothing more than pass on rumors and myths. Much of what I read later proved to be pure "bovine scatification". Here are the facts.

Near the end of World War II, the Soviet Union captured several German aircraft factories, much technical data and some production line jet fighters including Willy Messerschmitt's Me262. The design bureau of Artem Mikoyan and Mikhail Gurevich studied and improved his swept wing design.

The result was their prototype S (I-310) which first flew on 2 July, 1947. It was powered by the British RD-45 Rolls Royce Nene engine received through the 1946 Anglo-Soviet Trade Agreement. This prototype failed during low speed tests. It exhibited a tendency to stall and spin in very tight turns. Later experience showed that this was partly due to a CG (center of gravity) shift when the weight (of expended ammunition) from its forward bay decreased and the weight of fuel present in the aft tanks remained.

Numerous modifications, including boundary layer fences and rear fuselage air brakes, were incorporated in the second prototype, S-01, which flew on 30 December, 1947. This model was produced and used by the Soviet Air Force starting in October, 1948. It was supplied to North Korea and China and was also produced in Czechoslovakia and Poland.

In 1950 the MiG-15bis (the bis suffix meant "second version") was produced with the Klimov VK-1 engine increasing thrust by one thousand pounds to nearly seven thousand. This improved model was subsequently distributed to Albania, Algeria, Bulgaria, Cambodia, Cuba, Finland, East Germany, Hungary, Iraq, Morocco, Romania, Somalia, Syria, Tanganyika, The United Arab Emirates and Uganda. More than five thousand, including other variations, were built.

The first airborne encounter occurred 1 November, 1950, when a flight of allied Mustangs patrolling the Yalu River were fired upon by six Chinese MiGs.

The first airborne victory was on 8 November, 1950, when Lieutenant Russell Brown, escorting a flight of B-29s in his F-80, shot down a Chinese MiG who was diving away in confusion from his six-plane attack formation.

Even as the F-86 emerged, the MiG-15 had some obvious advantages. The F-86s flew as much as two hundred fifty miles up to "MiG Alley" using one third of their fuel. The MiGs were normally within fifty miles of their bases and could cruise at high speeds without fuel worries. Also, the MiGs had sanctuary in Manchuria across the Yalu River. Their standard tactics were to cruise above the Sabre's 48,000 foot service ceiling then dive and fire and zoom back up to safety, utilizing its superior rate of climb. In return, the Sabres would dive using their greater weight to attain a faster speed. Below 25,000 feet, where the F-86 was more maneuverable, a sharp turn would either allow the Sabre to get on the MiG's tail or the MiG would stall and spin.

Performing combat maneuvers at speeds greater than six hundred miles per hour could impose crushing G forces that would push a pilot deep into his seat. These forces made it difficult to fire a jet's guns accurately in a sharp turn, and it was rare for a flier to line up directly behind his wildly evading target for an easy shot. Moreover, G forces deprive a pilot's brain of blood, thus threatening to bring on unconsciousness. American pilots wore G suits that countered this hazard, but the communists did not. Time and again a Sabre would engage a MiG in a turning duel only to see the enemy enter a spin and crash due to either loss of control or blackout.

By the time the Viet Nam war rolled around the Russians had evolved the MiG-15 into the MiG-17.

It was modified with the VK-1F afterburning engine providing 7,500 pounds of thrust and a thinner wing swept forty five degrees. It was now capable of supersonic flight.

Arab countries used the MiG-17 against Israel before, during and after the Six-Day War in 1967 and, during

Operation Desert Storm, numerous MiG-15s and 17s were destroyed in Iraq.

On 21 September, 1953, Senior Lieutenant No Kum-Sok, a North Korean Air Force pilot, defected from Sunan (seven minutes from the 38th parallel) to Kimpo Air Base, South Korea, in a MiG-15. This gave the U.S. its first opportunity to evaluate the enemy's level of technology and provided valuable information about the pilots.

He reported normal Red air strength as four hundred Russians, four hundred Chinese and two hundred fifty North Koreans throughout the war. Losses were over four hundred Russians, three hundred Chinese and one hundred North Koreans. While total accounts vary, there were over eight hundred verified kills.

Between November, 1950 and December, 1951 all enemy MiG pilots were Russian.

In April, 1951 the Soviet Central Aero-Hydrodynamic Institute, a flight research center (located at what is today Zhukovsky airfield near Moscow), dispatched a special group of test pilots to a training base in Manchuria. They practiced precision formation, flying for a month, intending to box in a Sabre and force it to land. Obviously, it never worked.

On October 6, 1951 USAF 2nd Lieutenant Bill Garrett was shot down and ditched his F-86A in the, low tide, coastal mud flats and tidal pools along the Yellow Sea.

Garrett was rescued by an amphibious aircraft. His wingman and others who arrived at the scene tried to destroy the downed aircraft but Russian MiGs fought them off during an off and on 3 hour battle. The Sabres shot down 7 MiGs and the incoming tide covered the Sabre. Within hours a search team of 500 Chinese laborers recovered the wreckage (even as U.S. ships fired on the site). The dismantled pieces were loaded on trucks and taken toward Andun. The convoy hid in tunnels during the day and traveled by night for cover from the pursuing American aircraft. A few days later after reaching the airbase at Andun the jet was shipped to Moscow for evaluation. Ironically Russian engineers concluded that the MiG-17, about to go into production, was more advanced overall and therefore copying the Sabre was unnecessary.

Reverse engineering was done anyway in an effort to evaluate individual parts and systems. Components were removed, catalogued and then installed on test bed aircraft at the Soviet Institute.

Some items, such as the accelerometer (G meter), were adopted for future designs such as the MiG-19.

In July of 1952 Walker "Bud" Mahurin was shot down and captured in an F-86E. The advanced model Sabre incorporated a completely hydraulic control system including an all-moving horizontal stabilizer or "flying tail". It also had leading edge flaps to improve maneuverability at slower speeds.

Since, by this time, production of the MiG-17 was winding down the improved systems were not incorporated into Soviet jets until the MiG-19. And even then the leading edge flaps were not used due to the almost 60 degrees of wing sweep angle.

Possibly the most significant adaptation was the introduction of the G suit systems thus improving the performance of the most lethal system in a fighter jet—the pilot.

Lieutenant No gave instruction (through an interpreter) to Major Tom Collins and Captain Chuck Yeager for their 11 evaluation flights on Okinawa. Some of the more simple things included lack of nose wheel steering and humble environmental controls. Minimal cockpit heating is available at high altitudes (where temperatures can reach—75 degrees Fahrenheit) and vent air only for cooling up to 10,000 feet. (I routinely lost about five pounds of fluid during a summer airshow.)

More important was the aircraft's speed limitations. Critical Mach for the MiG-15 is .92 where the speed brake automatically deploys. Collins and Yeager wanted to know why.

After deactivating the auto speed brake feature, Collins attempted the first supersonic flight and was unsuccessful. He told Yeager about the jet's tendency to buffet and then pitch nose up at the highest Mach even with both hands pushing full forward on the stick. (At speeds in excess of 450 knots the tall control stick feels like it's stuck in a bucket of cement.) Yeager's solution to the problem was, at 50,000 feet, to roll inverted to forty five degrees nose down so that when the nose pitched "up" it would be pointing down nearly vertical. Yeager recovered at 3,000 feet over the water and the jet never reached Mach 1.

The guns were impressive. A single thirty seven millimeter cannon, which fired straight for only about one hundred meters, used its slow fire to shoot down bombers. The two faster twenty three millimeter guns were used for dogfighting and strafing. Fortunately, No's jet was fully loaded allowing for armament testing on the ground (into a revetment) as well.

The Americans were particularly interested in the MiG-15's gunsight. The F-86 used the Sperry AN/APG 30 radar ranging gunsight which was easier to use and much more accurate than the MiG's. It was extremely accurate up to a range of about 3000 feet and able to measure range and compute lead time while its target was maneuvering. We learned that the gunsight installed in the MiG had been designed in the 1930s.

In addition to his $100,000 dollar reward, No received a college education here in the U.S. and was integrated into society with, obviously, an assumed name. He is now known as Kenneth Rowe and has worked for many aircraft companies as well as on the faculty of Embry Riddle Aeronautical University.

YEAGER

Earlier in the year I had read Chuck Yeager's autobiography and was very interested in the chapter in which he described testing the MiG-15 on Okinawa. He described it as being "one of the most dangerous airplanes (he had) ever flown" and that got my attention!

At that point I had not yet flown my MiG and figured that some advice from him could possibly save my life in the future.

So, I called directory assistance in Grass Valley, California and, sure enough, got his number. (This was before his revived notoriety due to his commercials as a Delco battery salesman.)

His wife, Glynnis, answered the phone and, ever the careful call screener, seemed reluctant to let me speak with him but I turned up the country accent a notch and she eventually called him to the phone.

I made sure I was exceptionally polite while beginning to explain the nature of my call when he suddenly ripped into me with a vengeance. Right after I had said something about the jet being at Chino he called me everything but a nice guy. Even though he didn't know me he was cussing me out. He was ranting and raving about some guy named Maloney and where we could stick it. He informed me that he could fly a MiG any time he wanted to.

It seemed that he had a sore spot about an incident with the Planes of Fame Museum involving his not being allowed to fly a Mustang of theirs due to insurance problems. Ed Maloney ran the place and Yeager thought he had put me up to calling him to get him to test a MiG for them. Once he had his blood pressure under control, I explained that I had no connection with Maloney, did not want him to test the jet, and had called to merely ask his advice based upon his comments in the book. He loosened up a bit and said some things like, "Don't touch that damned TO&E (takeoff & emergency) switch 'cause it'll blow the ass end plum off the airplane". (It's used for, basically, an extra boost of power in an extremis situation such as running out of runway on takeoff.)

Granted, he did give me some gouge (naval aviator slang for scoop or inside information), vague as it was, but he was a real horse's butt in the process. His arrogance and condescending tone were totally uncalled for.

I took copious notes and thanked him for his time, sadly realizing that one of my aviation heroes had fallen from his pedestal and onto common ground.

That winter was spent doing interviews for magazines and even a segment on the popular television show, *Lifestyles of the Rich and Famous*. I thought how ironic that was since I was neither.

Regardless, the publicity was something that money couldn't buy and it thrust me into the limelight around the world.

The MiG and I were hailed from as far away as Germany and Japan.

Being the first at anything can have both good and bad sides, but the good seemed to far outweigh the bad. I hung up on a lot of cold-calling stock brokers and learned the value of an unlisted telephone number and a post office box address.

PITTS PROBLEMS

I initially kept the Pitts at the Milton airport due to a lack of hangar space at Pensacola.

Having heard that there was to be an open house at the airport that Saturday, I decided to fly out to the beach for some aerobatic practice for the duration of the festivities. I'd had kids try to step on the fabric wings before and I thought it prudent for the plane to be away from the area.

At the top of a loop the engine sputtered, which had never happened before. I leveled off and checked the instruments which gave no adverse indications, but my little voice told me to take it on back. I stayed at about 1000 feet as I skirted the Pensacola airport ARSA (a radar controlled area which requires permission to enter) and was over Escambia Bay when the engine suddenly stopped.

I tried a restart with no success and quickly evaluated my options.

I could either jump immediately and risk drowning due to parachute entanglement with no floatation device or stay with the airplane and try to ditch it near the shoreline.

The latter sounded better so I made for the Bagdad peninsula. I was amazed at how well the plane was gliding and soon remembered that there was an auxiliary Navy field, OLF Choctaw, not too far beyond the trees.

I had done many FCLPs (field carrier landing practice) and night landings there as an instructor and had a good idea of its approximate location. I couldn't see it but I knew it was close so I stretched the glide as much as possible, frequently getting the aural stall warning. When I was too low to jump and committed to clearing some tall pine trees directly ahead, I had a sinking feeling that I probably wouldn't make it. I had resigned myself that I had had given it my best shot when I saw an opening just past the trees and knew it had to be the runway. I had to miss the trees by staying in the stall until the last second and then dump the nose to get a smidgen of airspeed to allow a bit of a flare just before impact. It worked. I hit the runway hard which flattened both tires and hit the prop, but the little Pitts didn't flip on me and I walked away without a scratch. I really don't understand how that little plane glided as far as it did, but I do believe I know why. Once again, the good Lord was looking out for me and took me in His *Mighty Hands*.

A mechanic later discovered that the fuel filter was clogged with gunk that I'd picked up from some bad fuel at Milton T and the engine had died due to fuel starvation. I never bought fuel there again.

The plane was out of commission for several weeks so there's no way I could have practiced for the coming season. As it turned out, I never flew a single show in the Pitts. In fact, I planned to keep it for more cost efficient aerobatic practice but the differences between it and the MiG were just too great to be practical.

After flying it for many more uneventful hours I sold it to an attorney from San Diego who, along with his ferry pilot, ran it out of gas and crashed on their first leg out of Pensacola. Neither one was critically injured but the beautiful Spectrum Eagle was totaled.

I heard it was bought from the insurance company as a salvage project and was later rebuilt and flown.

By June the MiG had still not been certificated by the FAA so I had a little spare time for other endeavors.

Kim McCabe had introduced me to Slick Goodlin who happened to be a life-long friend of his father's. Since retiring from test pilot work, Slick had been in the used airliner business and had contacts all over the world.

Kim came up with a scheme for us to purchase some former MAP (military assistance plan) F-5s from Jordan after learning of Slick's relationship with Ali Gandour, Jordan's Minister of Transportation. Slick set up a trip that provided us with the potential to deal but we felt the Jordanian's prices were unreasonable.

We also had potential U.S. State Department problems regarding releasing the jets for sale as well, and they eventually ended up in Greece. It was a rough trip that took us from New York to Vienna to Amman to Zurich to Stuttgart to Baden to Frankfurt and back.

MACH 1

To say that Slick Goodlin was an interesting fellow is an understatement. He was depicted in Tom Wolfe's book and subsequent movie *The Right Stuff* as a greedy chap who wouldn't fly the Bell X-1 rocket plane past Mach 1 unless he was paid a substantial bonus. According to Slick, the crap perpetuated by egotists Wolfe and Chuck Yeager was either sour grapes or outright lies. He said that the project was taken over by the Air Force and that it was their decision to have a military test pilot fly the culminating Mach run. In fact, Slick had already created a sonic boom (or crack) over Muroc, albeit during subsonic flight. Slick documented the details in an address to the Society of Experimental Test pilots in Dallas a few years back. He gave me the original copy of that speech.

Dick Frost verified the story of Slick flying a structural demonstration flight for the Army Air Corps. It occurred on February 5, 1947, as Slick was diving the number two X-1. Upon reaching .79 Mach, he pulled a hard 8.7 Gs and then pushed over to zero G. A sharp crack was heard distinctly by the Bell people on the ground. Frost contacted Slick immediately and an expeditious, minimum-stress return to land was accomplished.

What happened was that the shock wave standing on the wing (present at or above approximately .75 Mach) was super compressed at 8.7 Gs and when Slick unloaded the wing to zero G, an explosive expansion of the air on top of the wing accompanied the rapid disappearance of the shock wave. This is similar to the noise heard when air rushes in to fill the vacuum created by superheating and ionization in the atmosphere—thunder.

Based upon historical fact, when Yeager flew the ninth powered flight on October 14, 1947, it was preceded by the fact that General Al Boyd wanted control of the program for the Air Force because he felt NACA (The National Advisory Committee for Aeronautics) and the contractor, Bell, were too slow and methodical. The "hell bent for leather" Air Force test pilots were aggressive to the point of being unsafe while the contractor test pilots were more cerebral and scientific in their approach. Without question, both had courage. For example, Yeager and Bob Hoover were great pilots, proven in combat, but not educated to the level of the likes of Scott Crossfield and Slick. (Slick was a combat pilot as well.)

In his book, Yeager even makes a point of belittling Neil Armstrong (a civilian test pilot) who, as we all know, just happened to be the first man on the moon.

The decision to transfer development of one of the two X-1s from NACA to the Air Force was strictly political and had nothing to do with bonus money for the contract pilot, Slick, as depicted in *The Right Stuff*. Slick told me that he was paid quite handsomely as it was. Slick flew five glide flights which preceded twenty one rocket-powered flights (not including at least six aborted prior to drop from the B-29).

Dick Frost and Jack Ridley, the two key engineers on the project, probably were more responsible for its success than anyone—especially Yeager. They solved controllability problems with the horizontal stabilizer by employing an earlier designed trimmable stabilizer mechanism—the flying tail. It was Ridley's idea to modify the horizontal stabilizer utilizing two air motors and a manually controlled jack screw to change the pitch as the rocket motors increased the X-1's speed toward transonic flight. The NACA engineers were far too conservative, thinking it would cause the X-1 to go out of control at the higher Mach number and proposed utilizing the adjustment only on the ground.

In addition to the pecker-matching between Bell and the Air Force as to whose pilot would fly the Mach-busting flight, there was another seldom referred to project occurring at the same time that made their bickering meaningless.

In, esteemed Marine Corps aviator and test pilot, Al Blackburn's book, *Aces Wild*, he tells, as Paul Harvey would say, the rest of the story.

> "The North American Aircraft Company was testing its XP-86 at Muroc during the same time period. The first flight of the XP-86 took place on Wednesday morning, October 1, 1947. Its pilot was George Welch.

He was confident that the sound barrier was a bunch of hokum based upon his knowledge of the German V-2 rockets which had gone in excess of Mach 4 thousands of times. At 35,000 feet and 320 knots indicated, he rolled into a forty degree dive pointed directly at Pancho Barnes Happy Bottom Riding Club. (Pancho had a standing offer of a free steak "with all the trimmin's" for the first pilot to bust the sound barrier.) A few thousand feet later, he saw the airspeed hang-up then jump to and peg at 450 knots where he reduced power and leveled off.

(Note that the XP-86 prototypes had no Mach meters.) His sonic boom rattled everything at Pancho's but there was no recorded proof.

The radar theodolites (radar-assisted optical tracking instruments) used to track the X-1 speed precisely were not routinely available from NACA to North American.

Two weeks after the first flight and having been instructed to back off, Welch again went supersonic on the fourth flight with Bob Chilton, his chase pilot, covering for him. The radar theodolite facility was finally utilized in November to verify the Sabres supersonic flight.

Dutch Kindelberger from North American had a "heart to heart" with Secretary of the Air Force Stu Symington who was under a lot of pressure from President Truman to ensure that Bell set the record.

Here's why.

Suppose a new fighter comes along (the F-86 Sabre), carries six guns plus bombs, can fly supersonic, and does it before the supposedly advanced technology rocketship. It makes the government look like idiots.

North American preferred contracts to records, so, with a wink and a nod, Symington and Kindelberger made a deal. The fact that the Sabre had flown supersonic was not revealed until some months later and, even then, the actual date was changed by six months."

Fate made Yeager the hero and winner of a free steak dinner. With his broken ribs, he knew his backup (Bob Hoover, admittedly a better pilot) could've flown the record breaking flight just as easily—twenty seconds at about 670 miles per hour.

Granted, it was an unknown in 1947 but let's put it into perspective by today's standards.

A jet afterburner is a thrust augmenter, like the passing gear of a car's automatic transmission. You select afterburner by pushing the jet's throttle all the way to full power, and then nudge it even further past a detent. The exhaust nozzles of the engine widen and a spray of raw fuel is injected into the exhaust blast. It's used for short spurts of maximum energy.

As you shove the throttle into burner you will eventually go past the mystical indication of Mach 1 on the airspeed indicator. That's all there is to it. I've done it in an F-5, an F-18 and even a MiG-17 and there's no beautiful aura of light and no perceptible feeling or sound.

It's just another number. Rather disappointing.

As Slick put it, "It's the greatest non-event in the history of aviation".

Admittedly though, it *is* cool to feel that burner light and hear the whaaboom! In the air, speed is life.

In addition to getting to Mach 1 second, Bell was also second to Mach 2. In 1953, Scott Crossfield, flying the Douglas D-558-2 Skyrocket, busted Mach 2 ahead of the Bell X-1A in which Yeager was also the pilot. Not convinced that Scotty had gone sufficiently beyond Mach 2, Yeager pushed the X-1A to Mach 2.4 (ignoring the NACA engineers warning of instability beyond Mach 2.3) and subsequently departed* the aircraft which is depicted in the movie *The Right Stuff* as the scene where Yeager cracks his helmet against the canopy. Pancho gave the steak to Scotty this time. Crossfield again bested Yeager by flying the North American X-15 to Mach 3.

Mach speed has become a non-event. The space shuttle orbiter exceeds Mach 20. In fact, the military has ceased their focus on speed and directed it to stealth. In their quest for stealth, stability and control characteristics are so effected that, without advanced computer technology, the newest generation of jet aircraft cannot fly, thus, lending credence to Scott Crossfield's remark about " . . . the difficulty of economically replacing such a highly sensitive, infinitely variable bit of protoplasmic servomechanism that can be produced by wholly unskilled labor"—the pilot.

Both Scotty Crossfield and Slick Goodlin are now, no doubt, flying under their own power in heaven. The countless contributions they made to aeronautics can never be calculated.

*Departed controlled flight, i.e. as to stall and spin.

CHAPTER 8

THE BANDIT

"FIGHTER PILOTS DO IT UP IN THE THIN AIR WHERE THE GROUND IS FAR AWAY. IF THEY GET TOO CLOSE, MOST EJECT. AIRSHOW FLYING IN A FIGHTER AT NEAR SUPERSONIC SPEEDS REQUIRES INTENSE CONCENTRATION AND IS TOTALLY UNFORGIVING OF ERROR."

When pilots are flying with the potential to engage in aerial combat, they use the code name "bogie" to identify an unknown aircraft and "bandit" to identify one known to be hostile.

Flying a MiG around the country, fellow pilots naturally came up with a most appropriate name, thus my call sign, Bandit.

Airshow sponsors had been calling continuously since the ICAS convention, keeping abreast of our certification progress. Many did not anticipate the lengths to which the FAA would make us go and were miffed with me for not being available. By August, however, I was ready for my first airshow.

That cross-country flight up to Canada was memorable due to an incident at Seattle. I had elected to fly the first trip without drop tanks and my range was significantly limited. I preferred to land at either Boeing or Paine Field but was forced to go to SEA TAC.

As luck would have it, even after a nice gentle touchdown, my nose tire blew on landing rollout and I was barely able to limp onto a taxiway. I was lucky to find a mechanic who kindly helped me find some jacks and pads and installed another nose wheel assembly when it arrived from Chino.

Even with the lengthy delay I made it to Abbotsford, British Columbia for my very first airshow on August 9th, 1987.

It was a very ad-libbed dogfight with a fellow named Ben Hall who had the only flying F-86A. We took off on the same runway simultaneously from opposite ends; much like two knights beginning a joust. We lifted off about the midpoint of the runway and accelerated to the end where we both turned outboard, away from the crowd. We spiraled up to 1,000 feet and the fight was on.

In retrospect it was a good show but I think the folks would've been thrilled just to see the MiG fly.

It was the first time in North America.

The next weekend I flew my first U.S. airshow for the Lynnwood Rotary Club at Paine Field in Everett, Washington.

Ben based his jet there as did Boeing who had an F-86 camera ship on site. A Boeing test pilot, Terry Kriha, flew aerobatics in trail with Ben and me and we finished up with some loose formation fly bys.

I had experienced a *Catch 22* in my attempt to get an aerobatic competency card which authorizes low level aerobatics at waivered sites such as airshows. I was told that I had to fly a low level show to get the card but I couldn't fly low level without it.

A local FAA inspector, appreciating my predicament, agreed to evaluate my aerobatics and greeted me with a card upon my return to the chocks there at Paine Field. That would be impossible under the current tightly regulated procedures.

For the remainder of the season I was on the road.

I knew I needed to develop something more than just a standard military type flight demonstration but there's only so much you can do with a jet with the MiG's thrust to weight ratio. The jet was graceful (mainly because it rolls so slow—even with full stick deflection) but I needed something special.

I learned quickly the importance of great narration and music with the act.

During an airshow in Denver, I asked wing walker and great aerial stunt man Johnny Kazian to narrate my act. He had some spare time after riding Jim Franklin's wing and kindly agreed. Johnny had a style all his own which always included a big "Oh Yeah" after something interesting. He did a fabulous job and, afterwards, other performers came up to compliment me on the improvements in my act. I didn't fly anything any differently . . . it was all Johnny.

Soon after, I hired Dan Lucas, a Pensacola radio announcer, to help me cut a tape with original music and the narration I had written. Dan read it superbly and the tape made a big difference.

Johnny was special but, generally speaking, most of the airshow performers I met were very nice people. Obviously they were talented, but we all liked to think that we had some special gift as aviators that allowed us to fly the way we did—upside down and close to the ground. Truth be known, and I'm about to shatter the airshow myth here, most of the performers, myself included, were just a little above average. Of course there are Bob Hoovers and Leo Loudenslagers and Sean Tuckers but, for the most part, we're just entertainers who happen to use the sky as our stage. I knew this early on as a Marine flight instructor. I watched them and said, "I could do that. How hard could it be?" So I joined the traveling troupe of showmen and became a part of the airshow culture.

I had a super smoke system on the jet and incorporated a trademark takeoff with a huge plume of smoke billowing up to capture the crowd's attention. I was unique and it was good.

My first show at a high elevation site was in Grand Junction, Colorado. All pilots know that density altitude makes a big difference in aircraft performance. In essence, performance at high elevations is drastically reduced compared to that at sea level. The worst conditions involve *the three Hs*; high, hot and humid. The humidity was reasonable but it was definitely high and hot. It was an excellent experience to do that show early on before I had the chance to become complacent.

I had flown non-stop from Chino with a 100 knot tailwind from the jet stream and orbited near the airport waiting for an

A-7 that was to "escort" me into the show for the media. He missed the rendezvous and, after waiting a bit too long after bingo fuel, I ended up landing with fumes. (Bingo fuel is the calculated fuel remaining, allowing just enough to proceed to the destination.)

Another reinforcement of piloting skill—Plan your flight and fly your plan.

I went from there to Halifax, Nova Scotia for the Shearwater airshow and was gradually getting more comfortable with the jet.

Years later while returning from a show up in Gander, Newfoundland and flying along the same route, the weather in New England was marginal and I had filed to Portland, Maine. The air traffic controllers at Moncton Center had done a nice job of keeping me in the clear but it was a different story once I was handed off to Boston. Even after advising him that I had no weather radar, the controller vectored me directly into a thunderstorm. I was IMC (in clouds) and never saw it coming. A microburst or downdraft within the cell was pushing me down. I was descending at 3,000 feet per minute with full military power and twenty degrees nose up. When I told him that I needed clearance to a lower altitude his reply was "Maintain 13,000". I reiterated that I needed lower due to adverse weather and his reply was the same. In my next radio transmission I really got his attention by saying that I was "going down". He asked if I was declaring an emergency and while I was thinking about it I broke out of the weather and the jet instantly started to climb.

I replied "negative" and told him I could now accept a clearance as I was out of jeopardy. He eventually handed me off to another controller and I landed safely.

I made a phone call to the Center supervisor and smoothed things over by explaining the details and all was forgiven.

The precipitation in that cell beat most of the paint off the leading edges of the airplane and I was very lucky to be alive. Cells like that have a tendency to chew up and spit out little airplanes.

In the future I asked for vectors to follow an airliner through or around significant weather.

One particular cross-country flight was thrilling for a number of reasons. It was my first long leg requiring maximum range and, since I was traveling from west to east, I decided to take advantage of the jet stream. I filed for flight level 470 (47,000 feet) and figured I had somewhere around a 100 knot tail wind.

At the halfway point I knew I had sufficient fuel to make it to my destination so I decided to go on up to 50,000 feet—just to test the jet's flight characteristics and, also . . . because I'd never been that high.

Center approved my request to climb (there's not much traffic up there) and I slowly worked my way up.

High altitude flying is extremely tedious since aircraft are much more control sensitive up in the thin atmosphere. Other than the sensation of balancing the jet on the head of a pin, the thing I remember most was the vivid sapphire blue color of the sky. It was spectacular and almost mesmerizing. As the indicated airspeed decreases at altitude, the cockpit gets much quieter, too. It was a very surreal feeling and one that made me feel close to the heavens—close to God.

I think that only in those precious moments that I've been privileged enough to see the aurora borealis in the northern night from the cockpit, have I been as thrilled at the color of the sky.

I truly envy the SR-71 Blackbird pilots that cruised at 60 to 80,000 feet for the view that they had. I'd love to see the sky turn from cobalt blue to black as they did.

MiG on the ramp

Since that flight, I've had a much greater appreciation for the poem *High Flight* by John Gillespie Magee, Jr.:

> Oh, I have slipped the surly bonds of earth
> and danced the skies on laughter-silvered wings;
>
> Sunward I've climbed and joined the tumbling mirth
> of sun-split clouds and done a hundred things
> you have not dreamed of;
>
> Wheeled and soared and swung high in the sunlit silence.
>
> Hov'ring there, I've chased the shouting wind along
> and flung my eager craft through footless halls of air.
> Up, up the long, delirious, burning blue
> I've topped the windswept heights with easy grace
> Where never lark, or even eagle flew.
>
> And, while with silent, lifting mind
> I've trod the high untrespassed sanctity of space,
> Put out my hand, and touched the face of God.

Magee was an American who joined the Royal Canadian Air Force in 1940 and went on to England to fight in the war flying a Spitfire. He was killed during a dogfight the next year at the tender age of nineteen.

On my way home at the end of the season I was making a fuel stop in Huntsville, Alabama to visit my Aunt Martha and Uncle Earney.

I had cruised at a very high altitude (around 47,000 feet) and, obviously, the outside air was extremely cold at altitude. One little anomaly that I hadn't foreseen on this particular day was that any moisture in the cockpit would freeze regardless of the cockpit heat setting. When I began my descent, the throttle quadrant was frozen and wouldn't budge. I hadn't deduced that yet but assumed that some FOD had found its way inside and was somehow binding the throttle mechanism as I tugged at it. (FOD is the acronym for foreign objects or debris.) I knew better than to force it but had to think fast about a solution. I deployed the speed brakes and informed the controller of my situation.

I knew that I had to descend gradually enough so as to not exceed red line airspeed but I had to get down quickly to avoid running out of fuel.

By the time I reached 10,000 feet (where pilots must normally slow to 250 knots or less for further descent) I had reached well over 600 knots and was bordering critical Mach. I was setting myself up for a long straight in glide where I planned to cut the fuel off and dead stick in. On my final attempt to reduce power the ice had thawed enough that I was able to pull the throttle back and I landed uneventfully.

My learning curve about the MiG had gone straight up thus far and I was ready for the airshow season to be over.

1988 introduced me to a few more friends.

I had met Jim Robinson briefly at Chino. He had purchased one of my MiG's sister ships to go along with the stable of warbirds he was collecting. Eventually Jim had two F-86s, a T-33, F-104, A-4, Hawker Hunter, MiG-15 and a MiG-21.

I stopped at Houston to refuel and figured I'd say hello while I was there at Hobby. Unfortunately I had another one of those pesky nose tire flats but Jim and his guys came to the rescue. He refused any compensation. That's the kind of guy he was. His family was well-off but he had built a lot of flight time by corporate flying on his own and he had very good stick and rudder skills.

Jim was a little wary of new friends and rightfully so. Everybody wanted something from him. We discovered that we had more in common than our MiGs and became good friends vowing to assist one another in our ordeals with the Feds.

Operating as the Combat Jet Museum, Jim had surrounded himself with top notch mechanics and pilots.

His chief pilot was Eddie Schneider, a former Navy pilot flying test for NASA out at Edwards. Eddie was first class.

Jim was also fortunate to have astronaut Hoot Gibson in his program, too, and with him, a wealth of knowledge.

I also met Chuck Scott, another former naval aviator and a pilot with Southwest Airlines, who was flying for the museum.

Jim had agreed to fly some of the jets up to Addison, Texas for a photo shoot with publisher Mike O'Leary. I volunteered to fly his MiG with Chuck and Eddie in a Sabre and Hunter.

We'd never flown together and were all slightly apprehensive about formating in marginal weather but the old naval aviator briefing went just like we all remembered and we felt at ease with one another by the time we strapped in. Chuck had the lead in the Sabre with Eddie in the bright red Hunter on the left wing and me on the right. Chuck was a solid lead which was essential in the instrument conditions we experienced most of the way. Somewhere before level-off I started to experience some symptoms of hypoxia (oxygen starvation) and told the guys what was up. Chuck immediately got us clearance for a lower altitude while I tried to figure out the problem. I was wearing my mask so I went to 100% oxygen to clear my head. Eventually I noticed that the canopy was not properly sealed and that was the problem.

We proceeded uneventfully and I really appreciated the coolness of my wingmen.

We flew the photo mission (which eventually appeared in some books with outstanding results) and then headed back to Houston. Returning in the thick clouds, even though I was never more than five feet from Chuck's wing, I could barely see his green position light. It was actually easier to see Eddie in the bright red Hunter fifty feet away.

After we landed I knew that I'd fly anytime, anywhere with those two. They were naval aviators extraordinaire and we became good friends.

There was a nice article in *Flying* magazine that spring. My friend, Bill Mayo, owned Pensacola Aeromotive (one of two, at that time, fixed base operators at Pensacola Regional airport which provide fuel, servicing, etc., to both local and transient aircraft). Bill managed to scrounge up some hangar space for both the Pitts and the MiG when there was none to be found. (I don't suppose it had anything to do with the fact that we were both Auburn men and former naval aviators in both fixed wing and helos.) He had told me that another friend of his was in the same issue of the magazine and, because of the coincidence, he felt we needed to meet one another. We flew up to a little grass strip in Chapman, Alabama in Bill's Baron on a rainy afternoon where he introduced me to the colorful character, Floyd McGowin.

Floyd had a spectacular spread surrounded by hundreds of acres of pine timber. His family had been in the logging business for years and provided them a very comfortable life. Floyd was also a former Marine who, although not a military pilot, had worked in Marine aviation as a ground radar officer in Korea. Quite a few guys owed their life to his GCAs (ground controlled approaches). He was an avid aviation enthusiast and had amassed an unparalled personal aviation library and built a spectacular facility.

The runway was manicured like a golf course and you could almost eat off of his hangar deck. The adjoining office was filled with aircraft lithographs and prints and thousands of volumes of reference books. He was in *Flying* with his beautiful SNJ that had been restored to museum quality. He also had a Stearman, a Great Lakes, a Cessna 185 and a Baron.

Floyd's love of aviation and generosity allowed him to become involved with the Air Force's Air Command and Staff College up at Maxwell Air Force Base in Montgomery and he sponsored a part of their Gathering of Eagles each year. Each class would select about a dozen extraordinary pilots from history and honor them for a few days in June. The pilots in return would provide lectures for the class and both educate and entertain them with stories of their exploits.

Floyd had met and maintained friendships with some of the most famous pilots in the world and I was very fortunate to be in his and their company.

On one particular occasion, Floyd suggested that we impress a couple of Maxwell's "Eagles" with our formation skills.

He was taking two Russian aces on a little tour of Mobile and the Museum of Naval Aviation in Pensacola. He thought it would be a great idea if I could intercept him on my way into Maxwell as he returned in his Baron. We rendezvoused enroute and the Russian chaps were astonished to see one of their own jets flying in formation with them just a few feet away.

Later that summer, at Oshkosh, I flew some formation passes with Chuck Scott in a Sabre and also with Hoot Gibson in a MiG-21. I flew a couple of passes on Chuck's wing and then broke off for Hooter to join on me. We made a beautiful pass at 300 feet and 300 knots with him really tight on my right wing. We were later accused by an aviation newspaper writer of having a mid-air as evidenced by some photos he had taken and published. Obviously, we didn't or we'd both be dead but the illusion of the photos was certainly impressive.

Hoot is a piece of work. I met him at a show in Denver, right after his brake bladders melted and he rolled off into the grass in Jim Robinson's MiG-15. We had a good laugh at Hooter's expense and later seriously discussed some of the peculiarities of the MiG. You'd never meet a nicer, more humble guy and he's deceptively brilliant. He commanded several space shuttle missions, became NASA's chief astronaut and was the first mission commander to dock with the Russian space station, Mir. I used to ask Hoot what he was going to do when he retired and his answer was always the same, "I want to do what you're doing—fly for the airlines!" I thought he was nuts.

Floyd McGowin & 2 Russian Aces

MiG-15 & MiG-21 flown by Astronaut Hoot Gibson

Marine Harriers & Hornets on my wings

A guy with his background could name his price and work for a host of major aerospace corporations. But not Hooter; nope. Hoot is a pilot, first and foremost. He loves to fly and that's all he wants to do. You've got to admire him for that. He eventually did become a pilot for Southwest Airlines.

I have another astronaut friend because of Hoot. Prior to one of his shuttle missions, Hoot was up at Oshkosh with his rookie second-in-command, Curt Brown. Curt fit right in. Another guy who just loved to fly and was easy to like. Curt became a mission commander himself and assumed Hoot's role as the best of the best. He was chosen to be the boss when John Glenn made his return to space and, prior to that (in 1994), Curt was kind enough to take one of my Bandit patches into orbit on STS-66. My little patch rode the space shuttle Atlantis for twelve days and 4.5 million miles. Thanks Curt. By the way, he's now a pilot for American Airlines.

Another memorable formation flight was a beautiful Marine five-ship at the Lake Charles, Louisiana air show. I had the lead with two Hornets on my right wing and two Harriers on my left. I brought them in for a steeply banked pass at high speed. It was cooler than cool.

I've also done some tame passes with an F-4 and an F-15 but I think my favorite was at Minot, North Dakota in July of '92 when I had a Ukrainian MiG-29 on each wing. It was wild to be flying a Russian jet with two Russians on my wing, each jabbering away to each other on the radio.

We communicated with some universal (?) hand signals and wowed the airshow.

Somewhere on the airshow circuit I bumped into my friend Ed Bowlin and his wife Connie. They were flying a couple of Mustangs around and they were also very easy to get to know and like. As a matter of fact, Ed was the one who planted the seed in my mind to reconsider flying with the airlines. He and

Connie were both Delta pilots and he said it was the "best part time job in the world". He told me I'd get tired of pulling Gs one day and, when I did, to give him a call.

As it turned out, Ed was good friends with Chuck Yeager and, when I was invited to fly the MiG up to Maxwell for a Gathering of Eagles, I told him about my previous telephone encounter. Ed explained that almost everybody that sees Yeager wants a piece of him and that he'd developed a crusty shell to ward of the leeches. I didn't think that excused his behavior during our phone conversation, but kept an open mind on Ed's advice.

He said he'd introduce us, remind Chuck of the story and make sure we got off on the right foot. He did and Yeager warmed up after a couple of days, eventually interested in climbing into my cockpit. He checked it over and pointed out what he could remember.

We posed for some pictures and ended up having some enjoyable conversation together that night. He's a really nice guy when he's had a few snorts under his belt; joking and surrounded by his peers. Since then, we've attended functions at the same place and the same time but he seldom offers more than a polite acknowledgment.

Ed allowed me to use him as a reference on my Delta application which I'm sure didn't hurt my chances for an interview. We worked together for several years helping to educate the Feds about surplus military jets.

He and Connie are both now retired from Delta and, sadly, have terminated their friendship with Yeager due to a lawsuit encouraged by his current wife.

As I mentioned, I've had the opportunity to meet so many world famous aviators through Floyd and, from aces to astronauts, they were mostly gentlemen.

One of the best was astronaut Joe Engle. When I met him and his wife at the Gathering of Eagles, they couldn't have been kinder.

Joe had made brigadier general before his retirement from the Air Force after which he settled down in Colorado Springs with a sporting goods store. One of the things we had in common was our love of the outdoors. We both enjoyed hunting and fishing and talked for quite a while about only that.

A few days later he was kind enough to send me some memorabilia from his missions. (Not the least of which was his testing of the shuttle orbiter's emergency detachment from its piggy back mount on the NASA 747. He also performed the first glide tests of the orbiter in that way.)

For such a pleasant, smiling and unassuming man, my tall friend had some very impressive credentials!

Chuck Yeager & me

188

PAUL T. ENTREKINPAUL T. ENTREKIN

I had an interesting encounter with another fairly famous astronaut named Alan Shepard. Al was coming to Pensacola for a function at the Museum of Naval Aviation. We requested that he pay a visit to my kid's school and offer a quick, motivational talk to an assembly. He graciously obliged and the principal asked me if I would offer the introduction.

So, before he arrived, I had a TV and VCR set up to show the kids a short clip from the *The Right Stuff*. (I should mention that just about everyone portrayed in the movie, except Yeager, hates it. Obviously, I didn't know that at the time.)

To my misfortune, Shepard walked into the assembly just as his character, portrayed by Scott Glenn, was peeing in his space suit before the launch.

I stopped the tape and, without missing a beat, announced to the school, "Ladies and gentlemen, the first American in space, Alan Shepard!" The kids were cheering as he took the stage and he leaned over and whispered to me, "Thanks a lot (expletive deleted)." We shared a laugh later, once he had thoroughly schooled me about the many fictional holes in Wolfe's book and film.

The MiG has opened doors, too, because we're naturally attracted to a fellow pilot who's willing to take a risk and push the edge of the envelope. Talk is cheap, so the camaraderie comes easy to that select few.

I met Duke Cunningham at the El Toro airshow in 1989. He was just walking around the flight line and came up and introduced himself while I was servicing the MiG. I recognized him as a Vietnam ace and we yakked for quite a while. Years later he would sign a print for me with the inscription, "One of the few MiG drivers I wouldn't like to smoke".

One afternoon I was at a cookout at the Troy, Alabama airport with my buddy Rick Kammer as the guests of our new friend Kenny Campbell. (While at Floyd's, we were taking turns flying the Stearman and SNJ when a T-34B showed up. It was Kenny coming to visit and we all hit it off right away. When he learned that Rick and I had instructed in the T-34C he insisted that we take his airplane for a spin and tell him what we thought of it. We were hesitant at first but eventually we flew it around the patch.)

Kenny was a very generous guy and invited us to the cookout being held by another warbird enthusiast, Wiley Sanders.

Wiley's a good ol' country boy who made his fortune by figuring out a process for salvaging old automobile batteries and then melting them down for the lead and plastic. He has more airplanes than anybody ought to and has enjoyed air racing for years.

His chief pilot, Earl Smith, was a real character, too, and can fly anything with wings.

Anyway, we were enjoying the fellowship with a bunch of other folks at the cookout while some of the boys were taking turns flying formation around the pattern. A group of T-34s flew by, each one doing an aileron roll on his pass. The last one was owned by a fellow who'd had it for years and, even though he'd had aerobatic instruction, made no bones about not enjoying aerobatics at all.

I figure he felt shamed into doing a roll, too, and when he did, he dished out in sort of a split S and stuck it straight into the ground. Rick and I hustled into my car and headed to the wreckage.

Nothing burned as the plane had disintegrated into hundreds of pieces.

We were the first ones there and immediately looked for survivors but found nothing but the crumpled remains of him and his passenger.

HOOVER

Later that year I was performing at the Oklahoma City airshow when I had the chance to meet a real airshow legend.

It was a really hot, dusty day and the nice folks there had provided a motor home for the performers to use to get out of the sun. It was air-conditioned with some soft drinks and light snacks inside so I moseyed in to cool down after my flight. I was surprised to find that the only person inside was none other than Bob Hoover. He was sitting there in his flight suit with his big panama hat on the table. With a great big smile that welcomed me he said, "Come on in young fella. Nice show!" I really appreciated the compliment coming from a pilot of his caliber but figured he was just being nice.

I noticed he kept grinning like a Cheshire cat and wondered what was up. After giving me a chance to relax he said, "I've got some good news for you. My good friend, Bob Goodrich, is the Director of Flight Standards for the FAA and he called me with some concerns about some fella flying the circuit with a MiG.

Since I told him we'd be performing together here, he asked me to do an informal evaluation on you and I'm happy to say you passed with flying colors! I like the way you use the jet's energy. It reminds me of the way I flew the Sabre."

Now, coming from Mr. Energy Management himself, I was humbled by the high praise. He must have quite an astute eye because he somehow knew that I wasn't adjusting the throttle. It was a matter of continuously trading altitude for airspeed or vice versa. (In Bob's act, in the Shrike Commander, in particular, he actually shuts down one engine, then the other, as he uses energy management to put the plane through a series of maneuvers.) It's not a terribly big deal, just a technique. It's the only way that gliders stay aloft. But then, they don't weigh very much either.

Mr. Bob Hoover is an easy fellow to like. He is so genuine and sincere and seldom forgets a face. Each year at the ICAS convention he would put his arm around *his protégé'* and we'd swap lies about the preceding season.

I'm thrilled that he finally wrote a book that's filled with his memoirs of over fifty years of flying. If there ever was a pilot's pilot, he's the one. It's ironic that the same FAA that held him in such high regard, later allowed a couple of loose-cannon inspectors to attempt to ground him by revoking his medical certificate because they arbitrarily felt that he was "too old to be flying airshows".

It took him two years of legal wrangling and a pot full of money but he finally beat the jerks.

It's no wonder that Yeager called him the best pilot he ever saw.

Bob was the first in a long line of airshow stars with which I became friends but none was as much a mentor as my good friend Leo Loudenslager.

Leo always had a smile for everybody but, more importantly, he has probably done more for the airshow industry than any individual. He was always at the tip of the spear when a big problem came along and he was innovative, too. Some of today's better competition aircraft designs are spin-offs of his Laser.

My folks and I helped him smuggle his dog, Bear, into the hotel at a show in Huntington, West Virginia. They're pretty good judges of character and they liked him instantly. Mom used to ask about him all the time.

Several years ago I listened to Leo and Wayne Handley solve all the industry's problems during a post-show hangar party in Roswell, New Mexico. They were both fountains of knowledge.

When we performed together at the Wilkes-Barre/Scranton, Pennsylvania show I was delighted to prop the Laser for him prior to his act. I wore the bruises on my fingers like a badge of honor for several days thereafter. Incidentally, he's the one who gave me the moniker "Mr. MiG".

Sadly, Leo was hit while riding his motorcycle, close to home, when a driver fell asleep at the wheel and crossed over the center line at eight o'clock on a summer evening. Leo was paralyzed from the chest down and needed a respirator to breathe but we all thought he would pull through.

It seems that he suffocated when his breathing tube became clogged and the nurse's station didn't hear the alarm. I heard the news on the radio from Paul Harvey . . . and I cried.

Others like Dave Hoover and Al Pietch are deceased now, too, but I'm proud to have known them. Many are still around though, and some, like Craig Hosking, do more movie work than shows but they are the best at what they do. Lots of us are airline pilots. Julie Clark, Bud Granley and Gene Soucey are all captains with major carriers.

Jimmy Franklin was one of the few who did airshows and movie work full time.

He and Eliot Cross (with Johnny Kazian narrating) had a dogfight routine called "Dueling Wacos" which was the best airshow act I've ever seen. Jimmy was killed in a mid-air collision during a performance with Bobby Younkin.

Prior to Jim's death Bud Granley endeared himself to Jim and his new wing-walker, Lee Oman, at an airshow. Lee was holding onto the Waco's axle when he slipped and was left hanging by a safety cable. He was unable to get back up to the plane and landing would have probably killed him so Bud came up with the idea of snagging Lee in the back of a pickup truck as Jim flew the Waco as low and slow as possible down the runway. Bud drove the truck while a couple of other guys grabbed Lee and cut the cable. It was a spectacular rescue.

Craig broke into the airshow industry with something unique, too. He modified a Pitts S-2B with a landing gear assembly on *top* of the wing and tail. He actually landed the plane, named "Double Take", upside down.

I talked at length with him after he moved from Salt Lake to California to immerse himself in movie work and he explained how tough it was to break into the motion picture industry as a pilot or "stunt" pilot. You have to be virtually "invited".

Craig also has a lot of helo time but is not immune to disaster. He and two crew members are lucky to be alive after crashing into the Kilauea volcano while filming for the movie *Sliver*.

I anticipated a substantial amount of work in the industry and was quickly contacted by Jim Gavin, a well-known aerial coordinator in Hollywood.

Only one project ever produced any revenue; an HBO movie called *Steal the Sky*—a 1988 film based upon the true story of Munir Redfa's defection in a MiG-21 from Irag to Israel in 1966. After that, the opportunities dried-up as Hollywood procured their own MiGs after the Eastern Block collapsed and prices for the jets plummeted.

Bobby Bishop was one of the first performers to get big corporate sponsorship. He had a deal with the Coors Brewing Company, calling his BD-5J microjets the Silver Bullets and operated two or three throughout the season.

I remember one show in particular that we flew together called the Ft. Erie/Buffalo Friendship Festival. We staged out of a remote airport in Canada and flew in a sort of horseshoe canyon set up over the river. It was really hairy with the dam and high tension wires on one end and spectators on either side. We couldn't fly over the crowd on the Canada side and couldn't fly over downtown Buffalo.

It was a really hard, high G pull to maneuver with limited depth perception over the water as well. Our references on the water were supposed to be unmanned boats so imagine our surprise when they turned out to be little three-foot florescent buoys instead. It's a wonder we both didn't fly into the water at our speeds.

The real kicker at that show was that when it came time to head to the hotel, I was informed that they had run out of rooms and I would be staying at the home of one of the show's *patrons*.

The patron turned out to be Lois Maxwell. Although the name may not be familiar, her face was unmistakable. She was the lovely Ms. Moneypenny of the James Bond movies, then retired and living in Ft. Erie.

She was a gracious hostess and made a potentially bad situation a real joy by sharing her beautiful little cottage.

Getting chronologically a little ahead of myself, this is a good time to mention more of Bob Bishop and our aviation business relationship.

Leo had enjoyed a great corporate partnership with Anheuser Bush's sponsorship of his BD-5J Bud Light Microjet. Following Leo's death, the aircraft was acquired by his ground crew, Bill "Big B" and Teresa "Little T" Beardsley, who intended to continue to operate under that sponsorship with BiG B's son, Bill "Burner" Beardsley as the primary pilot. Burner was still flying for Delta at the time and was not willing or able to fly a full schedule or airshows. I learned this during a casual conversation with Little T during the NAS Pensacola airshow in 2001. I offered my services and we had an agreement.

I went to Arizona the next spring to check out in the BD-5J under Bobby who also signed on with the Beardsleys. Unfortunately, the partnership was short lived due to Anheuser Bush cancelling their sponsorship.

Fortunately, Bobby had 2 other BD-5Js and had cultivated a relationship with the Air Force resulting in a contract to use them to simulate cruise missles. (The BD-5J presents the same radar profile as the Chinese "Seersucker" cruise missle.) So, there was still flying to be done for the former Bud Light microjet, too.

I quickly learned how quirky the little jet was.

The world's smallest jet at approximately 500 pounds (depending upon pilot, configuration and fuel load), 12 feet long with a 17 foot wingspan was powered by a 225 pound thrust Turbomeca engine and was capable of attaining up to 300 knots.

The jet was shrouded with problems from it's inception with double digit crashes and resultant deaths. The fuel system was squirrelly, requiring constant attention to maintain wing balance. Center of gravity was also a significant issue considering the multiple modifications necessary for various requirements.

I had already personally known 2 pilots who had crashed BD-5Js and died under mysterious circumstances. The causes were never positively confirmed as being either mechanical or physiological.

Bobby was and is the highest time BD-5J pilot in the world and was an excellent instructor. At 5 feet nothing, Bobby easily fit into the jet while most of us had to put it on like a pair of pants.

In April of 2002, I joined Bobby, Burner and our airshow friend, Chuck Lischer, at Trent Lott airport in Moss Point, Mississippi. The 4 of us were to rotate through these classified missions flying specified coastal and inland routes into Mississippi and Alabama in Bobby's 2 jets and the old Bud Light jet. We were also tasked with flying into the gulf simulating sea to land cruise missle attacks. We were typically at or below 500 feet above the water in usually hazy, marginal VFR conditions.

During a routine flight (in one of Bobby's jets) to Monroeville, Alabama, I noticed about half way that my wing fuel was not transferring properly. We had maintenance folks at Monroeville so I elected to continue to the destination which was equidistant to Moss Point. At altitude I adjusted power settings and was comfortable that the jet was maneuverable even with the significant weight difference between the two wings. I set up for a long final and flew a slightly faster than normal visual approach to compensate for the problem. Once over the threshold, I reduced power at about 10 feet and adjusted a slight nose up flare for touchdown. At that point, with no stall warning, the left wing stalled and dropped uncontrollably. I pushed the side-stick contol all the way to the right but the jet hit the runway hard enough to buckle the left wing and we skidded off the left side of the runway into the grass. I now know that if I had reduced to normal approach speed at altitude the jet would likely have quit flying as it did over the runway.

I sat momentarily dazed in the cockpit and quickly realized it would be good to secure the electrical system and egress the aircraft since jet fuel was spouting from the left wing.

Up until that time I had never bent metal on an aircraft.

We discussed the possible causes but came to no specific conclusions. The jet would have to be disassembled for the mechanics to determine a probable cause. For some reason, Bobby was leaning toward pilot error as a causal factor which was not only premature but incorrect.

The next day Bobby bailed out of the Bud Light jet when his engine caught fire. It was the second time he was forced to jump from a BD-5J.

Airshow pilot Debbie Gary wrote of two occasions where her fuel system caused a complete flameout while she was flying a BD-5J.

Four years later Chuck was killed flying an approach into Ocean City, Maryland flying the *same* jet I flew. He, however, exploded on impact.

So, yeah, there were significant problems with those jets, the most dangerous aircraft I ever flew.

BD-5J the Bud Light Microjet

GROUND ATTACK

On one occasion I was making a fuel stop at Martinsburg, West Virginia. While on final for a visual approach, the tower controller asked me to confirm my type of aircraft, which I did and he cleared me to land.

Martinsburg is a small, joint-use facility shared by Air Force C-130s and the controller, no doubt looking through his binoculars, must have suspected I was about to attack. (I still wonder where he thought I came from.)

I taxied over to the civilian ramp and, before I had even shut down the engine, a blue government pickup truck with sirens blaring and lights flashing screeched to a stop nose to nose with the jet. Two MPs with locked and loaded M-16s opened their doors, trained their rifles on me and shouted "Identify yourself!"

As the engine wound down I opened the canopy, took of my helmet, waved at the guys and replied "How y'all doin'?" They both stood with puzzled looks on their faces and I heard one say "He aint no Russian!" They lowered their guns and walked over to the jet where I explained who I was and we all shared a good laugh at the expense of the tower controller who had called for security in a panic.

At a Shreveport, Louisiana fuel stop, however, I met up with some airport security that wasn't so accommodating.

As a line boy directed me to a parking spot and into the chocks, a security vehicle pulled in front of me and a skinny little old fellow that looked like Barney Fife got out with a scowl on his face. I climbed out of the cockpit and smiled but before I'd said a word he put his hand on his pistol and said "Lemme see 'at driver's license boy!"

Figuring I was dealing with a less than brilliant chap, I told him my wallet was under my G suit, which I had to remove prior to a restroom stop which was my first priority, and that I'd show it to him as soon as I returned. He agreed to wait so I gave the line boy some fueling instructions and headed inside to make arrangements. At the service desk, I was informed that the old antagonist was a harmless but daily problem and that they could handle him with my cooperation. They radioed the line boy about our little plan and, just as I walked out, he gave the cop some reason for moving the cruiser. By the time he returned, I was strapped in and the line boy told him we needed to do an engine runup. Barney stood by patiently which allowed me to start, get my clearance and go before he figured it all out while still standing on the ramp and scratching his head in confusion.

By and large the shows continued to be fun, though.

I did a flyby at the Coca Cola 500 in Charlotte and "raced" a Budweiser stock car at the NAS Atlanta show.

I also finally got to fly my first home show at Pensacola Beach. It was a beautiful slick-calm day on the gulf even though depth perception over the crystal clear water and high temperature and humidity were significant density altitude issues requiring total concentration. I overcame the temptations to both marvel at the beautiful view and attempt to dazzle the hometown crowd as Byrd Mapoles, the Blue Angels and I watered the eyes of a couple hundred thousand of our friends.

RUSSIAN FIGHTER PILOT

Typically, airshow performers are frequently asked to do radio and television interviews to help promote a show. Most of us were hams anyway and really enjoyed that aspect of the business.

While flying in Seattle at the Emerald City Flight Festival to support the new Museum of Flight, I was asked to do a live spot on a noon television talk show at KIRO. Steve Raible was going to do a quick promotional spot with me right after an interview with actor John Davidson who was in town for a play. The station has to hustle during commercial breaks in order to swap guests on the set and mere seconds allow for a smooth transition. While waiting to go on, I was introduced to the producer who seemed to think that I was, perhaps, a real Russian pilot judging from the apparent authenticity of my flight suit. When she asked if I spoke any English, I took advantage of her naïveté` and played around with a feeble accent. The look of panic on her face was priceless but she was quickly relieved when the airshow representative and I fessed up to the joke. She thought it was a great gag and decided to play it on Raible, too. When it was my turn, they rushed me to my chair and proceeded to set up my microphone while the producer was giving the host a panicked heads-up that there might be a language problem. He had about fifteen seconds before the camera cue and he was really sweating when he started. I spoke in conversational English and he could tell that he'd been set up. We got a good laugh out of it and it broke the ice for a nice, fun interview.

Another time I used the Russian gag with equal success was in Amarillo, Texas.

I had arrived a couple of days early to stage the MiG and the sponsor had asked me to do a quick television interview next to the jet to promote the show. I told him that if he'd play along, we could con the gullible reporter and have some laughs. He agreed and we set the trap.

The girl was a relatively new reporter and she was fascinated with the opportunity to interview a *real* Russian MiG pilot. When she asked me a question, I would look at my accomplice who would repeat exactly what she said, only slower. I responded with a very broken accent which only further enhanced her excitement. After a few questions, I finally answered in simple English which left her with an absolutely stunned look on her face. She paused for a couple of seconds and then bopped me on the head with her microphone. It was a real hoot.

I've flown a lot of airshows that were far away from home, but the only reason I agreed to fly a show way up in Gander, Newfoundland was because my friend Gino Tessier was there.

We met and became great friends when he was flying with the Canadian Snowbirds and the Gander airshow was an excellent opportunity for us to get together again. So, I made the long trip over the coastal fjords of Newfoundland to see one of the most beautiful areas in the Canadian maritimes.

During the act I was at the top of a loop and as I looked through the canopy to acquire the ground I saw a really unusual sight. An Aeroflot airliner was landing on the other runway. As usual, I was on a discreet frequency to eliminate unnecessary radio chatter during the intense concentration required for low level aerobatics. I was later told that they were low on fuel so they were sequenced in at just the right moment. Something like that is normally strictly taboo during an airshow but it worked out okay.

Within a few minutes I was confronted by a couple of very excited Russian flight attendants who had dashed over to meet the MiG pilot. They spoke no English, were missing a few teeth, and were really shocked to find an American flying the jet with the red Soviet stars!

Another interesting individual I met on the circuit was Arthur Wolk, the epitome of a Philadelphia lawyer. Art had restored the only flying F-9F Panther and we flew a little "history lesson" together at the Kalamazoo, Michigan airshow. Art had no formation experience or training, which I didn't know (and never thought to ask), and it must've been hysterical to watch him trying to join on me for a fly by. He had no knowledge of radius of turn and a running rendezvous, so he was frantically calling for me to slow down. The next time we flew simultaneously was at the Willow Grove airshow near Philadelphia and this time I was prepared.

Art was to lead and this time I would join on him. That way he couldn't run into me and we could safely fly close together in front of the crowd . . . or so I thought.

During our section takeoff roll, I was on his right wing as we broke ground. As he lifted off, the habit of aligning on the runway centerline prevailed and he drifted over to within inches of me. The wake vortices from his jet very nearly forced me back into the runway and I had to hang on until we had ten to fifteen feet of altitude so I could slide further right and out of his way.

Even though I was, once again, ready to read my wingman the riot act Art never knew what happened because I didn't have the heart to hammer him after the ribbing he took from our counterparts when we returned.

It seemed he had attempted to taxi with a power cart still plugged into the Panther and everybody on the ramp saw it.

His piloting eventually caught up with him when he all but destroyed the beautiful Panther during a landing mishap shortly thereafter. Fortunately he survived but, although he was injured, that was the end of his jet warbird flying.

Occasionally during my tens of thousands of miles back and forth across the continent I had to contend with inclement weather.

At civilian airports it was easy enough to shoot an ILS (Instrument Landing System—precision landing), but I had no TACAN (Tactical Air Navigation—an exclusively military navigation system) for military fields.

While flying to NAS Miramar near San Diego, I encountered a marine layer that swept onto the field just as I was flying the approach. Since I was only flying from the nearby Chino airport and the field was calling VFR (Visual Flight Rules—basically clear) weather conditions, I took on only enough fuel for the trip. I did a missed approach, declared minimum fuel to expedite my handling and was handed off to a GCA (Ground Controlled Approach) controller. It was my first PAR (Precision Approach Radar controlled approach) in the MiG but I'd done hundreds of them before. The controller did a super job of getting me in under very near zero zero (no ceiling or visibility) conditions and seemed to lose her composure only briefly when she asked my aircraft type.

Controllers tended to do that when they almost always asked me to confirm that I was really in a MiG. That usually fostered a lot of questions which I was happy to answer even broadcasting on an airway.

One day while talking to Houston Center, I overheard a Continental jet being advised of my position. He asked if I was a real MiG to which the controller replied affirmatively. When the airline pilot asked if it would be possible to get a closer look, the controller queried me as to whether or not I was agreeable. We were both at altitude on a clear day with standard fifteen mile separation and I thought, what the heck. I maintained speed while he accelerated and eventually joined in a wide formation. He was close enough that I could see the faces in the windows and lots of hands waving as I wondered what he must've told those people.

By November of 1988 my initial airshow partner, Kim McCabe, had managed to find venture capitalists who he thought were willing to invest in our dream team, the Northern Lights. The only problem was that they weren't interested in airshows but felt that civilian-owned surplus military jets could probably turn a nice profit in the flight test arena. The first aircraft they acquired was a two seat Hawker Hunter which was specially modified like those used by the British Empire Test Pilot School to demonstrate stall and spin recovery.

The Hunter was particularly suited for that task with a uniquely stable swept wing. It was felt that the Navy and Air Force test pilot schools would benefit greatly from its use and that it could, therefore, produce substantial revenues.

In addition a two seat F-104 Starfighter, a Mach 2 capable jet, was purchased for high speed contracts. I wasn't too sure how the MiG would fit into the business but had committed to Kim to be a part of it all.

Our good friend and former squadron mate, Tom Archer, was hired as the only bona fide (trained) test pilot. He was the greatest asset to the business due to his flight test background and the credibility he brought to the mission. Unfortunately, due to a series of internal problems and the inability to compete with the big boys like Flight Systems, the business folded after only a short time. That's the kindest way I know how to put it without going into the specific problems of those who were managing the business.

Eventually both the Hunter and Starfighter and their later acquired sister ships were sold but the MiG and I just kept rolling along.

After Northern Lights went under, Kim worked himself into a crop dusting business and we left our dreams of a formation aerobatic team behind. Following a couple of accidents, one that left him severly burned and nearly cost Kim his life, he eventually took positions with different Middle Eastern companies flying helicopters in some very contentious locales. He could write a quite intriguing book himself.

Tom, one of the finest pilots I've ever seen, was hired by the FAA as a test pilot and has enjoyed substantial success testing the new commercial airliners that roll off of the Boeing assembly line in Seattle.

CHAPTER 9

BACK TO THE WOODS

With the new found freedom of being self-employed it was wonderful to get back to a favorite old past time.

After some quiet time in the woods I was rejuvenated. Just the mere pleasure of listening to the owls hoot, the cardinals sing, the turkeys gobble and to see the sun rise was enough to recharge my batteries for days.

Hunting, much like flying, has introduced me to some wonderful friends and one of my best turned out to be a local taxidermist.

I found Howard Smith at random in the phone book and after a few visits to his shop we discovered that we both just enjoyed each others company. He later said it was puzzling to him that I liked to sit around and watch his artistry without asking for something as many customers did. He figured I wasn't looking to steal any of his secret techniques and wasn't angling for an invitation to hunt some honey hole with him. We simply enjoyed each others company and have traveled, hunted and fished together over the many years since.

We had a terrific caribou hunt together up near the tip of Quebec on Ungava Bay where we slept in semipermanent shelters and hunted with the Inuit in freighter canoes.

The scenery was spectacular. We saw small herds of caribou swimming across bays where the tidal changes were nearly fifty feet each day. It was a great trip for a couple of country boys.

In 2004 we hunted moose in Alaska, too. After flying into the small town of Tok, about a 7 hour drive east of Anchorage, we were flown by bush plane to a small dry lake where we camped for several days. Howard took a good bull and we proceeded to do the skinning and meat packing. During that process one of the planes from Forty Mile Air flew over and rocked his wings indicating that he had seen our kill site. We knew he would return to take the cape, antlers and meat back to Tok for storage. As we were loading the Cub with meat sacks one of us happened to inquire about what was going on in the world. Having been isolated for the better part of a week we were just curious as to current events and hungry for a bit of news. The pilot mentioned nothing of much significance up to the point that he told us there was a big storm brewing in the Gulf of Mexico. After further inquiry and learning that a hurricane had Pensacola bore-sighted, we advised that we needed to depart forthwith to return home to our families. To their credit, the kind folks at Forty Mile Air managed to get us out that very day using two of their aircraft. We hurriedly broke camp and proceeded to get on our cell phones as soon as we were returned to Tok. Hurricane Ivan was indeed bearing down on the Florida panhandle.

While Howard made arrangements for the care and handling of his trophy I was tasked with trying to arrange transportation home. After several futile attempts to get our airline tickets changed I had run out of options and ideas . . . all save one. While driving toward Anchorage with Howard at the wheel and me urgently attempting to make transportation arrangements with spotty cell phone coverage, I broke the news to Howard that we were very likely not going to be able to get *into* a geographic area from which thousands of people were trying to flee.

At that point I looked Howard in the eye and said, "I believe we have one more possibility, though. Give me your hand, buddy." I closed my eyes and began to pray out loud. "Lord, we've done all we can to get home to our families who we know are afraid and need us there to help them cope with this storm. It's out of our hands, Father, and we sure could use some divine intervention. We know that whenever two or more are gathered in your name that you are there also so we implore you to bless our trip home." I picked up my cell phone and called Delta one more time. Instead of going through an exchange in Bangladesh or Delhi, this time I actually got a reservations agent in the USA. As the agent checked the computer he saw that there had just been two cancellations from Anchorage to Atlanta on the next available flight; irrefutable evidence of the power of prayer!

We checked into a hotel near the airport and spent the next several hours packing our hastily loaded gear into a means acceptable for airline travel. After our first real bath in several days, we grabbed a short nap and then were on our way.

All flights to gulf coast destinations were cancelled by the time we got into Atlanta so we rented the only vehicle available, ironically a van which was exactly what we needed, and headed for home. It was odd to be traveling southbound on Interstate 65 with no other traffic. The northbound lanes, however, were creeping along bumper to bumper. Within less than an hour of our exit off the interstate the southbound lanes had been converted to northbound lanes to expedite the hurricane evacuation. The good Lord had smiled upon us once again.

We got back just in time to get our homes ready and batten down the hatches as best we could. Hurricane Ivan, the most devastating hurricane ever to hit Pensacola, arrived just hours later.

Both our homes survived with minimal damage.

When I decided to book my first guided hunt in 1989 I picked an elk and mule deer combination near Bozeman, Montana at the Shelton Ranch.

It was about 120,000 acres of cattle ranch adjoining the Spanish Peaks with the Madison and Gallatin rivers running through. My guide was one of the ranch manager's two sons and that spectacular ranch had been his childhood playground. Bob Griffith was a college-aged cowboy, born and bred in the true spirit of the Montana west.

We had stalked a big bull bedded down on a heavily timbered finger late one morning after his herd had grazed and headed back into the darkness of the Ponderosa pines. As a last resort we tried to put a sneak on him but with the swirling breeze he was eventually spooked by our scent and I had my introduction to the stealth required to take a real trophy elk.

We were up early each day, traipsing through knee deep snow in the high country. The next day after glassing a valley for the better part of the afternoon we started back down the mountain for the truck. As we passed a stand of quaking aspen the woods came alive with what sounded like some spooked deer. We made it to the road and continued to look toward the trees when we saw what had really made all the racket. We had roused a huge seven by seven point bull from his bed and he just hopped up and trotted off to a quieter place and proceeded to make another one.

He was thrashing around stirring up the leaves and grass with his giant antlers when we spotted him. I was so fortunate to quickly dispatch him with one well placed round before he spotted us again.

I was stunned at his magnificent size and absolutely amazed when we tried to load him into the flatbed truck. The ranch liked to weigh the field dressed animal at the local game station to help the ranch biologist with his record keeping but we nearly got hernias heaving over 700 pounds of wapiti.

The next afternoon I took a beautiful five by five point mule deer buck as he stood magnificently on the skyline, surveying his harem of twenty or so does.

The next year I hunted the Shelton Ranch in Kerr County, Texas. The boys in Montana had said that there were some nice whitetails down there so I decided to see for myself.

Each day I saw tremendous numbers of deer with most bucks averaging eight points. I saw almost every deer behavior I'd ever heard of, too.

On the morning of the third day one of the ranch hands, Robert Manning, dropped me off at a tower stand which overlooked about ten acres of brush. The tower was about twenty five feet high with a roof and roomy enough for four but open on all sides. At first light I began glassing the area and within thirty minutes I spotted a beautiful nine point buck.

I watched him feed and amble around and quickly decided that he was a shooter. I was enjoying the sight of this beautiful creature but ready to take him at just the right time. I had put down the binoculars and had my rifle up with his chest in the cross hairs. I knew he was a dandy and wanted to wait for a perfect shot. He was nearly where I wanted him but he seemed to meander around what appeared to be a big rock that was obstructing my line of sight.

As I waited, that big rock stood up. It was the biggest deer I had ever seen! I instantly contracted a real bad case of buck fever but somehow managed to control my breathing and squeeze off a round. I saw him jump and then nothing. Like a phantom he had disappeared and I began to doubt the accuracy of my shot. Had I been too hasty in pulling the trigger? I figured that if I'd hit him where I aimed he would certainly be down after about twenty minutes so I took a compass bearing to the spot about 250 yards away and climbed down to look.

The grass, brush and mesquite were thicker than they appeared and it took me a while to find the spot. When I was sure I was close I began a spiraling search pattern. I soon started to convince myself that I'd missed. A few minutes later my persistence paid off when I found him. He was a 10 point buck well over 250 pounds (a whopper by Texas standards) and the biggest buck ever taken on the ranch.

Things were just getting better in 1990.

I continued to hunt and even had time to take in an occasional Auburn football game with my oldest son, Charlie.

I had also made friends with a couple of Delta pilots who shared my passion for hunting—especially turkey.

Tom Kanaley was a good friend of Floyd McGowin's and he graciously took me to his lease up in Andalusia, Alabama. Although I never had the benefit of his expertise in the cockpit, I learned a lot from him in the turkey woods about calling and tactics.

While cruising along on a long Delta trip, I started making small talk to help break the cockpit monotony. When the topic turned to turkey season being near, the captain, who'd thus far been rather quiet, turned around and said "You a turkey hunter?" The captain on that trip was Warren Price and we've been turkey hunting buddies and great friends ever since.

I suppose Tom and Warren were good teachers because I've been fortunate enough to take at least one of each of the four primary North American Wild Turkey subspecies of *Meleagris Gallopavo Silvestris*, giving me what's known as a "grand slam". A Gould's turkey in Mexico gave me a "royal slam" and Warren and I made a trip to the Yucatan peninsula to complete our "world slam" with an Ocellated turkey in the Mexican jungle.

I've even had the good fortune to take two birds with one shot a couple of times.

My good buddy, Gino Tessier, was with his family visiting in Pensacola so we took off one morning for my lease up in Alabama. The gobbling had been good but no birds had come in close enough for an ethical shot. We moved to a thicket near a freshly plowed field where I had previously seen some jakes (juvenile males) pecking for grubs. Sure enough, in a short time four gobblers showed up and I just knew Gino would bag his first wild turkey.

When it came time to pull the trigger, he felt uncomfortable and said he'd rather that I shoot. We didn't have time to dicker so I slipped the shotgun out of his hands and put the bead on the nearest bird. Two of the turkeys were definitely out of range and the other two seemed to be joined at the hip.

They stuck together like twins so I didn't take the shot since I really wanted to take only one. As they eased away I knew that I'd have to take both or neither so I squeezed off the three and a half inch magnum and dropped them. Gino jumped up hooting and hollering, not believing what he'd just seen.

At home, we cleaned and prepared our dinner and I shared one of the beards with him as a trophy for a hunt that neither of us will ever forget.

If you're a hunter, you probably wear some type of camouflage and if you wear camouflage, you've probably heard of the Mossy Oak brand. Due simply to timing, I happen to have hunted out of the same lodge (Bent Creek in Jachin, Alabama) with Toxey Haas, the fellow who came up with the Mossy Oak patterns.

Hunting at Bent Creek was challenging but a pleasure for two reasons. Obviously challenging because turkeys are hard to hunt but a pleasure because the lodge was comfortable with excellent food and, mainly, because of my guides. Two of the best turkey callers in the world, Larry Norton and Bob Walker, guided there.

Warren Price & me with our Rio Grande turkeys

Larry and I had hunted hard for my very first gobbler with no success. After the morning hunt proved fruitless, Larry decided we should check some of the green fields on the property. At one, we low crawled over briars, thorns and everything else imaginable that could stick you. As we crept up to take a peek, we saw that there were a couple of nice toms. We eased into a semi-sitting position, still concealed by the tall grass around us and I took aim at one of the turkeys. I started to push the safety off when Larry reached up and pulled down my barrel.

"What size shot you shootin'?" "Fours", I said, "Why?" "Them birds are a good forty steps away. Here, use my gun. I'm shootin' twos." I'd been learning a lot from Larry and saw no reason to argue. We traded shotguns and I placed the bead on that gobbler's neck, flipped off the safety and pulled the trigger. Normally, one would expect to hear an ear numbing blast . . . normally. In this particular case, due to our frequent trips in and out of the truck and in our haste, Larry had neglected to load his shotgun. The snap of the firing pin sounded like a fog horn to those turkeys and they were gone forthwith. I couldn't believe it. I was more stunned than mad that I had laid down a loaded gun in exchange for an empty one and missed the chance at my first gobbler. Larry felt awful. He wanted me to get that bird nearly as bad as I did but what really bugged him was knowing that he'd never hear the end of it back at the lodge. He was right. For the rest of that trip at least, he was known as Snap.

Bob Walker has hearing like Radar O'Reilly (from M*A*S*H). As we drove and stopped, listening for an answer to Bob's calls, he would point to sounds totally imperceptible to me. Maybe that's not saying a whole lot due to all the jet noise induced hearing loss I've experienced but his hearing was, none the less, exceptional. When he found a bird probably 400 yards away, we headed into the brush at a trot. He knew exactly where that turkey was and proceeded to perform a soft tree yelp and a fly down cackle that convinced that gobbler that there was a nice hen waiting for him just over the rise. He was a dandy and I was lucky to get him and even more fortunate to have hunted with Bob.

I've heard that nobody has come up with a better way to pass a spring morning than sitting quietly in the woods with a shotgun in your lap and hope beating in your heart.

CHAPTER 10

FLYING THE LINE

"SCIENCE, FREEDOM, BEAUTY, ADVENTURE, WHAT MORE COULD YOU ASK OF LIFE?" AVIATION COMBINED ALL THE ELEMENTS I LOVED. THERE WAS SCIENCE IN EACH CURVE OF AN AIRFOIL. IN EACH ANGLE BETWEEN STRUT AND WIRE, IN THE GAP OF A SPARK PLUG OR THE COLOR OF AN EXHAUST FLAME. THERE WAS FREEDOM IN THE UNLIMITED HORIZON, OR THE OPEN FIELDS WHERE ONE LANDED. A PILOT WAS SURROUNDED BY BEAUTY OF EARTH AND SKY. HE BRUSHED TREE TOPS WITH THE BIRDS, LEAPED VALLEYS AND RIVERS, EXPLORED THE CLOUD CANYONS HE GAZED AT AS A CHILD. ADVENTURE LAY IN EACH PUFF OF THE WIND. I BEGAN TO FEEL THAT I LIVED ON A HIGHER PLANE THAN THE SKEPTICS OF THE GROUND, ONE THAT WAS RICHER BECAUSE IT WAS FREER OF THE EARTH TO WHICH THEY WERE BOUND.

IN FLYING I TASTED A WINE OF THE GODS OF WHICH THEY COULD KNOW NOTHING. WHO VALUED LIFE MORE HIGHLY, THE AVIATORS WHO SPENT IT ON THE ART THEY LOVED, OR THOSE MISERS WHO DOLED IT OUT LIKE PENNIES THROUGH THEIR ANT-LIKE DAYS? I DECIDED IF I COULD FLY FOR TEN YEARS BEFORE I WAS KILLED IN A CRASH, IT WOULD BE A WORTHWHILE TRADE FOR AN ORDINARY LIFETIME."

Charles Lindbergh

I was enjoying the notoriety I experienced as "Mr. MiG" but writing articles and serving on boards of different organizations was terribly time consuming and financially draining.

The airline business was becoming more and more attractive.

In April of 1989, I was invited to interview with Delta Air Lines.

About a year prior I had been commuting home after pre-positioning the MiG at a show site, which I frequently did. It was much more cost effective to fly the jet to the next closest show site in advance and then fly home commercially, so I became a relatively frequent airline flyer.

On that particular flight I sat next to a gentleman who noticed my Auburn class ring and acknowledged with a smile and a "War Eagle". We introduced ourselves and began small talk about Auburn. He had also noticed my helmet bag as I stuffed it into the overhead bin so the subject eventually shifted to an inquiry about my occupation.

We had an enjoyable chat during which he also asked if I had ever considered flying for an airline. I told him I was really enjoying the airshow flying and would only be interested in flying for Delta should I ever decide to pursue an airline career. He inquired as to why and I proceeded to elaborate on what a wonderful carrier I thought they were. He sat there listening with a smile for most of the duration of our flight.

As we taxied into the gate at Pensacola he wrote his phone number on his boarding pass stub and fessed up that he'd been sandbagging me.

In addition to being an Auburn man, Richard Colby was also a DC-9 Captain with Delta. He said that if I ever decided to put in an application he'd be happy to take it in for me, for which I thanked him and we proceeded to have a good laugh about his sly silence.

A year later, after I'd changed my mind, I called him, curious as to whether or not he'd remember our fortuitous meeting. He did and invited me to his Gulf Breeze home where, following a brief visit, he once again graciously offered to hand-carry my application to Atlanta.

He asked me to let him know when I got any news, which I did when I was called for the interview. I figured his Atlanta phone number was an apartment or crash pad, but when I called and his secretary answered, "Chief Pilot's office", I knew I'd been had again. Richard later became the Director of Flight Operations for Delta, the "Chief" Chief pilot, and was Vice President of Flight Operations up until his retirement. He was unique for having an open door policy to the pilot group.

Many times when I went to Atlanta for annual recurrent training I would drop in unannounced and he always had a minute to talk about hunting, football or whatever. His secretary and others appeared surprised that even a lowly engineer was always welcome in his office

He was by far the best management executive I ever saw at Delta Air Lines.

I could never have dreamed how intensely Delta would change my life.

While flying the El Toro airshow I phoned home for messages and got one of my favorites of all time. Delta had called offering me a class date. I was going to be an airline pilot after all. I was about to substantially increase my pilot education to the doctoral level of advanced training—the equivalent of an aviation Ph. D.

The initial training was one of my greatest challenges. We had to learn every Boeing 727 system inside and out from an engineering perspective. *Flying* an airplane had absolutely nothing to do with the training and the self-induced stress was intense.

Everyone, with very few exceptions, dislikes going to training. Each time you fly a proficiency check in the simulator your job is on the line and, depending upon the instructor, can be a hostile environment. Twenty or more years ago undergoing new aircraft training could be an almost unbearable crucible.

While some instructors refuse to acknowlege that "the simulator doesn't fly like the real thing", it's the truth. Thankfully the training occurs only once a year.

Bob Gandt explained:

> "Before they let you fly any aircraft, whether you're a fighter pilot, airline pilot or astronaut, you go through the same ritual.
>
> Before you climb in and take off in any new flying machine, you first have to acquire an intimacy with every detail and nuance of the beast's peculiar personality. You stare glassy-eyed at electrical system schematics, at multihued diagrams of fuel and hydraulic systems, sit through mind-numbing lectures about maximum hydraulic PSI, minimum fuel pressure, limits of exhaust gas temperature and fuel flow and oil pressure."

This phase of training was as much fun as a root canal.

The current generation of computerized flight management systems (FMS) are called glass cockpits. Because most of the traditional flight data instruments—the round mechanical gyros and pitot/static airspeed and altitude gauges—were replaced with CRT screens (cathode ray tubes, as in computer monitors) they look somewhat similar to video games.

The airplane's computers, having received pre-programmed information from the pilot, then does things and goes places without the direct, hands-on participation of the pilot. Or so it seems.

Early on, during the transformation from analog gauges to digital cockpits, it was common for perplexed pilots to stare at their deceptively simple looking flight displays in total bewilderment, silently wondering, "What the hell is it doing now?"

Now pilots *interface* with the machine and occasionally cringe when they hear the ominous aural warning, "deedle deedle", announcing the onset of an abnormal indication.

Clearly I did not want to fail but, quite honestly, there were a couple of times that the self-induced pressure was almost unbearable and I thought seriously about quitting.

Like Auburn football, Marine Corps boot camp and flight school, I just couldn't bring myself to give up even though I felt I was in way over my head.

Two months later my class and I completed engineer training and were flying the line.

I'll never forget our new-hire coordinator, Tony Lotti, "presenting" my class with our Delta wings. They came in a brown paper bag along with our epaulets and name tags during class one day. I suppose I expected the milestone of becoming a Delta pilot to be, at least, a little bit heralded by some type of ceremony but even though it was a disappointment it didn't really matter. We had reached a highly sought after pinnacle in aviation. We were pilots for the best airline in the world.

In his book, *Fate is the Hunter,* this is what Ernest Gann had to say about flying the line:

> "Most line pilots deliberately cultivate an almost psychopathic modesty which would be intolerable if it were not for the large part genuine and salted with humor.

It would be inconceivable for a line pilot to approach his fellows at the end of a flight and announce that he had just executed a complicated holding pattern without a moment's delay, flown an exact instrument approach, and topped it all off with a perfect landing. Instead he would say, "Well, I barged around for a while not knowing where I was, as usual, and when I finally got the clearance through my head, I managed to locate the range station.

Of course, I still have a lot to learn about an ILS approach* . . . those needles just never come together quite right for me . . . but this time I persuaded them to meet in the right place, so we stumbled on down until, to my complete surprise, there was the runway right ahead. Of course, if I could have seen anything it would have been one of my usual rotten landings, but it was raining hard and the windshield wipers weren't operating and so I just sort of waited until the ship landed itself, which is what a man ought to do all the time if he had any sense . . .

This is, of course, an outrageous twisting of the truth. It is also ostentation. But that is the way it must be said if anything is said at all.

Likewise, should you enquire of a line pilot if he has ever been afraid, his answer is bound to be, "All the time". Which is another distortion of the truth.

Yet the tenor of such replies should repudiate those envious cynics who always hasten to label courage a virtue of indifferent value. Line pilots do not live in an atmosphere of heroism, for that is a very temporary condition better suited to wildly inspired moments in which the hero hardly knows what he is doing.

*An ILS (Instrument Landing System) approach utilizes two needles on the attitude indicator; the vertical needle indicates the aircraft's position relative to the proper course or localizer heading and the horizontal needle indicates the aircraft's position relative to the proper glide path. Alignment of both needles to a perfect cross hairs pattern indicates on course and glide slope.

> The pilots know what they are doing, right or wrong, always. They wear courage like a comfortable belt, rarely giving it a thought.
>
> But a line pilot is wary all of the time, which is an entirely different matter. To be continuously aware you must know what to be wary of, and this sustained attitude can only come from experience. Learning the nature and potentialities of the countless hazards is like walking near quicksand.
>
> Yet such is the swift tempo of airline progress that no pilot can long rest upon his past or everyday experience. He is almost continuously in school, studying new devices and methods . . .
>
> And then there are physical examinations to be taken at least three (now two) times a year . . . Consequently, the hours spent in the actual flying of an airline pilot's schedule and that given to attendant assignments are about equal.
>
> These extracurricular activities are never seen by their passengers, though upon them much of their intrinsic safety depends."

Gann wrote that in the 1950's but it is, essentially, still true today.

I was on reserve in Atlanta for a short time but soon had a regular line and my seniority steadily progressed. During a military career you become accustomed to competing with your peers for everything—grades, assignments—everything. You sized up the other guy, and then figured out how you were going to wax his tail. You had to beat somebody else for everything. Almost nothing is merit based for airline pilots. Seniority rules.

I was blessed to fly trips with some of the best airline pilots in the world. For years Delta has made a point of identifying the very best aviators available and hiring them through a thoroughly scrutinizing interview process. Physical, psychological and mechanical aptitude tests weed out all but the fortunate few. Personality is assessed by retired captains who determine, "Would I like to fly a trip with this guy?"

The beauty of the job is the flexibility. You can live where you want—just sign in for your trips on time. You can bid for certain days off, to fly certain aircraft, international or domestic trips or to go to certain cities; all, of course, seniority permitting.

As a commuter, which I was voluntarily since I was hired, I would bid for the most days off and to sign in late and get back early. This afforded me more opportunities to both get to work and home with minimal stays in Atlanta. Some pilots, mostly those who live near their bases, bid for the biggest equipment they can fly because bigger planes mean bigger paychecks. They also bid captain at their first opportunity usually becoming a reserve rat with little quality time at home. The system allows for them to be utilized generally at the convenience of the company and providing for as little as 10 days per month free of duty.

Bid what you want but want what you bid. Once again, seniority rules.

I enjoyed flying the "Jurassic Jet"; the indomitable Boeing 727. There were innumerable things I liked about it, not the least of which was the three man cockpit. There was much more interaction on the three holers (three engines—three pilots) than I've observed on a two man plane. You could always get along with at least one of the other guys which made for much more pleasant layovers. The 727 was a bear to land, thoroughly humbling to every pilot that's ever flown it and I like to think that, on occasion, I mastered the beast.

The greased-on landings were not uncommon to those who flew it with ample experience. We still navigated with charts and hand-flew all but the most weather restricted of our approaches. When it was retired in 2003 the last of the era of seat-of-the-pants airliners was over. The only thing consistent in the airline industry is change.

Captain Bob Falkins, Second Officer Kellie Waddell and I were the flight crew for the last Boeing 727 passenger flight in the history of Delta Air Lines. To commemorate it we set a U.S. and World Speed Record in ship #580 flying from Atlanta to Greensboro on April 6, 2003.

I knew I was going to miss it.

A great three day trip for me would be to sign in at noon giving me time to get to Atlanta with a backup or two, fly three legs, land at a great city (say, Seattle), have a nice meal with the crew and a good nights sleep, do it again the next day and arrive home on the last day with plenty of time to commute home.

A great month would be to do this once a week—twelve days at work (away from home for 48 hours per trip) and eighteen days off.

Let's do that math one more time and let me preface the following remarks by stating, for the record, that I very much liked my job but quickly tired of those who think that airline pilots always layover in Honolulu and make a million bucks a year.

Okay, the average person is at work forty hours a week and sleeps in his own cozy bed every night. There's a lot to be said for that . . . sleeping in your own bed, that is. I was at work over forty hours *a trip* and, believe me, hotels aren't all they're cracked up to be—even when we stayed at a Marriott.

I doubt that I could convince many that we were worth our hourly wage so I'll just make a simple comparison and leave it at that. If you're going to have brain surgery, you probably want the absolute best surgeon that money can buy. Right? He spent a lot of time learning his skills and as a result, he is paid accordingly. After all, your life is in *his* hands. If you're going to fly somewhere and the weather is marginal or even if it's clear and something goes wrong with the plane, you probably want the best pilots that money can buy. Right? We've spent a lot of time learning our skills, too, and as a result we were paid accordingly. After all, your life was in *our* hands.

Quoting George E. Hopkins in *Flying the Line*:

> "Airline pilots should be well paid solely for the skills they possess and the responsibilities they bear, and in an ideal world they would be. But in the real world people get paid what they are worth only if they have the muscle to command it."

I never truly thought that I'd enjoy flying a big transport aircraft (a glorified bus driver), but I did. The chemistry is not quite the same as in a military squadron but, more often than not, there were some super guys to fly with and some beautiful sights to see.

One night in the spring of 1997, cruising along at 39,000 feet, we finally saw the spectacular Hale-Bopp comet. Its brilliant light and the glow of its showering tail were visible for several days. As I watched with my chin on the glareshield, it lit up the night sky like a full autumn moon.

Another phenomenon occasionally experienced by pilots is St. Elmo's fire. When thunderstorms are in the vicinity and the air is electrically charged and excited, static electricity can build up on an aircraft. At night, with a pitch black sky, tiny arcs of the static electricity jump across the windscreen providing a mesmerizing dance of light. Sometimes, when the electrical charge builds up to and reaches a peak, the light will discharge back into the air with a near blinding flash and an audible bang similar to a lesser clap of thunder. The entire anomaly is relatively harmless but thoroughly entertaining.

During my first year as an engineer, on our way from the Edmonton, Alberta airport to our downtown layover hotel, we saw the northern lights flashing about the cold, crystal clear Canadian sky. I spent the entire twenty minute cab ride with my nose pressed up against the window enjoying the spectacular show.

Now in the twilight of my aviation career I can glance back and wax nostalgic about the experiences of my vocation.

Pilots, for the most part, cannot look into their past and point to something tangible; something built that will last. Our world is one of inner successes and accomplishments. Many of us fill that tangible void by creating our hallowed "shrines". Most pilots have one. We have walls of aviation pictures, paintings and memorabilia including cherished parts or pieces of an airplane; things we can really touch . . . and touch us as well.

As a young pilot with Delta Air Lines, I watched our company excel as a smallish, well-run, profitable airline that knew its market. Senior guys had more vacation than they could use and the biggest onboard problem was choosing between the steak and the lobster. Flight attendants actually enjoyed lengthy visits to the cockpit, made in no small part even more enjoyable by foot rubs from the Engineer.

On a layover our Engineers never paid for a beer and the after-diner pub visit was frequently followed by a trip to the Captain's room where he broke out the "survival kits" packed in air sickness bags provided by the recipients of those foot rubs.

Nobody ratted on anybody else. Conflicts were handled in-cockpit and you could actually go into a chief pilot's office and volunteer that you screwed up on something without fear of termination. Chief pilots back then were older guys who played a lot of golf and didn't spend an inordinate amount of time in the office.

As a Captain with Delta Air Lines, I observed a post multi-merger corporation managed by the same inbred corporate cronies who I wouldn't hire to mow my lawn because they'd hold too many meetings about how to use the mower. At every turn the Perfumed Princes have peed in the pool and then blamed us, the pilots.

But, I dwell on a few negativities and digress. How about a stroll down memory lane recollecting nearly 18,000 hours of logbook entries and experiences . . .

Consider:

Cruising mere feet above a table-flat cloud deck at Mach .86.
Punching out of the top of a low overcast while climbing 6,000 feet per minute.
The majesty of towering cumulus.
Rotating and feeling a quarter of a million pounds of Boeing 777 come alive.
Icebergs in the North Atlantic while crossing in the tracks.
The chaotic, non-stop babble of radio transmissions at LaGuardia or Atlanta.
The quietness of a Center frequency at night during a transcontinental flight.
The welcome view of approach lights appearing out of the mist, just as you reach minimums.
Being the co-pilot in a three-man cockpit.
Lenticular clouds over the Rockies.
Luxury hotels.
The camaraderie of a good crew.
Landings in the 727 when the only way you knew you had touched down was the pat on the back from the Engineer.
Brain bags crammed with charts and manuals.
CAT III autolands when you felt the wheels touch before you ever saw the ground.

The rush of a full speed brakes descent at barber pole when
    the controller asks if you can make it in a 727.
Being the Captain in any cockpit.
Max cross wind landings.
The excitement of the last leg on a 4 day rotation.

At night when I dream of flight, after having spent more than
10,000 hours of my life at the controls of a Boeing 727, I find
myself there tweaking the N1 power settings, responding to
the checklist or thumbing the autopilot for an altitude change.
It's easy to forget sometimes how much I loved it.

As an airline pilot I was, obviously, very interested in
technology which would foster safety and efficiency in
transport aircraft.
    During my conversations with Slick Goodlin, I had the
privilege to not only learn history from an aviation pioneer,
but to be educated in politics as well.

Slick's passion for many years was to champion the cause of
the late, great aircraft designer Vincent J. Burnelli. Slick was
Chairman and President of The Burnelli Company and did his
best to keep it alive
    " . . . despite almost five decades of political and financial
suppression by the military-industrial complex".
    Burnelli's may truly be the story of an American aviation
scandal. Quoting a *Miami Herald* article:

> "For fifty years the Burnelli, an original "lifting body"
> aircraft similar to the flying wing, has been relegated to
> the dustbin of U.S. aviation because of a U.S. president's
> fit of political temper.
>   Despite tributes to the design from such giants of
> early military aviation as Generals Billy Mitchell and
> Hap Arnold, bad luck so dogged its creator, Vincent

Burnelli, that he went to his grave broke in 1964. The last Burnelli was built in the late '40's.

And yet a small clutch of believers still cite the Burnelli as a stunning example of power politics in the military-industrial establishment, by which rival airplane manufacturers have kept the flying public shackled to inefficient, dangerous aircraft types that today girdle the earth."

Witness the design of the B-2 Stealth bomber with a design closely resembling Burnelli's. Also witness the staggering number of deaths by fire associated with the crash of a modern commercial jet (tube fuselage) aircraft.

Burnelli's aircraft carried twice the load, took-off and landed at half the speed and had greater range with equal fuel than a conventional plane.

In 1941, Burnelli went to the White House for the formal signing of an order for his aircraft by President Franklin D. Roosevelt. When Roosevelt casually inquired as to whom was financing the enterprise, he became enraged at the answer, threw his pen across the Oval Office and told Burnelli to get out.

One of the financiers, Sun Oil Company's Arthur Pew, was a backer of Roosevelt's arch rival, Wendell Willkie.

Soon after, a secret Army report was issued denigrating the Burnelli concept and it was shelved.

Slick actually flew a Burnelli aircraft in 1951 and was thoroughly impressed. Shortly thereafter, he became involved with trying to "un-do a grave injustice perpetrated on this country and the flying public in general".

Quoting his address on the occasion of his induction into the Niagara Frontier Aviation Hall of Fame, May 15, 1987:

"About 1970, I commenced getting rumors that the retired president of General Motors, Ed Cole, had started a company to develop a family of large airplanes for the purpose of delivering cars, parts and general cargo worldwide at vastly reduced rates.

I, then, heard that T. A. Wilson, present Chairman of Boeing, had learned of the rather extraordinary wind tunnel results from models tested at Michigan University. He flew to Detroit, met Ed Cole and a deal was struck whereby Boeing would build the airplanes under a joint venture with Cole's company, called International Husky. Then some publicity pictures of the aircraft, now called the Boeing 754, began appearing in the aviation press.

It was not surprising to me to see that the Boeing 754 was a direct steal from existing Burnelli patents. Shortly thereafter, I received a call in my London home from a European airline president who was in Seattle picking up a new B-727.

He said that Boeing's Vice President of Sales, Clarence Wilde, had introduced him to Ed Cole. The two of them took him to a hangar to see the airplane of the future which, they advised, he should sign up for right away! My friend took one look at the mock-up and exclaimed, "Good God, it's a Burnelli! What about Burnelli and Slick Goodlin?" Wilde and Cole replied, "Oh, they are being taken care of."

What was meant by that is yet to be determined.

Anyway, I wrote to Ed Cole and Clarence Wilde saying we were delighted that they had discovered Burnelli's brilliance and that Burnelli would be glad to negotiate a normal license arrangement.

About six weeks later, I got a letter from Boeing stating that, while they had investigated the Burnelli design, they had decided not to proceed with the project. The fact that Boeing decided to cancel the project after spending some millions on it, became even more astonishing when a disgruntled engineer sent me a couple of pages out of the Boeing 754 manual which disclosed the enormity of Burnelli superiority. With similar power, the twin engine Burnelli type B-754 had a maximum containerized payload of 160,000 pounds while the B-767 could only carry less than half, 72,000 pounds, non-containerized. In short, the Burnelli type could carry more than double the payload and fly it 1,200 nautical miles further than the B-767!"

It could revolutionize commercial aviation and maybe, just maybe, save your life. Burnelli's genius was in designing an aircraft whose fuselage itself contributed to flight: thus a "lifting body".

Again quoting Mr. Goodlin:

"Airliners today are simply derivatives of early planes, like the Boeing 237 and the Douglas DC-2, which embrace the conventional technology of the late 1920s and the 1930s, i.e. the irresponsible practice of hanging engines and landing gear onto fuel tank supporting structure in combination with excessively high takeoff and landing speeds on overstressed tires. Add to these design flaws a fragile fuselage, devoid of crashworthy features, and there is a perfect recipe for disaster.

By 1935 the industry and government agencies were fully aware that these fatal flaws, inherent in the conventional designs, were totally eliminated in the well-proven Burnelli lifting body design.

Outstanding in payload and performance with low takeoff and landing speeds, the Burnelli UB-14, on January 13, 1935, demonstrated to the world its unparalleled structural integrity in a spectacular crash at Newark, New Jersey. Though it hit the ground at 135 mph and cart-wheeled across the field, the fuselage remained intact, no fire ensued and the occupants walked out unscathed. How could this happen? Simply, because the Burnelli fuselage is comprised of the bulk of the aircraft structure which provides a safety cage for the occupants.

The engines and landing gear, the major fire sources, are attached to the main structure and isolated from the fuel tanks in outer wing panels. The engines are mounted close together on the fuselage, eliminating the serious asymmetrical thrust problems associated with conventional airliners which have engines mounted way outboard of the centerline thrust.

In 1936, the Boeing technical chiefs Ball, Minshall and Lauden announced in Los Angeles:

"Fuselages of the present type would disappear and all equipment and load would be housed within the center section of the wing."

This is a precise description of the Burnelli configuration. In 1937, Donald Douglas stated:

"When the need for a really large transport arrives, as it inevitably will, we shall build a flying wing."

At the same time, Lockheed's chief engineer stated:

"The next step is the vanishing of the fuselage itself. Sky travelers will ride in a giant wing with plenty of head room, plenty of space to stroll."

Both of these men predicted that the flying wing transport would be a reality by 1947. Indeed, it could have been and should have been but craven politics intervened to stifle the natural evolution of Burnelli's advanced lifting body technology."

ALPA, the Air Line Pilots Association, itself has been involved with and supported the Burnelli concept. In 1961, the head of ALPA's engineering and air safety department, Theo. G. Linnert wrote to the FAA:

> "The advent of the UAL DC-8 accident in Denver has again highlighted, among other things, the need for development of high lift devices and other means which would enable transport aircraft to takeoff and land slower.

> We believe that much of the damage incurred by the DC-8 in Denver was due to the high kinetic energy which is a product of speed and mass. If the plane had a slower landing speed, we believe the damage would have been reduced and, possibly, a fire would not have occurred or would have been smaller and easier to subdue or control.

> This Association conducts evaluations of new air line aircraft and, in this regard, we have had the opportunity of doing some design and flight evaluation of an airplane which approaches the flying wing design concept. We refer to the Burnelli transport. We were favorably impressed with its design features which permit slow flight with high gross weight, considering the low horsepower. The design of the airplane also permits considerable inflight inspection of the control system, power plants and landing gear. The advantage of this is obvious from the safety standpoint. Knowing that your Bureau is working on many projects relating to increasing the safety and efficiency of aircraft, we respectfully request that the FAA include some studies for aircraft design which would embody low takeoff and landing speeds and still permit economical operation. We believe the Burnelli type design has these features and an updated version of the airplane should be considered."

Can severe crashes be fire-free and survivable?

March 1st, 1978. A Continental DC-10 waddles onto LAX runway 6 right.

It is wet and the huge jet weighs in at 430,000 pounds, very near its maximum takeoff weight. Near V1* (156 knots) there was a loud noise as a left main landing gear tire succumbed to "weight, friction and the laws of centrifugal force" followed by the failure of the other three. The DC-10's speed was near 68 knots as it exited the runway and the left main gear failed, rupturing a fuel cell. Two people died and 31 others were injured escaping the fire.

In theory, a Burnelli would never have needed to reach such a high V1 speed and, even in the event of a crash, a fire would not have occurred.

Well into his 80s, Slick continued to carry the banner for Burnelli. Upon his passing he was still waiting for justice to be done. From what I've read Burnelli's lifting body design seems workable and an advance in both technology and safety. Perhaps it's time for the concept to be readdressed.

*V1 speed is the calculated indicated airspeed short of which an abort or rejected takeoff is considered safe and beyond which takeoff is imminent.

CHAPTER 11

A NEW DECADE

"THE MOST DANGEROUS MAN ON EARTH IS THE MAN WHO HAS RECKONED WITH HIS OWN DEATH. ALL MEN DIE; FEW MEN EVER REALLY LIVE."

John Eldredge
Wild at Heart

MIGHTY HANDS *AGAIN*

Before long, I was able to get weekends off and continued to do ten to twelve airshows per year where interesting things continued to happen.

I was performing at the Robins Air Force Base airshow in Macon, Georgia. I kept the jet at my buddy, Earl Arrowood's hangar with his Sky Warriors T-34s and had hired an avionics technician recommended by Ed Bowlin to replace some instrumentation. I had been flying with the stock attitude gyro and compass for years and it was time to upgrade.

The attitude gyro is the primary instrument used during instrument meteorological conditions. It provides an artificial horizon and tells you your pitch and roll attitude. A standard western gyro is divided with the top half blue or grey, indicating the sky, and the bottom half black or brown, indicating the earth. Essentially it stays erect during flight and indicates the plane's attitude around it.

The Russians decided that they would be different. Their gyros were blue on the bottom and brown on the top. If you can imagine rolling your aircraft upside down and flying inverted, that's what my gyro looked like in normal flight. Furthermore, when you pull *back* on the stick to climb, the pipper (aircraft reference index) in the center of the gyro would go *down* into the sky. Conversely, when you push *forward* on the stick to descend, the pipper would go *up* towards the ground. If that sounds confusing to read, imagine the confusion inflight.

In actual instrument conditions I simply disregarded it and used my VSI (vertical speed indicator—it indicates rate of climb or descent in hundreds and thousands of feet per minute) and turn needle—it indicates rate and direction of turn including level flight. Fortunately the bank angle on the Russian attitude gyro did, at least, correspond to the direction of turn.

The directional gyro had a fixed but adjustable compass card with an airplane index in the center which rotated to point to the compass direction corresponding to the flight path. For example, with the compass card adjusted so that north was at twelve o'clock and you were traveling east, the airplane index would be pointed to 090 degrees at three o'clock. That was easier to get used to than the attitude gyro but screwy none the less.

Anyway, this avionics tech had been taking his time doing the work and I was getting frustrated. His delays had cost me two shows and I was determined not to miss Robins. I gave him an ultimatum and he miraculously finished just in time.

Although unsolicited, he had reconfigured my instrument panel and I must admit it looked nice.

I flew the jet down to Macon uneventfully and the next day proceeded to fly the first day of the weekend show.

I had just finished a maneuver and was doing a tuck under roll reversal to reposition. I was heading south and was 3/8s through the roll at about 200 feet when a loud pop got my attention. Four big thumb screws held the panel in place and one had backed off under pressure. The panel was misaligned and forced into place with the instruments not properly seated and the aircraft vibration and G loading had finally caused one of the nuts to come loose. I was looking outside but the movement of the panel and the sound caught my eye and it appeared that the entire panel might drop onto my feet.

Had that happened I would most likely have lost control. I instinctively reached with my left hand to stop the panel. With the stick in my right hand already at full right deflection, the motion of my left arm had rotated my shoulders slightly causing a slight pull by my right.

This all happened in the time it took for me to complete another 2/8s roll so I was then inverted. At that point I had to make a split second decision. I had to either push forward on the stick to climb or continue the momentum with a rolling pullout. Most pilots will choose the latter which is what I did but, in hindsight, I probably should have pushed out. I knew it would be close.

Everything seemed to go into slow motion as I tried to *will* the MiG to roll faster. Once past 90 degrees I pulled as hard as I could but I could clearly see the leaves on the trees rising toward me and realized that I probably wouldn't make it. I was afraid but had a sense of peace, feeling that I'd done all I could.

As I tensed for the inevitable impact, I once again felt as if some *Mighty Hands* had reached down to pull me upward. Again, it was surreal that I was still alive, still flying and extremely puzzled as to why.

It was my good fortune that the terrain was rolling downward and I had followed that contour and actually disappeared beneath the trees from the crowd's vantage point. Even though I was shaken, I realized that the panel had moved as far as it would and everything was back under control so I continued the performance.

As I taxied toward the ramp the adrenaline was still surging in my system and it wasn't until I shut the engine down that I noticed the G meter which indicated a positive ten, maximum deflection on that gauge. I have no doubt that I pulled substantially more.

The lesson learned here was how a *split second's* inattention during low level, high speed aerobatics can be fatal.

Another friend and fellow Delta pilot, Chris Smisson*, had seen what happened and, of course, realized that my recovery was way too low. He met me at the aircraft and I related to him what had happened.

That was the closest I ever came to tying the "low altitude world record" and there is absolutely no other explanation as to why I am alive today other than divine intervention.

There is a well known aviator's axiom; *Flying consists of hours and hours of boredom, interrupted by moments of stark terror.*

Apropos.

*Chris was killed a few years later at the Eglin Air Force Base airshow during his first ever attempt to race a jet truck.

Ready to fly

FIRST WORLD RECORD

I was scheduled to fly at the NAS Whiting Field airshow and very anxious to perform at the place I had learned to fly. I still had some friends serving as flight instructors there and was thrilled to have the opportunity to fly a close to home airshow for them and my kids. Since it was Whiting's 50th anniversary, I wanted to do something memorable for the show. So, I contacted the National Aeronautic Association to request a sanction to set a speed record. The NAA is the recognized governing body relating to record-making aviation and space events in this country. Each record is defined by a class and category for different types of aircraft.

With all the paperwork complete, on July 6, 1993, I flew from the Charlie Brown Airport in Atlanta to Whiting Field in 25 minutes and 30 seconds, setting a city to city national and world speed record. (Unfortunately, the "official" time was 30 minutes and 30 seconds. I think the timing error was due to the Whiting tower's mistake in not stopping the clock until I touched down. Crossing the tower in flight was the correct method.)

I flew at 10,000 feet most of the way and wondered which would melt first, me or the wings. The temperature in the cockpit was close to a hundred and twenty degrees with only ambient vent air to provide any cockpit cooling.

I calculated my fuel burn so as to take on the least amount possible. Less weight equaled more speed. I could have reduced the time even more by building up speed in the pattern at Charlie Brown and then departing abeam the tower for an air start. When I called on the ground for my clearance, though, ATC gave me a straight-out departure on course and directly to 10,000 feet so I decided to just takeoff, raise the gear and flaps and accelerate to maximum speed. The throttle was full forward the entire time. My average speed was a little over 500 miles per hour. The fuel plan worked out perfectly because I passed the Whiting tower on fumes.

Nobody has ever flown that route any faster . . . in anything!

I received the awards at a ceremony in Washington, D.C. at the National Air and Space Museum the next spring. The FAA administrator, James Busey, presented me with the National Record NAA award and the World Record award from the FAI (Federation Aéronautique Internationale). The ceremony was relatively small, mostly just the recipients, so the part I enjoyed most was visiting with my friends. Hoot Gibson was there to receive an award on behalf of his space shuttle crew and Patty Wagstaff received one as well for donating her Extra 260.

Dinner afterwards with Patty and her husband Bob was the perfect ending to a great evening.

CHAPTER 12

DESERT STORM

1991 was noteworthy to a lot of Marines. Desert Shield and Storm managed to disrupt our lives, some more than others.

(Now) Colonel Tony Gain was General Norman Schwarzkopf's Chief of Operations and based at Riyad with CENTCOM (Central Command). He aged dramatically during the war and was so affected by it that he retired shortly after his return. He was selected for promotion to brigadier general but turned it down. Since he had endured combat in Vietnam as both an infantry rifleman and later as a platoon commander, one can only speculate as to the stress and trauma associated with the staff responsibilities in the Gulf war.

Having maintained a reserve commission just for the purpose of being available in case "the balloon went up", it didn't surprise me when I was activated.

As soon as it was evident that the Marines would deploy, I began contacting guys in some reserve squadrons to attempt to get myself into a flying job. I waited too long because their mobilization was very quick and there just wasn't time.

Instead, the Marine Corps decided to utilize the expertise in my tertiary MOS (Military Occupational Specialty). They were forming a new battalion of IRRs (individual ready reservists) and I was slated to be the Air Officer and my duties would include forward air control with RECON.

We are now aware that several SEALS and RECON Marines were killed in Iraq lasering for bombs and missiles. I wasn't crazy about going to war as a grunt but figured that it was better than watching it on CNN.

I was told to get a full compliment of utility uniforms and stand by to report to Maxwell Air Force Base in Montgomery.

I got an outstanding regulation haircut and put all my personal affairs in order and waited.

Unfortunately the war was over almost before it started and the order came to stand down the battalion. I wasn't happy about it but powerless to do anything so when the opportunity came a few months later to retire from the Marine Corps reserve, I accepted.

During all the commotion to get the reserve squadrons activated a lot of paperwork had slipped through the cracks. My old squadron mate, Gene McCarthy, had been working as a special agent for the DEA (Drug Enforcement Administration) since we left active duty and he was involved in Operation Snowcap down in Peru.

The Peruvians were having a difficult time controlling the various drug lord's cocaine processing in the jungle and our DEA was there in force to help. Everyday was a firefight complete with mortars and close-in combat. Our buddy Kim McCabe had managed to contact Gene down there and asked if he wanted to go to war. Gene said that he was already in a war but would rather be flying.

Gene had stayed in the IRR like me and jumped at the chance to get out of the jungle. (The IRR is the Individual Ready Reserve—a component of the Marine Corps reserve that does not require drilling or active participation.) Kim "updated" Gene's NATOPS jacket, making him current and eligible for combat duty. (NATOPS is the acronym for Naval Aviation Training Operations.)

In a dazzling display of paperwork chicanery Gene was an up to date, fully qualified Marine Cobra pilot once again.

Kim and Gene were best friends and I envied them being in the same unit going to do what we'd trained our entire careers to do—go to war.

Gene was returning from a night escort mission in Saudi Arabia flying low level on night vision goggles. He was in the gunner's seat, with another guy at the controls in back, when they flew into a sand dune that they couldn't see with the goggles. Major Eugene T. McCarthy was my friend and comrade and I miss him.

Author Pat Conroy, upon eulogizing his father, Colonel Don Conroy, touched some things that pretty much define the characteristics of all Marines. Granted, not all of us are "The Great Santini", but we draw from many of the characteristics that embodied Colonel Conroy. For that reason and in Gene's memory, I will recount some of what Pat Conroy had to say.

> "The children of fighter pilots tell different stories than other kids do. None of our fathers can write a will or sell a life insurance policy or fill out a prescription or administer a flu shot or explain what a poet meant. We tell of fathers who landed on aircraft carriers at pitch black night with the wind howling out of the China Sea. Our fathers wiped out antiaircraft batteries in the Philippines and set Japanese soldiers on fire when they made the mistake of trying to overwhelm our troops on the ground.
>
> Your dads ran the barber shops and worked at the post office and delivered the packages on time and sold the cars while our dads were blowing up fuel depots near Seoul, were providing extraordinarily courageous close air support to the beleaguered Marines at the Chosin Reservoir and who once turned the Naktong River red with the blood of a retreating North Korean battalion.

We tell of men who made widows of the wives of our nation's enemies and who made orphans out of all their children. You don't like war or violence or napalm or rockets or cannons or death rained down from the sky? Then let's talk about your fathers, not ours.

When we talk about the aviators who raised us and the Marines who loved us, we can look you in the eye and say "You would not like to have been America's enemies when our fathers passed overhead." We were raised by the men who made the United States of America the safest country on earth in the bloodiest century in all recorded history. Our fathers made sacred those strange, singing names of battlefields across the Pacific: Guadalcanal, Iwo Jima, Okinawa, the Chosin Reservoir, Khe Sanh and a thousand more. We grew up attending the funerals of Marines slain in these battles. Your fathers made communities like Beaufort decent and prosperous and functional; our fathers made the world safe for democracy."

While Gene was substantially more modest than The Great Santini, essentially, we are all cut from the same tartan.

Saepius Exertus, Semper Fidelis, Frater Infinitas . . .

Often Tested, Always Faithful, Brothers Forever.

CHAPTER 13

NORTHWEST TERRITORIES

By the end of the year I was preparing for my upgrade at Delta to First Officer on the 727. When the opportunity presented itself, though, I went hunting in the Canadian Northwest Territories and, man, was that ever an odyssey.

It all started with a series of commercial flights that ended up in Norman Wells.

The place is a tiny oil town built mainly of portable pre-fab structures. It was a remote stop-off point for hunters and oil workers.

From there the other hunters and I that were booked by our outfitter were taken by float plane to a base camp about a hundred miles into the McKenzie Mountains. There was a nice lake there and we landed to stretch our legs and meet the outfitter.

We then continued on to a valley farther north. After about another hour of flying we circled a little pond where we could see the guides and horses waiting for us.

I was rather apprehensive as the pilot set up for his approach. Much to my surprise, he set that little Pilatus Porter down on less than two acres of water and we were soon on our way to camp. Four hours later, we snuggled into our sleeping bags about 80 miles south of the Arctic Circle.

The trip there had taken three days.

My guide was Jim Doran. I had met him in Montana on my elk hunt and was impressed with his abilities. We were about the same age, had similar interests and were both former college football players. (Jim had played at Nebraska.)

The next five days were spent glassing our valleys for big caribou bulls. I was fortunate to locate a herd of thirteen moose bedded down with a big dominant bull leading the group. We looked at him through the spotting scope for a while and sized up our best avenue of approach. We hustled the mile or so through the brush and managed to sneak up a mountainside that kept us downwind and above the herd.

Having watched our progress through their spotting scopes, the other hunters later told us that we had stalked within about fifty yards of a grizzly that had watched us with keen interest.

The mountainside was exceptionally steep and, worse, covered with loose shale which made the climb treacherous. We managed to be quiet enough that the moose were not spooked and I settled my rifle onto my pack for a solid 200 yard shot. I was amazed that the first bullet only made him flinch even though it had hit him squarely in the boiler room. I hit him twice more until he finally stood up, took a couple of steps, and I anchored him with one last shot.

Unless the atmospheric conditions and sunlight are just right, it is unusual to be able to see the flight and impact of each round but I remember seeing the swirl clearly.

We took some pictures and then started the long, laborious, task of preparing the meat and hide to be packed out. We had some strong horses, but it took two to carry the cape, antlers and all the meat. Each antler palm alone weighed over twenty pounds.

One of the two pack horses was a big, spirited horse named Fugly. He had a mind of his own but was really stout. Most likely he had some draft horse or Belgian blood in him and his oddest characteristic was his compulsion for human food.

All the horses wore hobbles around camp but he always seemed to find his way near the cook tent around dinner time. On one of his days off while we were out hunting, he got into the cook tent and ate or destroyed all of our food. He was obviously the guilty party because he was covered with flour. We had a caribou quarter hanging nearby which we subsisted on for the remaining few days.

I still had a caribou tag to fill and we hunted hard to find a good bull. As a last resort we took a chance and climbed to the top of a mountain known to have a basin at the top much like a volcano. We went through a cloud layer at the top which forced us to wear our rain gear. I think I got just as wet from the sweat inside my rain suit as I would have from the moisture in the clouds. We got to the top and crept up to a point where we could see into the basin and, sure enough, there were two nice bulls bedded down on the other side. There was no way to get closer than 400 yards. We took a few minutes to get our breath before I was comfortable and ready to ease off a shot. The bull managed to stand and then fell over with his legs straight in the air. I had held very high to compensate for drop but couldn't do much to compensate for the swirling wind. There was considerable luck involved but I finally had my mountain caribou.

On my return trip I stopped in Edmonton, Alberta to visit with my buddy Holmes Patton and to clean up and briefly recover from the rugged time near the Arctic Circle. I stored the meat and antlers in the Delta cold storage room at the airport and then headed to Holmes' for a few hours of food and fellowship.

By far, though, the best thing that happened to me in 1992 was the birth of my second son, Logan.

Guide Jim Doran & me with my Alaska Yukon Moose

Canadian Mountain Caribou

CHAPTER 14

LIFE GOES ON

"LET THE PEOPLE FEEL THE WEIGHT OF WHO YOU ARE AND LET THEM DEAL WITH IT."

John Eldredge
Wild at Heart

By the end of the year I was, once again, getting involved with administrative duties involving the MiG.

I was selected to be the jet representative on the International Council of Air Shows' Performer Safety Committee. It involved dealing with individual safety issues that occasionally arose with performers.

Of all my contributions to the airshow industry, this is the one of which I am most proud.

Our chairman at that time was Bob Davis and he was a great guy to work with. Tough and thick-skinned, he intercepted a lot of the political malarkey and allowed us to make good decisions.

Our toughest case involved a female pilot. She had plenty of experience, marketed herself well and was known throughout the industry. She had changed aircraft a couple of times, trying to find that niche that we all looked for, and ended up with a very high performance and highly modified Pitts. We (the performer safety committee) had been given a heads-up that she was having trouble with her inverted ribbon cut. We were told that her approach was unstable and that she was coming way too close to hitting the ground. The problem persisted throughout one entire season and, eventually, even esteemed airshow pilot Sean Tucker got involved. Sean had seen her fly, too, and expressed his concern. We were in the process of trying to counsel her and even threatened some type of sanction when she finally did hit the ground at a show. Luckily, she was not injured but the plane was badly damaged. Without a show plane, she eventually tried her hand at air racing in a sponsored warbird but couldn't qualify in the big Sea Fury and has since sort of disappeared back into her airline job.

When my two year term was up I recommended Jack Ekl, at Leo Loudenslager's suggestion, to take my place. Jack was a former Blue Angel and flew for Southwest Airlines when he wasn't flying Leo's Bud Light BD-5J. I'm not sure I did Jack a favor, but Leo encouraged him to take the job. He said I left things in good hands.

That high profile exposure made it easier for me to get to know many of the "big wigs" in ICAS, not the least of which was the President, T.J. Brown.

I had met T.J. on the airshow circuit and found him to be very friendly. He was leading the Holiday Inn/Coca Cola Aerobatic Team which consisted of some former Air Force pilots. Each was very talented and they had a great reputation. Three of the four, T.J., Mike Vanwaggenen and Buzz Lynch also had test pilot backgrounds and they were very excited by the MiG.

Seeing my success, T.J. became interested in acquiring a jet, too, and found himself a partner to buy a surplus F-86 Sabre. Shortly thereafter, he approached me about teaming the MiG and Sabre together for a dogfight act which I already knew would be a tremendous success.

In order to purchase the Sabre, T.J. had become partners with Jim Gregory, a Jacksonville, Florida businessman who owned some Taco Bell franchises. Jim was a likable guy with a Navy background and the work-up flights proved him capable of flying formation aerobatics.

We had a complex routine involving two-ship aerobatics followed by a vertical split at show center and then a mock dogfight.

It was well done and I was happy to be involved with T.J.'s operation. I had checked T.J. out in the MiG so as to have a backup pilot for both jets. Jim and I were to be the primary pilots whenever possible with T.J. covering when either of the two of us couldn't fly.

After Jim received an aerobatic competency check by an ACE evaluator on T.J.'s team, he and I flew our first show together at Marine Corps Air Station Cherry Point, North Carolina and our second at Aguadilla, Puerto Rico. The formation was fine but after we split, apparently Jim was getting too low. I didn't find this out until months later because no one who observed it said a word to me at either show. (To my knowledge, he only displayed poor headwork on one occasion and that was not considering wearing a flotation device during our first over water flight.) Jim flew all but a couple of his work-up flights on T.J.'s wing and T.J. flew on mine when we practiced so my actual flight time directly with Jim was limited.

The trip to Puerto Rico was challenging since the primary VOR navigation stations were unreliable out in the Bermuda Triangle. We both had portable GPS units (Global Positioning System—the newest generation of navigation aids utilizing satellite downlinks) and were able to find the southernmost island in the Bahamas, Great Inagua, to refuel. It was not much more than a Coast Guard station with a runway that looked like it had been mortared. Both landing and takeoff required an interesting dance of maneuvering around the potholes.

Jim had a few minor problems on our cross-countries but I just attributed it to being rusty.

We were booked to fly the Marine Corps Air Station El Toro show in California but I came down with a nasty head cold a week or so prior. Just to be safe, we activated our contingency plan for T.J. to take my place. As luck and Murphy's Law would have it, T.J. got sick *at* the show and there was no way that he could fly either!

Rather than cancel entirely, T.J. asked Jim if he would be comfortable to fly a similar routine as a solo. Jim eagerly agreed so T.J. gave him a thorough brief on what to do.

It was a crystal clear southern California day with a quarter of a million people watching. They even had some live television coverage.

Jim was pumped and ready to show what he could do . . . and he did.

After takeoff, we would normally make one turn in the pattern to clean up and build some energy. Jim didn't, and entered his first maneuver without enough airspeed. He pulled an estimated five to six Gs (four was normal), evidence of just how pumped he was, to enter a loop with a roll on top.

By the time he finished the roll, he had lost so much energy that he was doomed. *Accustomed to being the wingman and, therefore, relying on his lead (me or T.J.) to maintain the proper parameters*, Jim probably never even looked in the cockpit for airspeed or altitude indications or he would have seen that he was both too low and too slow.

Because he pulled so hard and entered the maneuver without enough airspeed (typically 300 knots minimum), there was no way that he could complete it. Had he realized his predicament at any time prior to committing the nose below forty five degrees on the back side, he could have rolled-out and recovered. He didn't, and continued to pull even though he had topped out at only 2500 to 3500 feet; 1500 feet lower than normal.

It's estimated that he might have made it with another two hundred feet or so, but he entered accelerated stall and impacted the runway directly on the centerline.

The airplane exploded and Jim's body was thrown clear.

The pretty black jet named "Sabre Dance" was destroyed and Jim was killed instantly.

Because the mishap occurred on a naval installation, NIS (the Naval Investigative Service—now NCIS) was involved and, during their background check, they discovered that Jim had obtained his pilot's license under fraudulent circumstances. It seems that he actually attrited from flight school after coming close to getting his wings and afterwards somehow managed to take the military competency exam to get his civilian pilots license. Since then he had accumulated a significant amount of flight time and to his credit he remembered a lot of the lingo from flight training. He fooled us good but, ultimately, he was the fool.

Obviously, Jim had the wrong perspective about airshow flying.

I had a lot of time to reflect on the incident, what led up to it and my own culpability in not realizing that Jim was ill prepared.

I had hitched my wagon to T.J.'s rising star. As the president of ICAS he had been the driving force behind policies which made it more and more difficult for the average Joe to be an airshow performer. The ACE (aerobatic competency evaluator) program replaced the performer safety committee and took the responsibility for certifying performers from the FAA (which, with their lack of expertise, they were glad to be rid of) in an unprecedented way. The result, intentional or not, basically pulled up the rope behind those of us already grandfathered in. It was implemented purely for economic reasons.

In hindsight, T.J.'s method of getting Jim qualified should have gotten my attention.

I was caught up in the concept of the jet team and not around for most of Jim's training which, I now believe, was probably pencil whipped. It was an exercise in hypocrisy.

In an ironic twist of fate, T.J. was killed four months later while flying an L-39 in Russia, preparing to buy jets for our formation team. No one knows for sure what happened but it is suspected that the passenger, a Russian officer who had asked for a flight demonstration, became frightened and grabbed the control stick during a low inverted pass.

T.J.'s funeral was somewhat odd. He was a graduate of the Air Force Academy so his memorial service was held at their beautiful chapel. It was surprising to see such a small number of people there, considering his standing within the airshow industry, but perhaps that made it more intimate. T.J. didn't make it on time, though. Yep, he was late for his own funeral. FedEx reportedly had a problem with delivering his remains.

What I remember most vividly, though, was a magpie which had somehow flown into the chapel and perched near the apex of one of the spires, trying to find a way out through the stained glass.

To me, it was as if the magpie embodied T.J.'s spirit. He had come to see the service and was now anxious to go fly.

MiG-15 & F-86 flown by Jim Gregory

POLITICS

Woe unto you, when all men shall speak well of you!
Luke 6:26

In a vain attempt to discourage me, some of the folks who had considered operating jets in the past told me that they had "crunched the numbers" and that there was no way that a jet act could make it on the airshow circuit.

One of those individuals was Frank Sanders. Frank had survived a few airshows and done some air racing for about twenty years. He had a warbird restoration and maintenance business in Chino where he had renovated and modified a Hawker Sea Fury for air racing and designed a smoke generating system that mounted on a jet's missile rail which he called the "Sanders Smokewinder"—a play on the sidewinder missile that would normally occupy that spot. Maintenance and design were his forte. Flying was not.

Frank was a cerebral sort who liked to write papers. One, concerning stress, contained many references to both the psychology and physiology of flying. It was filled with medical facts about which Frank knew only what he transposed. He did do a good job of assimilating the information to make his point to the reader, right or wrong. And that was the essence of my beef with Frank. Essentially, he fancied himself a preeminent airshow pilot and was wary of anyone who might overshadow his domain or expose some of his thoughts as bunk.

Frank anointed himself as a safety guru within the airshow industry and, as such, could be out of school in his judgments. For example, he was highly critical that a former military pilot with a split helicopter/fixed-wing background, like me, would be foolish enough to think himself capable of flying a MiG although he, Frank, had no substantial training whatsoever.

(In fact, I had more fixed-wing than rotary-wing time.) He seemed to take some perverse enjoyment when those with more experience or better qualifications made a mistake.

By the next year those number crunchers who had said, "You can't do that" were saying, "How'd you do that?" Frank was one of them.

Like a fool, I shared all the details and found myself with competition in the form of the Red Knight the next season.

Frank teamed up with Rick Brickert to display a T-33. Since there was almost no competition, there were plenty of shows for both of us, but I guess Frank just didn't see it that way.

That year at the ICAS convention, I couldn't understand why people were taking such a wide berth around my booth and I hadn't booked a single show after the first three days. Finally, a guy representing the Point Mugu airshow stopped to talk and told me about some comments Frank had made in one of the seminars.

Frank, conveniently, didn't happen to mention a name but warned everyone that there was a very unsafe pilot trying to do airshows in a MiG. Of course, everyone associated what he was saying with me but he was cleverly making reference to another guy who was flailing around the west coast, scaring the hell out of himself. Frank made no attempt to clarify who he *wasn't* talking about either.

I immediately went to the Executive Director, Rick Nadeau, who made a somewhat apologetic disclaimer at the general meeting and I managed to salvage the season.

That was a good lesson for me in the politics of business and I soon came to know who the "Frank Sanders" in the industry were.

Ironically, Frank ended up killing himself flying the T-bird. Go figure.

He was giving a media ride in the T-33 at an airshow in the southwest. Post crash analysis determined that the aircraft was over stressed to the point that an aileron actually departed the jet. The poor observer in the back seat who had entrusted his life to Frank never had a chance.

I had met Rick Brickert a year or so prior when we were both on the FAA's Warbird Technical Advisory Committee chaired by Ed Bowlin. Rick was brash and arrogant but reined it in a notch around those of us he considered to be his peers. Later, he developed quite a reputation at Delta as a pain-in-the-butt boy captain on the MD-88.

Rick was debuting the Pond Racer, an experimental aircraft made of composite materials with two Nissan automobile engines. Bob Pond, the owner of the Planes of Fame Museum in Minnesota, had funded the project to help introduce a new top speed racer at Reno.

The old warbirds were getting tired and this was an attempt to determine a viable replacement.

Rick had been flying some of Bob's planes at airshows and, since he was an experienced air racer at Reno anyway, was a logical choice.

During a race at Reno, Rick maydayed that he had a problem and departed the course. It is speculated that he was trying to land on the desert floor when he was overcome by smoke or fumes in the cockpit. There had been some kind of fire onboard and the composites were emitting toxic fumes.

Rick did not appear to have been wearing his oxygen mask when the rescue personnel got to him.

Sadly, two of the "experts" were history.

It is said that imitation is the sincerest form of flattery. Such was the case when I noticed another pilot's photo in *ICAS News*.

He was a new performer, flying a MiG-17, who had written an article to enlighten us all as to how to go about obtaining sponsorship and marketing. (Interestingly enough, he was independently wealthy and was initially "sponsored" by his own business at that time.) He sported a black flight suit, like mine, with CCCP and Soviet Fighter Weapons School patches on the shoulders, like mine, and a name tag with Soviet wings, like mine. What a coincidence! The only difference was an Air Force scarf. Marines wear T-shirts.

Amused with his arrogance, I gave him a call both to introduce myself and to offer my assistance as a fellow MiG pilot and performer. Although he initially denied knowing anything about me, he knew I had his number. It was a hoot.

His show became noted for his night pyrotechnics act—potentially catastrophic and rare for that reason. I think he got the idea after burning up his first MiG on a post maintenance flight. (Essentially, during a "prudent" engine change, a stainless steel fuel line was damaged and a hairline crack which was created went unnoticed. When the line was pressurized on takeoff, it sprayed fuel into the aft section and caught fire during activation of the afterburner.)

He was luckier with the second one and did extremely well with eventual sponsorship from Red Bull although he recently succumed to cancer.

Several of my fellow MiG pilots have not had adequate respect for the jet and it has bitten them. Pilot induced oscillation (PIO) is easy to enter due to a lack of baffles or foam in the fuel cells which prevent sloshing. Rocking the wings at slow speeds can result in a departure. (i.e. departure from controlled flight—a spin.)

Fuel management has scared some, too. Essentially, you're at minimum fuel at takeoff, especially without drop tanks. A clock is the best fuel gauge in this generation of MiGs and inattention to the engine's running time has caused some interesting unscheduled landings.

There are other reasons, I'm sure, that there are still only a very few MiG-15s and 17s flown regularly.

CHAPTER 15

GONE BUT NOT FORGOTTEN

Now I'll use this bully pulpit to share my passionate views on the debacle of our country's quagmire with our unaccounted-for military personnel. Having been there myself, it is a topic I hold near and dear.

For many years I've worn a P.O.W./M.I.A. (Prisoner of War/Missing in Action) bracelet. It's indicative of my commitment to those men still missing in action and unaccounted for and an outward symbol of my support for their cause.

Time has shown that men unfortunate enough to be captured and become prisoners of war become political pawns or worse. Negotiations take place and many are repatriated. For an unlucky few, however, fate takes a nasty twist. Some have been known to be used for medical experimentation and died miserable deaths. Others were subjected to confinement for the rest of their lives because it would be impossible for the enemy to save face after denying their existence. It is known that some men in particular are alive and being kept as prisoners of war. (I highly recommend the book *Bohica* by Scott Barnes.) There are men held captive from the Vietnam War as well as the Korean. Most of the Korean War prisoners were taken to either China or the Soviet Union while the Vietnamese kept or killed theirs. It has been documented that some are still alive today.

Marion Sturkey does a brilliant job of explaining the history of Vietnam's POW negotiating in his book *Bonnie-Sue*.

"Vietnam embarked on an intense campaign to normalize relations with America. Recognizing the

275

extreme United States' interest in the fate of servicemen still listed as missing-in-action in Indochina, the Vietnamese government *discovered* the skeletal remains of twelve of these missing men. Amid much ceremony, these remains were returned to the United States' custody. Later, there was a series of such *discoveries*. The Vietnamese government then promised further searches for American remains.

In return for their good faith, the Vietnamese asked the United States to dissolve its trade barriers, reestablish diplomatic relations and accept Vietnam as an equal member in the international community of nations. The Vietnamese say that they have always told the United States all they know about the Americans killed or missing during the war. Further, they say they treated American prisoners of war (POWs) humanely and turned all of them over to the United States after the fighting.

Those who now accept Hanoi's explanation could profit from a reality check. As late as the 1970s, Hanoi had claimed that none of its soldiers were even fighting in South Vietnam. Of course, the United States was also maintaining that no Americans were fighting in Laos or Cambodia.

What—or who—can we believe?

With respect to Vietnam's treatment of POWs, Jeremiah A. Denton, Jr. has a story to tell. For those who may not have heard of him, Denton was a United States Navy pilot who flew the A-6 Intruder. On July 18, 1965, Denton was catapulted from the flight deck of the USS Independence for a bombing sortie over North Vietnam. He got shot down, captured and jailed in the infamous "Hanoi Hilton". Almost eight years later, Denton was the senior officer among the first group of POWs to be released. On February 13, 1973, at Clark Air Force Base in the Philippines, a C-141 rolled to a stop. Denton was the first POW to exit the aircraft. With hundreds of television cameras recording the moment, he walked to a waiting microphone and announced:

We are honored to have had the opportunity to serve our country under difficult circumstances. We are profoundly grateful to our Commander-in-Chief and to our nation for this day. God bless America!

In writing, Denton later told of the interrogations and brutal beatings that lasted for days; lasted until he lost consciousness from the pain. He told of the screaming POWs who were dragged away for interrogation and who were never heard from again and who were never repatriated. Between senseless torture sessions, Denton, himself, had been kept in solitary confinement for four of his eight years in Hanoi and his guards often kept him locked in a coffin for sport. Back in America, Denton would eventually be elected to the United States Senate from his native Alabama.

His fellow POWs, including George Coker, a former Pensacola class 43-63 classmate of mine (Sturkey's), vouched for Denton's revelations of torture in Hanoi at the hands of Vietnamese guards and interrogators.

Dieter Dengler, another pilot, had been captured after being shot down in Laos on February 2, 1966. He escaped and was plucked from the jungle by a helicopter over five months later on July 20.

His written account of the subhuman treatment he received at the hands of his Vietnamese captors, first published in 1979, defies all human reason.

Humane treatment of POWs? Be your own judge.

During the war, Hanoi also had maintained that it never failed to disclose the names of American POWs. As late as 1972, Hanoi stated that it held only 368 American captives. However, North Vietnam repatriated 591 POWs during February of the following year. Almost to the very end, North Vietnam had denied that it held the additional 223 Americans. In view of this eleventh hour disclosure, many wondered if North Vietnam kept additional POWs as "bargaining chips". If not, had other POWs been killed while in captivity?

The answer depends on whom you elect to believe. Hanoi has always maintained that it has given full accounting with respect to American prisoners. Conversely, based on debriefings of POWs who were released, the United States initially stated that many POWs were left behind. Yet, the United States government later said it believes that the American prisoners in question are now all dead—case closed. Where does the truth lie?

Bit by bit, the answers seep out. In the early 1990s, the Vietnamese government, desperate to curry favor in the United States and gain economic aid, allowed Theodore G. Schweitzer access to previously secret records. The Vietnamese thought Schweitzer was researching a book that would cast favorable light on their country. However, Schweitzer was actually a covert agent who worked for the United States government. In Hanoi, he computer-scanned and photographed Vietnamese records, war photographs and the military ID cards of many former American POWs. He also computer-scanned the North Vietnamese "Blue Book", a chronological registry maintained by the North Vietnamese that listed all Americans captured in North Vietnam. Many of the men listed in the Blue Book had never been repatriated to the United States.

Schweitzer also computer-scanned records and photographs of American airmen who had been killed when they were shot down or who had died while trying to avoid capture.

Knowledge of the fate of many of these men previously had never been acknowledged by Vietnam.

During his months in Hanoi, Schweitzer met and was photographed with General Giap (the primary Vietnamese military leader during the war), who is still revered. Schweitzer's aid for the research project was Lieutenant Colonel Nguyen Van Thi, a General Political Directorate (GPD) officer. According to Schweitzer's records, the GPD officer confided to him:

"Our government does not want America to know that our darkest secret is that we killed many Americans in cold blood. They were tortured to death in prison or simply killed outright from fear they would try to escape. And our leaders are afraid to admit this. They were tortured to death here in Hanoi."

Schweitzer released his photographs, computer records and interview documents to the United States government. He later contacted technical author Malcolm McConnell who used Schweitzer's data and published "Inside Hanoi's Secret Archives: Solving the MIA Mystery" in early 1995. In his book, McConnell also disclosed the results of research work in Moscow in 1993 after the collapse of the Soviet Union. At the "Center for the Preservation of Contemporary Documents", a researcher had stumbled across a transcript of an address to North Vietnam's Politburo on September 15, 1972, during the war. According to the transcript, Lieutenant General Tran Van Quang told the Politburo that there were 1,205 American POWs. (Remember that six months later the North Vietnamese would repatriate only 591 POWs.) Quang noted that the United States did not know how many American POWs were held in North Vietnam and he added: "In accordance with the decree from the Politburo, we keep secret the number of POWs".

After the Quang transcript became public, the American media accepted it as genuine. The Vietnamese government, still pushing for American economic aid, labeled it a forgery.

(The Vietnamese failed to suggest why someone might have forged such a document and why anyone would want to plant such a document in Moscow of all places.) After a lengthy silence on the issue, the United States government took the position that the transcript was not genuine.

Again, where does the truth lie? Who knows? For many, the only reality that matters is that American servicemen listed as missing-in-action, just like their comrades on The Wall in our nation's capital, are gone.

The long war in Indochina somehow gobbled up all of them.

(Thanks to president, Bill Clinton) Vietnam got what it wanted: diplomatic recognition, the right to negotiate trade and investment treaties and a green light for the United States companies, which had been waiting, to pour dollars into Vietnam. At a press conference in Hanoi, Le Mai, the Vietnamese Deputy Foreign Minister, was ecstatic over the economic windfall. Strange—he had nothing more to say about further Vietnamese efforts to locate Americans still missing in Indochina."

I remember vividly the day I filled out my first combat SAR (search and rescue) authenticator card in the squadron ready room. How would I be recognized during a rescue attempt?

I wrote down four things that would be only known to me in war—my son's nickname (Tunaman), the color of my Corvette (champagne beige), my college sport (football) and my instrument (drums). There was a small photo stapled to the card in which I wore a flight suit with no name tag or squadron identification. My fingerprints were irrefutable.

I remember thinking that I had faith; faith that every effort would be made to recover me. *I would never be left behind.*

CHAPTER 16

BEAR HUNT

I had always wanted to hunt dangerous game—something that could also hunt *me*. I did a lot of research and eventually booked a brown bear hunt in Alaska. My buddy, Warren Price, decided he'd go, too, but just to fish and take in the scenery and some photos. I would hunt the great hunter, *Ursus Arctos Horribilis*.

Our area was on the Alaska Peninsula just south of Iliamna. Our campsite was on Lake Iliamna and the shoreline was littered with the carcasses of thousands of salmon that had spawned and died. The tributary streams were filled with arctic char and grayling and Warren and I wasted no time tying on our Mepps spinners and catching them upon our arrival.

There were lots of tracks and scat near and around our campsite and I chanced to see a sow and her cubs while fishing during our first day out.

Confidence was high but we had to hunt hard to find a trophy bear. I had been led to believe that the bears were abundant there and an eight-footer would be typical. As it turned out, I was lucky to find one.

We spotted the bruin from camp while glassing one morning and the chase was on. We were led on a trek across the tundra that covered several miles but we stayed downwind and eventually caught up as the beast ripped apart a beaver lodge.

I set up on some higher ground that I figured would eventually be within shooting range and waited for the bear to pass by. A shoulder shot with the .338 sent the bear down immediately. Another shot was fired for insurance and we then started the laborious task of caping the hide.

My guide, Charlie Hostetler, stuffed the hide into his ruck sack and we began the hike back to camp, alternating carrying the bear. The tundra was soft and mushy and the farthest either of us could go was about a hundred yards before collapsing. There was probably near two hundred pounds of unfleshed bear in that pack and we each dreaded our turn.

As we approached the lake I got an idea to try floating the pack back to camp. Charlie was afraid that it would sink but I was convinced that there was enough fat and hair to allow it to float. It did, and towing it along the shoreline in our hip waders was a whole lot easier than hauling it.

It was good to see the float plane arrive a few days later because the weather was about to take a turn for the worse. The Alaskan wilderness can be unforgiving of an inept sportsman and we felt a real sense of satisfaction in having conquered it.

Alaska Brown Bear

Because I am an indiscriminate saver of things—a tendency acquired after a childhood of having little to save—I have tucked in a drawer of my gun cabinet a stack of paper. Now several inches thick, this little stack of paper contains, to the best of my knowledge, every hunting license I ever bought.

I can't remember exactly how or why it began, whether there was even a conscious desire to save them or just some indefinable reluctance to throw them out. At the end of each season I'd just toss the old license in the drawer. Each was a document authorizing me to do one of the things I love most. Over the years things like this just have a way of adding up, a lot like the years themselves.

I have no idea how many of those old licenses there are nor the slightest interest in sorting or counting them. In fact, I can't recall a single occasion that I've done so much as casually thumbed through them. There's never been a need to. If I can't remember every last place I've hunted, I can call to mind most of them, and so I have a pretty fair idea of what's in that stack without bothering to look.

Preserved in there are, among other things, the records of various personal "firsts"—my first hunting trip out west, the first time I turkey hunted, the first deer I ever got. Hefting that stack of many years, I can honestly say that I've never begrudged or regretted a single penny of the cost.

The wilderness has offered me solace, breathing space and a sense of wonder. Collectively, the places map out a territory I think of simply as "hunting country" and those old licenses have been my passports to it.

When the season is finished and the passports expired, I add a few more scraps to the growing stack of paper. There's no sentiment or ceremony, just a lingering question: Why have I kept track of a lifetime's worth of useless paper?

Only now, well past the midpoint of my hunting life, have I gotten some glimpse at the answer.

In some small way, I've come to see that bundle of old licenses as a tangible record of a life lived with a certain kind of deliberateness. They are a log of my travels to hunting country, a stack of postcards sent to myself from the edge of the wild, signifying a choice about what is valuable to me and why.

When the day comes, as it inevitably must, when I can no longer hunt, I wonder how thick that stack will have grown. I wonder if my sons, too, will have similar stacks with the same destinations at the same time as mine. Then, I might at last sort through them and contemplate the map they make.

CHAPTER 17

HANGING UP MY SPURS

"SUCCESS IS GETTING WHAT YOU WANT.
HAPPINESS IS LIKING WHAT YOU GET."

I had enjoyed a wonderful partnership with the MiG for several years but it seemed that my little voice was telling me that it was time to move on. The fact that so many friends and acquaintances had died doing airshows certainly had an impact on my thought process, but it was far from being the primary reason.

All of us performers tend to believe that it can't happen to us. If we dwelled on the possibilities, we'd be terrified to fly.

Unfortunately the accidents do happen, though, and not necessarily due to pilot error.

Machines break and don't always give any preliminary indication that something is about to fail.

Physiological factors also come into play as our bodies don't always give advance warning that we have a problem that is about to occur.

I wasn't concerned with the latter so much as the possibility that a forty year old airplane would eventually become tired enough to break regardless of the quality of maintenance it received.

Besides, it just wasn't as much fun as it used to be. That was primarily due to the fact that I had so little control of my airline schedule that scheduling airshows required extremely innovative time management.

All in all I figured that we both needed a break.

The National Naval Aviation Museum in Pensacola had become one of the best in the country and, as a benefactor, it seemed appropriate that the MiG be retired to such a quality facility.

I had some preliminary talks with the museum's director, Bob Rasmussen, and was planning for them to display the plane. The only prerequisite was that I retain ownership of the jet. This way if the jet should ever appreciate to some magnificent value, it would give my heirs (the kids) the option to sell it. It was a win win deal for both.

Prior to that decision, I had decided to make my "swan song" performance at the NAS Pensacola airshow. I had been solicited by one of T.J.'s old partners to sell him the MiG and he came to the show in an effort to convince me to sell the jet to him. He really wanted my MiG because of its significance of being the first one certificated in the country and he also knew that it had been well maintained and was fully operational.

When I flew the MiG to Pensacola, I landed and was taxiing clear of the duty runway and heading for the ramp. I was unaware that my brake pucks were severely worn on *both* main landing gear and they finally failed, either heating the rubber bladders or puncturing them with the keepers until they ruptured.

As I entered the ramp and attempted to turn, I realized my predicament. To make things worse I was headed directly for Blue Angel number 5 with no way to steer or stop the jet.

Fortunately the ramp was slightly up hill and I wasn't taxiing too fast. The jet eventually coasted to a stop and I hopped out and placed a chock I carried behind one of the wheels. Then I started the process of getting replacement parts overnighted right away.

I missed the Friday show but was able to fly the next day even though the weather was marginal.

Since it was to be my last show, I asked to wait and fly after the Blues (which is normally unheard of, particularly for their homecoming show) in hopes of clearer skies. I had a good rapport with the team and they were gracious enough to allow me the last slot. The weather cleared just enough for me to fly a modified high show and I had a hollow feeling in my stomach as I returned to the ramp and put the MiG "to bed" thinking we'd flown our final show together.

The jet stayed on the NAS ramp for almost a month as I waited for some incentive from Rasmussen. Our negotiations had concluded after his indication that I would have to pay an exorbitant fee to insure the jet against liability while it was in the museum. He said the museum's legal counsel had told him that they could not accept liability for an aircraft they did not own. When I enquired as to what liability there could possibly be, his only answer was a potential fire. I argued that there was absolutely no way that an aircraft with no fuel, minimal lubricants and no battery (source of electrical ignition) could possibly cause a fire! Also, there were other aircraft on loan to the museum from other sources which was common practice among museums. Clearly, I was being strong-armed for an outright donation which I declined. I left Rasmussen with the ultimatum that the deal was as initially agreed or not at all and that I would await his reconsideration.

After no contact, I deduced he was disinterested in a loaned aircraft and I reluctantly agreed to sell.

I ferried the MiG to Conroe, Texas and began what turned out to be an odyssey with the buyer. I checked him out in the jet and flew home.

Within days of my inquiring about the supposedly forthcoming payment in full, he indicated that his financial situation was such that he was unable to pay as agreed.

Even though he had income as a retired Air Force pilot and currently flew for Continental, he had planned on cashing in some investments and, he said, a loan from his brother which didn't come through. We then agreed that he would be responsible for all insurance, maintenance and other fees associated with operating the jet and I would have full access to use it for airshow performances or other contracts while he made regular payments over a specified period of time.

He eventually managed to pay off the debt although our relationship soured over time.

The end of one of the most noteworthy jets in U.S. aviation history was abrupt and unfitting of such an aircraft.

I was told that following a fuel stop in Little Rock, Arkansas, the pilot took off fully loaded and later said he "thought" the aircraft was having acceleration problems. He then attempted, after being airborne, to put the aircraft back on the runway. He did not use the longest runway available at the airport (which probably wouldn't have mattered much anyway) and was, not surprisingly, unable to stop on the runway remaining. He went off the end and on an excursion through the grass and into some trees which, apparently, did only minimal damage to the exterior of the plane.

I was in Atlanta at the time, studying for my upgrade to the 767 and took a break long enough to watch the evening news where I happened to see the report. The film I saw showed a jet still in pretty good shape so I presumed it would be repaired and flying again soon.

I learned a couple of years later that with the aircraft being grossly underinsured to save a few dollars and likely looking for a way to recoup some of his investment, the guy let the insurance company have the jet for a pittance of what it was worth. The insurance company promptly sold the jet for parts and it was subsequently dismantled. I understand the cockpit section of the fuselage sits in a small museum somewhere in the Midwest.

I believe the entire aircraft could easily have been cosmetically restored to museum quality for a small expense and I would gladly have bought it myself had I known.

In addition, I've also flown a MiG-17 owned by a retired airline pilot who bought the jet and found himself in over his head. He also owned a former Swiss Venom and thought it exciting to do a dogfight with the two jets. I helped him out for a couple of years but eventually had to part company because of the safety aspect of his poor aerobatic abilities and significantly deficient business acumen. "Captain" Curt, as he called himself, was both dangerous and unreceptive to criticism.

CONDITION ZERO

September 11, 2001

0846— American flight 11 hits the North Tower of (Eastern time) the World Trade Center in New York City.

0903— United flight 175 hits the South Tower.

0937— American flight 77 hits the Pentagon

0942— The FAA (Federal Aviation Administration) issues the execution order for SCATANA (Security Control of Air Traffic and Air Navigation Aids*) grounding all U.S. air traffic and diverting all international flights inbound to U.S. airspace.

*An emergency preparedness plan facilitated by the FAA, DOD (Department of Defense) and the FCC (Federal Communications Commission) designed to bring U.S. airspace to *Condition Zero*—no aircraft allowed airborne except for waivers to specified law enforcement, air ambulance and military flights.

0945— Shutdown of U.S. airspace begins

1003— United flight 93 crashes in Pennsylvania

1215— Skies are empty of all commercial and private flights

Within minutes of receiving our clearance revision from Denver Center we had descended from cruise altitude, flown our approach and landed in Denver. Everything in the cockpit was exceptionally professional, as one would expect from a Delta crew. The flight attendants were notified that we were diverting and to ready the cabin. Our engineer made a PA to the passengers informing them that, although *we* had no in-flight emergency, it was necessary for us to land and further updates would be provided at the gate.

We speculated what the problem might be but quickly deduced by the radio traffic that it was indeed a national situation. Our 727 had no means to communicate with the company other than our two radios and they were busy acquiring weather information and other necessary data.

When the gate agent opened our door and briefed us, we de-planed the aircraft and everyone gathered in the gatehouse to watch the TV monitors and see for ourselves what had happened. It was surreal.

A little more than two years later, on January 24, 2004, after a lengthy process of application and acceptance, I became Federal Flight Deck Officer P----in FFDO class 413A.

To qualify it was necessary to pass an extremely complex security background check and a battery of tests, not the least of which was a mental evaluation by a psychiatrist.

After many months of debate, controversy and resistance by the Federal Air Marshals, the FFDO program was finally implemented the previous year. We traveled at our own expense (as FFDOs still do) to Artesia, New Mexico where we were trained at the Federal Law Enforcement Training Center. The training was outstanding and that is all I am at liberty to say.

The terms of our special deputation were specific. It was clear that we were not employed by the newly formed TSA (Transportation Security Administration), DHS (Department of Homeland Security) or any branch of the Federal Government. We were also given no special dispensation or remuneration by our airlines. The additional responsibilities of flying armed were not compensated in any way.

It is a tribute to the dedication and patriotism of my peers that the program continues today to offer an additional level of safety and security to the air-traveling public.

Part of our oath of office includes the promise that we " . . . will perform the duties of a Federal Flight Deck Officer with integrity, professionalism, and impartiality. So help me God." That impartiality part is of particular interest because I can guarantee you that anyone who breaches a cockpit door with a FFDO on the other side will be greeted by at least 3 well-placed rounds (2 and 1 as we used to say—2 center mass and 1 in the head) and possibly more on their way to the deck. Deadly force is the only force used. No wounding shots.

In keeping with that policy, a sailor in SEAL Team 6 on May 1, 2011, terminated Osama bin Laden who was responsible for masterminding the 9/11 tragedy.

Perhaps country music recording artist Toby Keith said it best in some of the lyrics from his song *Courtesy of the Red, White and Blue* (*The Angry American*):

" . . . justice will be served and the battle will rage:
This big dog will flight when you rattle his cage.
An' you'll be sorry that you messed with the U.S. of A.
'Cos we'll put a boot in your ass, it's the American way.

Hey Uncle Sam put your name at the top of his list,
And the Statue of Liberty started shaking her fist
And the eagle will fly and it's gonna be hell,
When you hear Mother Freedom start ringing her bell.
And it'll feel like the whole wide world is
raining down on you.
Ah, brought to you, courtesy of the red, white and blue."

NEXT WORLD RECORD

I mentioned I was in Atlanta undergoing training for the Boeing 767 when the MiG was damaged. The venerable old 727 had finally been retired from Delta's fleet and I was one of the 3 most senior first officers. As a member of the National Aeronautic Association I hatched the idea for Delta to garner a little good publicity for the 727's last passenger flight.

Captain Bob Falkins was in charge of all 727 training and he, second officer Kellie Waddell and I were being scheduled to fly the final rotation from Atlanta to Greensboro, North Carolina and back. After I applied for and received a sanction to set national and world speed records from Atlanta to Greensboro, Captain Falkins graciously allowed me to fly that leg so that he could be at the controls for the final touchdown in Atlanta.

On April 6, 2003, I flew the route in 37 minutes averaging 486 miles per hour. After some photographs and a brief celebration with a large cake commemorating the event we boarded our Atlanta bound passengers and flew our jet into the annals of aviation history.

Bob Falkins, one of Delta's most outstanding captains, retired shortly thereafter and I went on to eventually fly the queen of the fleet—the Boeing 777.

Like my friend Patty Wagstaff, I've experienced many realms of flight. I've flown helicopters (Hueys, Cobras, Jet Rangers and the enormous CH-53 Sea Stallion), fighters (F-5, F-18, F-104, MiG-15, MiG-17 and MiG-21), and experimentals (BD-5J microjet, Christian Eagle and Pitts Special) logging time in nearly 40 different types of aircraft.

From flight test to flight instruction, airshow aerobatics at 50 feet & 500 knots, 50,000 feet & Mach 1+, more than 18,000 hours of my life have been spent airborne—launching from terra firma and from the pitching decks of ships at sea, and recovering often times at night or with zero visibility.

Patty has thrived on the gypsy lifestyle whereas after 20 years of signing autographs, television appearances and show promotions, government and motion picture contracts, I'm content and seek no more aeronautical adventure.

I thoroughly enjoyed jumping out of airplanes and shooting rockets from them. Spotting for naval gunfire from a battleship, transporting movie stars and dignitaries and even hanging by a carabiner from a "spie rig" under a helo has been a blast.

All are, to some extent, adrenaline-producing challenges of managing time and the ever present risk factors with the heightened awareness of split-second decisions. I have been blessed to have these experiences and am blessed still to be able to describe them.

These days I seem to spend an inordinate amount of time pursuing my enjoyment of servant leadership.

As the only drummer in our church orchestra, dedication to regular attendance is mandatory. Our music ministry is awesome and it is a privilege to participate in the many programs we provide each year—In Excelsis Deo at Christmastime, our Pensacola Easter Pageant, Alleluias by the Sea, international mission trips and much, much more.

Serving as president of my Rotary Club was rewarding as well and I have continued to serve in some capacity on our board of directors.

Of no less importance but of tremendous sentimental significance are my roles as a Scout leader. For many years I have endeavored to give back to Scouting because of the jump start on life I was given by my adult leaders as a Boy Scout. The moral and ethical values imparted by Scouting are critical to the development of adolescent boys.

The largest youth movement in the world, Scouting has 28 million people in over 200 countries. During the time in their lives where they are experiencing dramatic physical and emotional changes, Scouts learn to lead by following the guidance of adults worthy of emulation. The male role modeling is superior.

Espousing patriotism (duty to Country) and spiritual reverence (duty to God) the Scout Oath offers a simple roadmap to physical, mental and moral wellbeing. I have tried to do my best to help impart those values to boys and young men by serving in many local, district and council roles such as Scoutmaster, District Chairman and as a member of the Council Executive Board.

I've led a council contingent to the Philmont Scout Ranch (high adventure base near Cimarron, New Mexico) as well as one to our National Jamboree.

The countless hours of effort are far exceeded by the reward of seeing the positive influence on the lives of Scouts. I am honored to serve.

It was also a tremendous blessing to be able to watch my youngest son, Logan, excel as an Eagle Scout as well as on the football field like his big brother.

Number 78 in your program; number 1 in our hearts!

Troop 10 Scoutmaster

Logan & me

CHAPTER 18

THE 10 YEAR CYCLE

"A MAN DON'T START TO LEARN UNTIL HE'S ABOUT FORTY; AND WHEN HE HITS FIFTY HE'S LEARNED ALL HE'S GOING TO LEARN. AFTER THAT HE CAN SORT OF LAY BACK AND ENJOY WHAT HE'S LEARNED, AND MAYBE PASS A LITTLE BIT OF IT ON."

Robert Ruark
The Old Man and the Boy

In 1962, when I was 8 years old, we had a revival at Beth Haven Baptist Church in Valley Station, Kentucky. The evangelist was a charismatic man named Lloyd Bartowell who captured my attention and held it for 3 days. His preaching stirred my heart and motivated me to be baptized, which I was shortly thereafter. I felt wonderful about being *reborn* and wondered what challenges and blessings being a new Christian might bring.

I promised the Lord that I would attend church regularly.

Ten years later, in 1972, I was a freshman at Auburn University and a walk-on football player. The practices were intimidating and, on my own, I was faced with my life's greatest combination of mental, spiritual and physical challenges. The chances were slim that a drummer in the band who had never played high school football could ever make the team at a Southeastern conference powerhouse. I prayed that God would give me the strength to do my best and He did. I played for 4 years, including 3 bowl games, and lettered.

And I promised the Lord that I would attend church regularly.

It was 1982 and I was a captain in the United States Marine Corps. Flying a Huey helicopter on Okinawa where my squadron was deployed for 6 months, my crew and I were tasked with transporting a general around the island on a particularly miserable, rainy day.

As my co-pilot and I were enroute to pick up our VIP, I decided that because of the deteriorating weather conditions we would take a circuitous route around the island, flying at low level above the water so as to avoid the significant inland terrain that varied from sea level to several hundred feet. Once the general was onboard he made a point of informing us that he was late for his meeting and that he did not want us to "spare the horses" in getting him to Camp Schwab. When Marine generals tell their charges to do something, those Marines are programmed to reply "Eye eye, sir" and just get it done. With a quick glance at my co-pilot I decided, against my better judgment, to take the most direct route. As my co-pilot diligently attempted to navigate us around steep terrain and man-made obstacles such as power lines, I flew and flew and flew until I just couldn't see the ground anymore. Resigned that I had no choice but to transition to instruments and plead a *mea culpa* to the general, I readied myself for the general's potential tirade about my ineptitude as a pilot and the almost certain butt chewing I would receive from my operations officer after we returned to our base.

Moments later, I saw the windscreen become tinted with green as we hurtled into a box canyon toward our death and the cliff wall ahead.

Almost instinctively, I put the aircraft through some sort of maneuver that I doubt could ever be replicated and somehow avoided hitting the cliff. I vividly recall cringing and anticipating the inevitable impact followed by the surprising realization that we were amazingly still alive. I had the most surreal feeling that a pair of *Mighty Hands* had somehow reached down and scooped us away from harm gently whispering to me "Not yet, son. Not yet."

Stunned but amazingly still in possession of some of my faculties I realized that, while we had somehow cheated death, the odds were not in our favor.

The rain was torrential and dripped inside the helicopter through the seams around the plexiglass overhead. Instruments spun and tumbled as we tried to contact a controlling agency for assistance. When I finally had the presence of mind to stop climbing, I managed to level the aircraft and decided to head a few miles in any direction so as to ensure that we were over water and not terra firma. A gradual descent eventually allowed me to stop in a hover over the sea and do a pedal turn until we again saw the island. Although the visibility was good, the weather aloft had deteriorated to a ceiling of maybe 100 feet so I basically hover taxied to the island where we eventually found our way back to the general's helo pad and deposited him and his aide where they could soon thereafter change out of their, no doubt, soiled trousers. Upon landing at his headquarters, although probably unhappy about missing his meeting, he was appreciative that we had returned him alive and was cordial and smiling as he departed.

I shut down the helo and spent a few minutes reflecting with my co-pilot and crew chief as we all wondered how we were still breathing. I said a silent prayer of thanks as I re-started the engines and returned to our base.

And I promised the Lord that I would attend church regularly.

During the airshow season of 1992, I was flying my MiG-15 at Robins Air Force Base in Macon, Georgia. This was the first flight after an avionics technician had replaced some instrumentation on the jet since I had not had a previous opportunity to do a post-maintenance check flight.

Following the completion of an aerobatic maneuver I was doing a repositioning turn known in aviator parlance as a tuck under break. I was at approximately 50 feet above the ground and moving at close to 300 miles per hour. And I was upside down, halfway through a roll.

With particularly poor timing, the instrument panel (which had been improperly re-installed) somehow decided that *now* would be a good time to release itself onto my feet and lap. Without getting into an in depth discussion of aeronautics and physics, it's enough to say that my reaction to the situation was purely instinctive.

Even with all the skill I could muster, momentum and gravity were winning the fight as I, once again, found myself bracing for what I hoped would be a painless death as I made a smoking crater in the earth.

And again, I was miraculously pulled from an imminent death by what can only be described as divine intervention—God's *Mighty Hands*.

After landing and opening the canopy I took a moment in the cockpit to smell the air; sweet with the scent of peach blossoms and I marveled at the illogical reality of still being alive.

And sitting there on the ramp at that Air Force base in Georgia, I promised the Lord that I would attend church regularly.

Somehow breaking with this habit of 10 year intervals, although I hadn't yet figured out this 10 year cycle thing, one might suppose I wasn't due for another crisis until somewhere around 2002. However, the most devastating event of my life would take place at the end of 1998.

There is nothing, absolutely positively nothing worse that can happen to a person in his lifetime than to lose a child.

On the afternoon of Tuesday, December 8th, I returned home from the annual International Council of Air Shows convention which is held in Las Vegas. When I called to check for messages on our answering machine at home, I had been aggravated by multiple calls from Catholic High School indicating that my son Charlie was absent on Monday and had not called in. I wondered if he had taken advantage of the fact that dad was away on a business trip and decided to play hooky. Even though Charlie wasn't prone to get into trouble, I knew that he knew that I would deal harshly with such nonsense.

As I walked in the front door I could hear the sound of the television coming from our great room in the back of the house. I followed my usual routine, whatever that was, after returning from a trip and it was a few minutes before I finally walked into the back room. I saw Charlie from behind, seemingly asleep in the easy chair with his leg propped up on the arm. I instantly determined that he must have been truly ill, tosseled his hair and said "Son, if you feel that bad why don't you just go upstairs and go to bed." I walked over to the telephone to check messages and then to the TV to turn it down. Then, as I walked back toward the chair that Charlie was in, my world changed forever.

Charlie was dead. He had taken his own life either late Sunday night or very early Monday morning by holding a pistol to his chest and squeezing the trigger. It was the long term solution to a short term problem; apparently that of being rejected by a girl. An act of justification by an 18 year old boy.

There was no pattern of depression. Even though he did leave a note, it was clearly an impulsive action taken after very little thought.

Just the day before, on Saturday, he had taken the SAT, got a haircut and then went to a party with some friends. What would cause a perfectly normal, well-adjusted teenager to take his own life? No one saw it coming. Except for a few vague, last minute calls to a couple of girls there was no real indication of his intentions. He was a senior looking forward to college. His final season had recently ended and he loved playing football. Friday nights were a joy for all of us. He had many friends. He and I were completely unabashed when it came to public displays of affection. We hugged and kissed often and never hesitated to say that we loved each other.

Charlie had a captivating smile and a jovial demeanor. He laughed easily and often and, in spite of my genes, was particularly handsome. His future was bright and unlimited.

I found that Charlie left me many gifts with which to carry on. One of those gifts was grace. I see life from a totally different perspective now and realize that many important things really aren't. The greatest gift of all, though, was the realization of the depth of my faith. I didn't curse God for allowing this to happen. On the contrary, I praised Him for giving me the assurance that Charlie was with Him and that I would see him again. I understand that I was just his earthly father.

Charlie was on loan for a little while.

So, I thanked Him for that and I promised the Lord that I would attend church regularly. I have and was ordained in 2002.

Charlie & me

He has solved it—life's wonderful problem,
The deepest, the strongest, the last;
And into the school of the angels
With the answer forever has passed.

How strange that, in spite of our questions,
He maketh no answer, nor tells
Why so soon we were earth's honoring laurels
Displaced by God's own immortelles.

How strange he should sleep so profoundly,
So young, so unworn by the strife!
While beside him, brim full of Hope's nectar,
Untouched stands the goblet of life.

Men slumber like that when the evening
Of a long weary day droppeth down;
But he wrought so well that the morning
Brought for him the rest and the crown.

'Tis idle to talk of the future
And the rare "might have been," 'mid our tears;
God knew all about it, yet took him
Away from the oncoming years.

God knew all about him—how noble,
How gentle he was, and how brave,
How brilliant his possible future—
Yet put him to sleep in the grave.

God knows all about those who loved him,
How bitter the trial must be;
And right through it all God is loving,
And knows so much better than we.

So, right in the darkness, be trustful;
One day you shall sing, "It is well."
God took from his young brow earth's laurels
And crowned him with death's immortelles.

CHAPTER 19

PURGATORY

When I first began writing this memoir I was resolved to keep as much of my own and my family's "dirty laundry" (which, of course, we all have) as private as possible. I learned early on, though, as potential editors reviewed my treatise, that an author owes a certain debt to his readers to be, at the very least, reasonably transparent.

I have intentionally, however, not included some mundane but potentially insightful family dynamics because, as the dedication states, my original intent was to give my children a better look into what has made their dad who he is.

It would be outright dishonest, though, to exclude a profound chapter of my life that, while ending in a positive light, had a negative impact of seismic proportions.

In Andy Andrews' wonderful story *The Travelers Gift*, his character David Ponder is enlightened by Abraham Lincoln, "Sooner or later, every man of character will have that character questioned. Every man of honor and courage will be faced with unjust criticism, but never forget that unjust criticism has no impact whatsoever upon the truth. And the only sure way to avoid criticism is to do nothing and be nothing!"

Further, in her eloquent commencement address to the 2008 graduating class at Harvard, renowned author J.K. Rowling, borrowing paraphrase from Theodore Roosevelt, said of her own life "Failure was a stripping away of the inessential. Rock bottom is a solid foundation upon which to re-build one's life.

It is impossible to live without failing at something unless you live so cautiously that you might as well have not lived at all."

Crisis during the spring of 1998 were but harbingers of Charlie's death later that year.

Mom had endured coronary bypass surgery, was diabetic and suffered from emphysema even though she continued to smoke until her death. Following Mom's funeral, with my lengthy absences from home having taken their toll on our marriage, Julie asked me to leave in April. Whether it was military deployments, air show seasons on the road or the monthly grind of being gone several days at a time as an airline pilot, my wife had paid an extraordinary price.

Although it did, it should not have come as a surprise to me that eventually she felt that a life on her own was preferential to a life waiting for me.

We agreed to a separation which lasted for several years. It was clear after a time that our marriage was truly irretrievably broken and so we divorced.

Our relationship remained uniquely amicable and it was not uncommon for us to enjoy meals together as a family. We created quite a conundrum for our friends, acquaintances, aunts, uncles, cousins and the like.

As a matter of fact, she once literally saved my life.

I had contracted a nasty bug with flu-like symptoms which necessitated that I remain in very close proximity to the bathroom. While seated therein, I felt the simultaneous urge to vomit which I did with such force that I actually ripped an artery in my esophagus spewing blood all over the bathtub. My last conscious act was phoning Julie.

She somehow managed to get me loaded into her car and raced me to Baptist Hospital where Dr. Wayne Cartee diagnosed my Mallory-Weiss tear and managed to cauterize the vessel with an endoscopy. I could easily have bled to death.

We were an enigma to all who saw our interactions together but felt we had a comfortable relationship that couldn't help but be of benefit to our children and a good example to others.

Typical of male bravado, I announced to all concerned that I was now a confirmed bachelor destined to never marry again having been there and done that. In spite of all that hot air, though, and in keeping with God's plan, inevitably I met a remarkable woman to whom I was drawn.

I was teaching a Sunday school class for singles and couldn't help noticing the bluest eyes I had ever seen. A very easy friendship ensued with casual conversation about our mutual alma mater, Auburn.

We eventually began a dating relationship which, while relatively private, was certainly no secret.

About that same time my odyssey of betrayal and humiliation began when a female acquaintance that I had known for several years decided that I was off limits to anyone except her.

Our relationship originated when we met on a plane enroute to Atlanta during one of my routine commutes to work. After I helped place one of her bags in an overhead bin, we sat next to each other and exchanged pleasantries and small talk until she became engaged in some paperwork relating to her job and I read the magazines I had brought from home. Upon our arrival in Atlanta, she left behind (apparently unnoticed) a very nice pen on the seat divider. As employees customarily do, I waited until all the passengers had de-planed and then headed to the pilot lounge to change into my uniform.

With a few minutes to spare, I recalled that she had said she was headed to a passenger lounge to wait for her connecting flight so I decided to try to find her there and return her pen on the way to my gate.

Upon locating her in the Crown Room she was grateful and offered her business card saying that if I ever had a layover in her town she would gladly repay my kindness with dinner which sounded fine to me.

A few months later I did, indeed, have a layover where she lived and took her up on her offer. I learned that she had planned to move to the Pensacola area and would need some help in the usual welcome wagon ways. Which areas were desirable to live, where to find a good dentist, physician and dry cleaners were all areas of necessity. She traveled for a living, too, and spent the better part of each week on the road.

Eventually her routine changed, involving the opportunity to periodically work out of her home by teleconference.

I had wanted a dog for several years after having met my buddy Warren Price's dog, Boss, a yellow Labrador retriever who stole my heart in about 30 seconds. Warren's son, Lantz, had a Lab (Rue) that was related to Boss and when that dog sired a litter with a female in Ocala I was one of the first in line to get a puppy.

With my airline schedule it would have been nearly impossible to have a dog without frequently putting him in a kennel.

During discussion of this quandary with my friend, she considered that it might be possible for her to help puppy sit from time to time. With reasonable coordination of schedules, I was able to get Angus to substantially enrich my life.

UNCONDITIONAL LOVE

After Boss had rested his chin on my leg and gazed up at me with his gorgeous brown eyes, I was truly enamored with the sweet disposition of the Labrador retriever.

About three years after my encounter with Boss I was at the home of Maggie; actually, in AKC records, Attagirl Fetchemup Mags, watching her litter of pups romping around their whelping pen and doing what puppies do. I had this idea that I'd know the *right* puppy when he came to me and looked at me with those soulful eyes as if to say "Hey, where've you been? I've been waiting for you!" That didn't happen, though. Instead, I noticed a big drowsy pup off to himself in the corner of the pen, lazily watching his brothers and sisters. I went over and sat down beside him on the floor among the newspapers and toys scattered about.

He managed to muster enough energy to plop his tiny head with big floppy ears and his enormous paws into my lap and then gazed around watching all the commotion with only his eyes. His tiny eyebrows would bob up and down and his eyes rolled from side to side but he hardly moved his head at all. I was drawn to the laid back puppy and pulled him close. I did manage to ask him "Are you the one?" After which his little yellow eyelashes began to droop and he promptly dozed off.

I brought a small carry on bag lined with a fluffy beach towel which seemed to comfort him on the short flight from Orlando to Pensacola. He whined once in the airport which I deduced to mean that he needed to relieve himself. In the airport restroom he seemed more than content to potty on some paper towels.

I left the bag partially unzipped so that I could keep one hand in contact with him during the flight. He was a perfect little gentleman.

Only months old, he went along on his first hunting trip. Logan and I were invited to a dove hunt with my good friend Howard and some of his family. Logan was only 8 and was there to fetch the birds when they fell. Little did he know that the outing would turn into a competition between him and Angus as they raced out into the field to retrieve the downed birds. When the hunt was over we were making our way back to our truck when we came across another hunter looking forlornly out into a small pond. Almost in the middle floated

PAUL T. ENTREKIN

a downed dove and he lamented being unable to get to the bird. He looked at Angus, then looked at me and inquired "You think that pup would go get my bird?" "I dunno", I said. "Let's see." So I picked up a small stick and threw it about 30 yards out to where the dove bobbed around. All I had to say was "Go get it" and Angus was in the water, swimming for the very first time.

Logan & my best friend Angus

He swam straight to the stick and then saw the dove which he rightfully determined was far more interesting. He gently mouthed the bird and swam straight back dropping it softly into my hand as soon as I said "Give". I handed the bird to its owner who smiled brightly and complimented Angus on his skill. I beamed like a proud poppa.

Beyond his hunting prowess, though, the small fuzzy puppy who grew to a whopping 110 pounds truly became my anchor. There were many lonely nights when he was my pillow, my confidant and my very best friend.

Angus, like me, has a love language that can best be described as tactile. When he is touched he feels safe and loved. Even when he chooses a place to nap he is always very close by, usually finding a way, even contorting himself if necessary, to touch me. Standing, he employs the "Labrador lean".

Every return home I'm greeted like I've been away for an eternity. He bounds around the dining room table and then seeks one of his toys to fetch and show me what a good boy he's been. His large rudder of a tail can sweep a low-sitting table top clean of its contents. And woe betide the unsuspecting guest in our pool who dives in and doesn't surface in what Angus feels is an appropriate time. He's very likely to jump in and *rescue* the surprised swimmer at the point they appear. He's quite the lifeguard.

With no doubt in my mind that most dogs *do* go to heaven, I look forward to the time when I see him and my sweet German Shepherd, Heidi, wagging their tails at the pearly gates as if to say "Hey, where've you been? We've been waiting for you!"

My friend was as enamored with him as I was and eventually decided that she wanted a Lab, too.

What followed was a mutually beneficial relationship that had the potential to develop further. Over a period of a few years, however, it was obvious that there were more differences in our personalities than similarities and it was apparent, at least to me, that a long term permanent relationship was not in our future. For the foreseeable future, though, we continued to maintain the status quo where she watched my dog when I traveled and I similarly watched hers.

It was clear to me that our relationship was not exclusive and when I decided to pursue a relationship with my future wife my "friend" quickly became my nemesis; truly the bane of my existence.

In the months prior, I had often suggested that my church might be a substantial benefit for my un-churched friend. I think she finally came on a semi-regular basis just to see who I was associating with there. Once acquainted with those within my circle at church, she began to cultivate relationships in an effort to offer her special insight into my character, telling some at the expense of her own reputation that she was my "mistress" and that since we had seen each other prior to my divorce being final she and I were mutual adulterers. She even made an appointment with the pastor in an effort to discredit one of his deacons.

Fortunately for me, most, including my pastor and friend Robert Mills, fellow deacon George Scarborough, my dear Scoutmaster Vick Vickery, District Scout Executive Cary Wilson and the loyal members of my Rotary Club (of which I was president at the time) particularly Bob Kent and Charlie Nye, were able to see through her façade and kindly disregarded her attempts at slander.

A final showdown was inevitable and it materialized just before Christmas when, unwilling to answer her phone calls, she crawled through the dog door at my home to see if I was there. The ensuing argument and my insistence that she leave the house forthwith was the terminus of that relationship . . . or so I thought.

In the weeks that followed I would learn that she had begun efforts to demean my reputation that reached far beyond anything I ever could have imagined. It was a classic case of a woman scorned.

She had contacted the local police and told them that her handgun was missing and that she suspected that I had taken it with the intent of coming back to murder her and attempt to make it look like a suicide. I'm not kidding! Following her incident with the dog door, she had persuaded one of her two boyfriends of several months (of whom I knew nothing about) to aid her in a story to police that I had crawled through *her* dog door. (Fortunately, I was on the phone with my future wife at the time she crawled through mine.) The story was manifested in charges being filed against me for burglary.

So, shortly into the new year I was awakened at 3:00AM by a knock at the door. I answered in my bathrobe and was surprised to see 4 deputies and 4 city police officers with very serious looks on their faces. In my sleepy stupor, the first thought that came to my mind was that something awful had happened to one of the kids. That wakes you up very quickly. Momentary consideration, though, made me realize that they don't send 8 cops to tell you that there's been an accident. (I guess they thought I was a real bad dude.) I was promptly escorted to the county jail.

Being incarcerated, albeit for only a matter of hours, is among the lowest of emotional lows. Even though I had suffered at the hands of the Syrians years before, then I was belligerent and at the service of my country. I was steadfastly in the right and willing to die. Now, I was under the persecution of representatives of my own country. I didn't understand why and I was devastated.

Only hours later, I was in church with my head still reeling over what had transpired.

In a small town and with the aid of arrest records being published in the local newspaper, it didn't take long for the phone to ring. It was my dear friend, our Minister of Music

Bob Morrison, calling to say that one of the ladies at church had seen my name and wanted to know what was up with one of our deacons. We met later that day for a milkshake and I shared the entire story with him. He was wonderful and vowed support during this tumultuous time.

I could write countless pages regarding the mundane details that took place over the following year. You, the reader, would then have to determine whether my perspective was either philosophical conjecture or reflective overview. Let's suffice to say that the following is perhaps a combination of both.

My resolve to fight the charges tooth and nail to clear my good name was absolute.

Most of us are taught to believe and have faith in our judicial system. We subscribe to the principles in the final words we recite in the pledge of allegiance that say " . . . with liberty and justice for all" and that everyone has the right to be considered innocent until proven guilty by a jury of our peers and that we are entitled to swift and unbiased justice. Well, it ain't necessarily so.

Think about it. If an accused was just that, *accused*, and not considered to have committed the violation of the law, they wouldn't be arrested to begin with. Clearly, for an accused to be arrested they must be presumed guilty.

I won't get into a debate on the law because, like most of us not affiliated with the legal profession, I can only speak to my own treatment and experience. Since my journey through the legal morass, I can honestly say that I have completely reversed my position on how accused individuals should be treated and have come to subscribe to the philosophy that it is better for 10 guilty people to go free than for 1 innocent person to be falsely detained.

As a sworn Federal officer, actively engaged in law enforcement (as a Federal Flight Deck Officer) I had every faith and confidence in the system of which I was a part. With character beyond reproach, absolutely no criminal record and having been screened and vetted through one of the most complex governmental security processes, I was initially certain that I would be given the benefit of the doubt in a he said—she said scenario, which this was.

In the eyes and minds of some state prosecutors, though, I came to experience that every accused person is a potential notch on their gun. Enough notches and they get a cushy job with a high-paying law firm. Some even view the truth as an irrelevant distraction. With regard to one's own legal counsel, to some you're just a paycheck. The deeper the trouble, the bigger the check and the longer the process can be drawn out equals even more dollars. Again, with some the truth has no bearing.

The civil judge who oversaw multiple hearings regarding that aspect of the case once implied that I was perhaps obtuse and then condescendingly inquired as to whether or not I understood the meaning of the word. Clearly his arrogance proved that he, in fact, was the one who was obtuse.

One of the two judges who presided over the criminal aspect of the case (and later recused herself because the state prosecutor inferred that she might be impartial due to the fact that she attended the same 5000 member church as I) rightfully offered me an apology saying "Mr. Entrekin, you are entitled to a fair and speedy proceeding and you have had neither." She later confided to a mutual friend that she was, indeed, predisposed to drop the charges due to the hearsay nature and total lack of substantiating evidence in the case.

Due to my civic connections of Scouting, Rotary, church and others, I have become friends or acquaintances with several judges in our community. They are stellar individuals but each would be the first to tell you that they put their pants on just like the rest of us each day. They are elected or appointed to ascertain the truth somewhere within the arguments of each side and apply the law. The same is true for friends and acquaintances that are attorneys.

The bottom feeders, though, are a blight on their profession and serve to foster the stereotypical perception that lawyers are a necessary evil.

My foray into the world of the judiciary was enlightening, eye opening and to some extent frightening.

Exacerbating the problem was that one of the aforementioned "boy friends" was a local city cop*. He, no doubt, was of invaluable assistance throughout the entire process.

That's a really low point in a person's life, isn't it? One would tend to think that things can't get much worse, right?
Well, they did.

Rewind the clock to November of the previous year.

Turning fifty, I had decided that I should have a really solid baseline of my health established. During my semi-annual flight physical I asked the doctor what he would recommend. Should I have a colonoscopy; a CAT scan? His suggestion was what he referred to as an "executive screening". It was just a blood test that took what seemed like a pint so that the lab can run tests on every aspect of your physiology.

*During the discovery process, in another touch of irony, my attorney was retained by this officer's wife when she filed for divorce (his second). Although bound by attorney/client privilege prohibiting his liberty to discuss details, my attorney did divulge that (in his words) "the guy was a real dirt bag." We were also aware through depositions of her and both boyfriends that the cop had moved in with her while he was married.

PAUL T. ENTREKIN

330

When he got the test results he gave me a call so that we could go over them and he could explain what everything meant. Clearly, he had not reviewed them before we met and his initial comments were glowing. When he turned the page, though, his furrowed brow and the comment that we needed some more tests got my attention. He explained that my thyroid numbers were out of the normal range and that he would request some lab tests to be more specific.

At that time I was completely asymptomatic and confident that there was just a mistake.

Within weeks, though, reality was a harbinger of substantial proportions.

I lost 25 of my 185 pounds and had very little energy. I finally understood why for the past couple of years my face always appeared red in photos and why I had to have the thermostat set at a temperature cold enough to hang meat. In the winter I could chuckle at those around me lamenting the cold weather while I never so much as shivered.

I had lots of tests and scans done and sought the opinions of an oncologist, endocrinologist and surgeon. Surgery eventually won out as the best option.

So, much like 1998, the year 2005 was not the best of times for yours truly.

How many times have these scenes played out in the lives of so many others? How many others have made either a bad choice or a mistake?

Let's say you go for a drive at night to get some milk for tomorrow morning's cereal and suddenly find yourself on black ice and skid off the road into a ditch. That is a *mistake*.

But, if you've been warned by the TV weatherman that conditions are not conducive for safe driving and you go anyway, that was no mistake. That was a *choice*—a bad choice.

I agonized for months over my precarious legal predicament and felt sorry for myself over my unanticipated health concerns. Had I made a *mistake* somewhere in my choice of relationships or had I made an exceptionally bad *choice*?

What I learned from all this is that while we all make mistakes and we all make bad choices, knowing the difference between the two is absolutely essential.

Even though, over time, this woman had eventually divulged that her previous relationship history involved a great many men (more than 40) since her divorce, years before (over her own, self-professed adulterous infidelities), I truly felt that encouraging her to begin a spiritual relationship with the Lord was something I could and should do. Despite her ill repute and knowing her to be cunning and deceitful, I could never have anticipated the depth of her character flaws and lack of integrity. Those internecine traits were revealed so late in my acquaintance with her that it was obvious I had truly made a very bad *mistake*.

She had managed to obtain phone and credit card records, routinely stalked both Lisa and me (evidenced by neighbor's accounts of seeing her car near our homes) and we both experienced her following us on several occasions. Our friends were cornered in grocery stores or wherever she could bend their ear and the real irony was that she was doing these things while I was being prosecuted and labeled by her as a sociopath. She was a master manipulator of the court system and she was obsessed. By all indications this was eerily similar to a *Fatal Attraction* scenario.

I soldiered on as the weeks turned into months with one continuance after another. There were emotional highs when I was told the state prosecutors had her number and were willing to drop the charges followed by emotional lows when I learned that she had somehow convinced them again to perpetuate the sham. The incessant proceedings were physically and financially draining but there was a tenacity in me that, as in years before, would not allow me to simply quit.

My personal scripture became James 1:12; *Blessed is the man who perseveres under trial, because when he has stood the test, he will receive the crown of life that God has promised to those who love him.*

And so I persevered.

Many friends and supporters all did their best offering guidance with such sayings as "God never gives us more than He knows we can handle" and "You're just being tempered in the fire, like steel, and He'll make you stronger." Somehow when you're in the middle of that fire there aren't a whole lot of words that make you feel much better.

There are some words that *did* make me feel better, though.

There is a wonderful scripture that depicts a very Godly woman in the book of Esther. From chapter 4, verses 12-16, we can learn that following God has a way of putting us in the right place at the right time. What we do with the opportunity is up to us. Esther followed God's leadership but didn't know until later it was God that had influenced her.

The basis of the story is that, as King Xerces wife, she prevented the holocaust of Jews in Persia. She was counseled by Mordecai that "You are where you are for a time such as this."

Sometimes seizing the opportunity requires risk taking. Making the right decision may be costly whether the toll is reputation, friendships or money.

God had a purpose for my experiencing these challenges.

After more than a year of legal wrangling and countless thousands of dollars, not to mention the emotional costs, my legal counsel finally advised that I accept a deal to plead no contest to a misdemeanor charge. I was spent in more ways than one and, against my inclination to fight, I complied. While I was *transformed* I was never *conformed*.

The sum of moral integrity is character. Mine was intact because I knew my thoughts and actions when no one else could see. Even though my reputation had possibly suffered in the eyes of some, those who love me never faltered and those who judged me just have to deal with the insecurities of their own shortcomings.

I did, indeed, emerge from the fire of those trials forged stronger and ever faithful of God's grace knowing that even though I am unworthy of His sacrifice I am truly blessed.

CHAPTER 20

ROCKY CREEK

As my body healed and my strength returned, I found that the constants throughout the entire ordeal were not only my faith but also the sweet soul with those piercing blue eyes. Proposing marriage to Lisa was one of the easiest decisions of my life and it has proven to be one of my best.

Following my years of wanderlust which, I suppose, is typical of most pilots, I've become a real homebody among who's greatest joys is being among God's creations, helping things grow and nurturing His critters. To that end, Lisa and I at long last found what may be our little slice of heaven on earth. Having had the opportunity to travel the world and see and experience many beautiful places, as I eluded to early on in the book, there's truly no place like home. I'm most comfortable here in the south, reasonably close to old friends and family despite the fact that I've seen some landscapes across the country that would be gorgeous to experience every day.

We were blessed to find a place nearby Pensacola that was virtually untouched and ready for us to sculpt. On Rocky Creek, the terrain is rolling and filled with hardwood timber and some pines among spectacular rocks and boulders. The topography is quite unlike any in this region. Having cleared and planted pasture as well as creating stream fords and a bridge for the abundant creeks, we recently completed our barn which will be used primarily to, we hope, accommodate and foster rescued horses that need rehabilitation until they can be placed in permanent homes.

This also fulfills a lifelong dream for me to have a place where deer, turkey and other wildlife are prevalent.

The Lord has forged our faith in the fires of trial and tribulation and we feel blessed to have emerged the stronger for it. After closing some doors and a window here and there, He has flung the barn doors wide open for us, offering peace and solitude.

Let the next chapter begin!

Lisa & me

Epilogue

In January, 1998, I had composed the bulk of this book and, except for editing, it was essentially completed. For some reason I just felt that there was something missing so I kept the manuscript locked away, apprehensive to go to print. It is now clear to me that the book most certainly was not finished. I realize that there was another 10 year life altering period of profound importance yet to come that would be essential to my story.

Of my greatest accomplishments, I consider those things *not* said in anger that I could have and those times that I have both figuratively and literally had the crosshairs of vengeance in my hands and, whether by conscience or character or both, did *not* pull the trigger.

I have taken the high road—the road *less* taken . . .

> "I shall be telling this with a sigh
> Somewhere ages and ages hence:
> Two roads diverged in a wood, and I-
> I took the one less traveled by,
> *And that has made all the difference.*"

Robert Frost

Life is full of ugly lies. Life is full of beautiful truths.

AFTERWORD

As you've read in this book, I first met Paul in Sunday school. He had been recruited to teach the singles class I was attending. I was quickly drawn to this handsome man with a ready smile. Paul has one of those smiles that can light up a room. He's confident, but not cocky; and has the self-assuredness that comes from knowing where you've been, how you got there, and where you're going. As I heard his testimony and interacted with him at church, I knew that I wanted to get to know him better, so I started finding reasons to talk to him. We compared stories about where our jobs had taken us the previous week and how our Auburn Tigers had performed. Most intriguing were the many ways that he and my dad are alike. We still laugh and shake our heads at their many similarities.

As our friendship developed, I discovered Paul's unique background in the same stories that you've now heard. I was fascinated by his can-do spirit and triumph over adversity. His humility was apparent. Unlike many individuals with so many accomplishments, he sought no recognition for himself. "No guts, no glory," he often says, and in no one's life have I ever seen this manifested as much as in Paul's. His quiet confidence comes from a deep faith. He has been forged from childhood through adulthood and has never lost confidence in God's omniscient wisdom. He seeks ways to give recognition to others; whether it's writing a heartfelt letter or a quick email or nominating someone for a Rotary or Scouting award. Most importantly, however, he always gives glory to God, whose *Mighty Hands* have carried, directed, shielded and cradled him throughout his life. Now I see "No guts, no glory", in a different way. The glory belongs to God!

On Paul's fiftieth birthday, one of the gifts I gave him was a gold bag with fifty cards, each numbered and in its own envelope. On each card was written a word or phrase describing something that I loved or admired about him. You've seen these qualities in action as you've read this book—patriotism, courage, faith, tenacity, integrity . . . and forty five more virtues. These virtues live within all of us and are affected by the circumstances of our lives. What we do with them is up to us. Do our circumstances make us stronger, or do they discourage us? Do our life events define us, or do we define our life events?

Paul often says that he's not been lucky; he's been blessed. Blessed by an awesome God who knows our every step and our every path, even if we don't have a clue. Blessed by a God who knows the difference between our needs and our wants. Blessed by a God who can take disappointment, grief or tragedy and turn it into triumph. Whose *Mighty Hands* and grace give us victory over adversity.

During adverse times in my own life, I've found great comfort in two particular Bible verses. The first is Matthew 12:20 (NIV). *A bruised reed he will not break, and a smoldering wick he will not snuff out.* When we feel like a fragile reed, bruised by life's circumstances, it seems easy to turn away from God or to be angry at Him for allowing such things to occur. We just want to give up, to blame somebody. God knows. He understands, and he loves us anyway—more than we can possibly comprehend or imagine. If we turn to Him, we will find His grace sufficient for anything that comes our way. The second is Psalm 32:7 (NKJ). *You are my hiding place; you shall preserve me from trouble; you shall surround me with songs of deliverance.* Sometimes we just need to collapse into God's arms. To know that His *Mighty Hands* are there to comfort us.

One of the things I enjoyed about Paul's Sunday school lessons was that he would always close by giving us a nugget of truth—a "take away" of sorts. Something from the lesson that was quick and easy to remember. Out of every story in this book, he would want you to take this away: that God's grace is sufficient to give us victory over adversity. That it's all about *Him*.

Lisa Entrekin

ACKNOWLEDGMENTS

Stephan Wilkinson, prolific motor sports writer, who guided my initial steps toward publication. Your frankness and honesty was the impetus that forced me to dig deeper as a writer.

My dear friend Floyd McGowin, again, provided a compassionate but critical eye to my initial manuscript and helped nudge me out of my comfort zone to reveal those ugly truths.

Tony Gain, Steve Bacon and Howard Smith; three men of courage whose brotherly love, while never worn on their sleeves, is clear and present. I love you guys, too.

Robert Mills (approaching 6 feet 7 inches, a man to whom everyone looks up) and Bob Morrison (at 5 feet 7 inches, a giant among men); my spiritual guides and ministers throughout some of the most trying times of my adult life.

My best friend Angus, who has given his unconditional love, brought joy into my life when there was sadness and made the good times even better.

My former wife, Julie, who tended the home fires.

Byrd Mapoles, whose sage advice and guidance helped me through the minefields of the airshow business.

Vick Vickery; my mentor in Scouting.

Warren Price, *El Kokono Verdugo*; the best turkey hunter I ever saw and loyal friend who never fails to call in early December each year.

Carolyn MacGregor and *The Tuesdays* for teaching me the power of prayer.

Dan Sivley who planted the seed to be a gyrine jet jockey.

Tom Deshazo who helped to make that seed grow.

Don Miller; my mentor in Masonry.

Richard Colby and Ed Bowlin who made my aspirations to be a Delta Air Lines pilot a reality.

My father and mother-in-law, Vic & Diane Goeller, for their warmth and perpetual senses of humor. You deeply enrich my life.

And my sweet wife, Lisa. You are truly the wind beneath my wings.

CURRICULUM VITAE

Paul T. Entrekin

Titles & Degrees

President & Chief Pilot, Entrekin Aviation
Major, United States Marine Corps, retired
Captain, Delta Air Lines, retired
Honorary Admiral, City of Decatur, Alabama
Honorary Kentucky Colonel
Honorary Lieutenant Colonel Aide-de-Camp, State of Alabama
Honorary Lieutenant Governor, State of Alabama
Honorary Alabama State Trooper
United States Naval Aviator
Bachelor of Science Degree, Auburn University
Knight of the Rose Croix, Royal Order of Scotland
32nd Degree Scottish Rite Mason

Aviation & Type Ratings

Airline Transport Pilot (Commercial)
Airplane Multi-engine Land
Airplane Single-engine Land
Rotorcraft-Helicopter
Instrument-Helicopter/Airplane
Boeing 757, 767, 777
Flight Engineer, Boeing 727
MiG-15, MiG-17, BD-5J
Level 1—(Unlimited/Ground Level) Aerobatic Competency
FAA/ICAS Aerobatic Competency Evaluator

Federal Flight Deck Officer, Transportation Security
      Administration—
Department of Homeland Security
Supersonic Rating, Canadian Air Force
Military Special Instrument Rating

Achievements

United States and World Record Holder (National Aeronautic Association and Federation Aéronautique Internationale) Speed Over A Recognized Course, Atlanta to Pensacola—505.51 mph, MiG-15bis, 7/6/93

United States and World Record Holder (National Aeronautic Association and Federation Aéronautique Internationale) Speed Over A Commercial Air Route, Atlanta to Greensboro—486.60 mph, Boeing 727-200, 4/6/03

*World's **First** Civilian MiG Pilot/Owner*
*World's **Highest Flight Time** Civilian MiG Pilot*
Eagle Scout, Boy Scouts of America
Varsity Track Letterman, Decatur High School
Varsity Football Letterman, Auburn University

Honors & Awards

Civilian:
Paul Harris Fellow, Rotary International
National Aviation & Space Wall of Honor
Carl Schwuchow Memorial Scholarship,
      Decatur High School Band
Scholarship, William Jewell College
Scholarship, University of South Alabama
James E. West Fellow, Boy Scouts of America
Order of the Arrow, Boy Scouts of America
God & Country Award, Boy Scouts of America

Cliff Dochterman Award, Boy Scouts of America
Daniel Carter Beard Masonic Scouter Award
Good Shepherd Award, Boy Scouts of America
District Award of Merit, Boy Scouts of America
Distinguished Commissioner Service Award,
     Boy Scouts of America
Big Game Hunter Award (x6), National Rifle Association
SCI Gold Medal qualifier—Rocky Mountain Elk (typical)
SCI Silver Medal qualifier (x3)—
     Rocky Mountain Mule Deer (typical)
     White Tail Deer (typical)
     Mountain Caribou
SCI Bronze Medal qualifier—Québec-Labrador Caribou
Grand, Royal and World Slam of North American
     Wild Turkeys

Military:
United States Marine Corps Aviation Safety Award
Bell Helicopter Outstanding Military Achievement Award
United States Marine Corps Rifle Expert (x7)
United States Marine Corps Pistol Expert (x7)
Honorary Plank Owner, USS Iwo Jima (LPD 7)
Order of the Red Max, U. S. Navy
     Training Squadron Three (VT-3)
Multiple Individual & Unit Decorations

Organizations

Society of Experimental Test Pilots
Ancient Order of Quiet Birdmen
Order of Daedalians
National Aeronautic Association
Marine Corps Aviation Association
Association of Naval Aviation
National Air & Space Society
National Naval Aviation Museum Foundation

Air Line Pilots Association
International Council of Air Shows
Experimental Aircraft Association
American Helicopter Society
Classic Jet Aircraft Association
Legion of Valor
Fellowship of Christian Athletes
National Football Foundation and College Hall of Fame
Auburn Football Lettermen Club
Auburn Alumni Association
Pensacola North Rotary Club, Rotary International
National Eagle Scout Association
Alpha Phi Omega
Boone and Crockett Club
National Rifle Association
National Wild Turkey Federation
Sons of Confederate Veterans
Sons of the American Revolution

"ALL GLORY IS FLEETING"